I0160601

POP GOES THE METAL

Hard Rock, Hairspray,
Hooks and Hits

STEPHEN H. PROVOST

STEPHEN H. PROVOST

DRAGON CROWN

Dragon Crown Books 2020
All rights reserved.

ISBN-13: 978-1-949971-14-9

Dedication

To my parents, who let me listen to whatever I wanted,
and trusted that I'd turn out OK.

STEPHEN H. PROVOST

Contents

POP GOES THE METAL

POP GOES THE METAL

The author at the Rock & Roll Hall of Fame in Cleveland, 2019.

POP GOES THE METAL

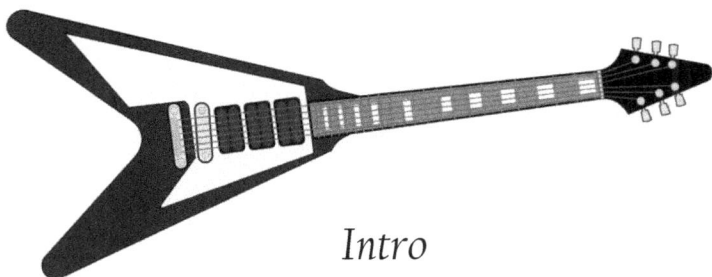

Intro

Hello Hooray

When I young, my parents used to drive me down to the local record store set me loose to browse through the racks. The Wherehouse was out on Ventura Boulevard, which would later be Tom Petty's hangout of choice for "all the vampires living in the Valley."

The San Fernando Valley, that is: the same one mentioned in Frank and Moon Zappa's "Valley Girl."

That's where I grew up, at least for six years during the heart of the '70s, from Richard Nixon's re-election through his resignation and the end of Vietnam. Then on through the birth of disco and *Saturday Night Fever*; *The Rocky Horror Picture Show* (which melded the glam-horror vibe of Alice Cooper with the gender-bending of Bowie) and *Star Wars*.

I hated disco, by the way. All of it. The Bee Gees' falsetto. John Travolta's stupid white jacket. (No, I didn't see the movie; the poster outside the local theater was bad enough.) Mostly, I bemoaned the lack of a guitar — preferably electric — which was like a ticket to nirvana to anyone with *real* musical taste.

I lived next door to the L.A. Dodgers' left fielder on one

side and *The Tonight Show*'s music director on the other, but when I wasn't at school, I spent most of my time in my room, listening to music and sorting baseball cards. Hanging out at the mall wasn't my thing: too many people. But I did like going to the record store, where I could check out the latest releases and agonize over how to spend my saved-up allowance.

I could've gone to another record store, Licorice Pizza out on Topanga Canyon, but The Wherehouse was closer, so we usually went there.

I remember one trip in particular. It was 1976, and my limited record collection included The Beatles' *Rubber Soul* (a Christmas gift from my aunt), *Elton John's Greatest Hits*, and *Their Greatest Hits* by the Eagles, released earlier that year. I was still a fan of Elton, and I thought I'd probably end up getting *Captain Fantastic and the Brown Dirt Cowboy*. But I wanted to look around first.

I walked up and down the aisles, and as I did, a couple of other albums drew my attention. My reaction to the first one was, "Huh? Really? You've got to be kidding me?" I picked it up for a closer look: The four band members on the cover wore dress suits, but their faces looked like they belonged to clowns who'd escaped from a circus in some alternate dimension to audition for *The Godfather*.

The album was called *Dressed to Kill*, and the band's name was Kiss. They had a cool logo, where the S's in their name looked like lightning bolts. But the band members themselves looked ridiculous. I flipped the album over, looked back at the front again, and quickly decided it was the most idiotic thing I'd ever seen. I'd never heard of these guys, and I had absolutely zero interest in their album.

I put it back and moved on to the racks against the back wall, where I came across an LP called *Desolation Boulevard* by

POP GOES THE METAL

Sweet. This one really tempted me, because I'd gotten hooked on the band's latest single, "Fox on the Run," which was playing a lot on the radio.

I used to sit in my room with a cassette recorder and wait for it to come on the radio so I could record it. This took a lot of patience, and even more luck, because I had to hope that 1) no one would slam a door in the background while the song was playing and 2) the DJ wouldn't talk over the end of the song and ruin it.

The second thing almost always happened. I hated DJs for it. I didn't listen to the radio to hear them talk, anyway. The only time I wanted to hear a DJ say anything was *after* the song was finished. What was the song called? What was the name of the band? Most of the time, though, they didn't say. More often, they launched into some B.S. product pitch or weather report, or announced the station's call letters — which I already knew because I'd been listening all day waiting for "Fox on the Run."

And because they talked over the end of it, I'd have to wait a few more hours for the rotation to come around again.

I liked "Fox on the Run," and *Desolation Boulevard* was just about the coolest name for an album I'd ever heard. When I picked up the album to check it out at The Wherehouse, I thought the cover looked like someplace in L.A., but I didn't know it was Sunset Boulevard in West Hollywood, which was just over the hills from where I lived and, it turns out, was the capital of the rock 'n' roll world before it moved to Seattle with the birth of grunge. It was barely 20 miles away.

I looked at the long-haired band members in the foreground of the cover shot and wondered whether the two in the middle were guys or girls. I *thought* they were guys. Not that I cared; it just bugged me that I couldn't be certain. I'd seen a poster of Bowie in the mall and wondered the same thing.

I didn't end up buying *Desolation Boulevard* — not because of the gender thing, but because I had just enough cash for one record, and I didn't know enough of the other songs to risk plunking down $5.99. "Fox on the Run" might have been the only good song on the disc, and then I'd have to start saving my money all over again. It wasn't worth chancing it.

I went back to that rack couple of times and picked up the album as I debated buying it, but I finally put it back and decided to go with the album I'd come to buy: *Captain Fantastic*. I'm glad I did: It's a killer album. But I wish I'd had enough money to buy the Sweet record, because it is, too.

I bought a few records at The Wherehouse over the next couple of years. One I remember in particular was *News of the World* by Queen. My mother had heard the song "We Will Rock You" on the radio while we were driving down Highway 101 and told me she thought it was pretty good, but when I asked her the name of the band, she said she thought it was by "The Champions" and wasn't sure if the song was a good influence because she was sure the band was a bunch of hooligans. Why else would they be singing, "We will *rob* you!" over and over again?

Ah, parents. I shouldn't be too hard on Mom: At one point, I thought the Fifth Dimension was singing about the age of aquariums, and I had no idea that Led Zeppelin's *In Through the Out Door* meant anything other than entering through the door marked "exit" at the supermarket.

I did figure out on my own that Mom had heard the lyrics to "We Will Rock You" wrong, and that she'd gotten "The Champions" from the name of the song that was paired with "We Will Rock You" on the single: "We Are the Champions." I bought the album because I liked the song, too (my mom might not have had the best ears, but she had good taste, at least on that occasion), and because the album art was, as they said at the time, "bitchen." A giant robot who was murdering members of the band? Nice!

By that time, I'd even decided to give Kiss a try, after all. I'd learned that my friends thought they were "cool" — which was, for me (like most impressionable teens), enough incentive to rethink my initial opinion. I picked up an album called *Alive!* because it included two records for just a little more than a typical single album cost. After listening to "Rock and Roll All Nite" and "Parasite," I was hooked.

Let the Music Do the Talking

Kiss didn't stay popular with my group of friends for more than a year or so after that, but I bought every album they put out over the next 40 years, anyway. It wasn't the makeup; it was the music. They weren't Beethoven or even the Beatles, but the songs were heavy and catchy. That's a combination I hadn't heard too often, and it's a combination that clicked for me.

It would click again and again with bands like Sweet, Cheap Trick, Def Leppard, Poison, and others. I didn't classify the music in my head as belonging to any particular genre, I just knew I liked songs that featured electric guitar, killer riffs, big choruses and strong melodies. Now I know that kind of music goes by a number of names: Pop metal, glam metal, and — in reference to its '80s heyday, when bands went all-in with big hair, spandex and eyeliner — hair metal.

I like the phrase melodic metal, because to me, the melody is what binds it all together. It sure as heck isn't the lyrics. No one's going to confuse "Nothin' But a Good Time" or "Cum on Feel the Noize" with "Imagine" or "American Pie." This is, for the most part, feel-good, party music. That's not to say the lyrics were always shallow, but tunes with a deeper meaning tended to get lost or dismissed amid the party-all-the-time anthems. Listen to Poison's "Something to Believe In" or Van Halen's "Right Now," for example. Yes, these songs really were recorded by the same bands that put out titles like "Unskinny Bop" and "Hot for Teacher."

But regardless of their message, if you remove the lyrics, you'll be left time and again with catchy, memorable, and powerful music that sticks with you. At least, it does with me. That's why, whatever you call it, I love this music, and it's why I decided to write this book.

It isn't intended to be an encyclopedic history. It's an overview that traces the evolution of pop metal from its origins through its ultimate triumph in the 1980s and beyond. What made pop metal king, and why did its reign come to such an abrupt end in the early 1990s? Those are the questions that led me to write this book. Some bands played more of a role in answering those questions than others, so I'll apologize ahead of time if your favorite artist isn't mentioned or perhaps gets just a few lines. Also: If you're looking for material on bands like Slayer, Anthrax, Metallica, and Megadeth, you won't find it in the pages ahead. No disrespect to any of those bands; they simply don't fall within the scope of this work.

I hope what you're about to read brings back a few good memories or turns you on to some music you may never have heard of. Imagine yourself looking through the racks at the Wherehouse, Tower Records, Licorice Pizza or whatever record store you frequented in your youth, and finding something there that stays with you forever.

That's what this book is about. Enjoy.

PART I:
VERSE
Setting the Stage

STEPHEN H. PROVOST

Welcome to the Jungle

Style vs. Substance

Two things happened in the world of music during October of 1969 that appeared to have nothing at all to do with each other.

On Oct. 11, an infectious bit of pop called "Sugar, Sugar" finished a four-week run at the top of the Billboard singles chart on its way to becoming the year's top-selling single. Eleven days later, on Oct. 22, the album that would close the decade atop the Billboard album chart hit the stores. It, too, spawned a hit single, which rose to No. 4 on the U.S. chart, but no one would have called it "pop."

The songs couldn't have been more different, and neither could the musicians that produced them.

The band behind "Sugar, Sugar" wasn't even really a band at all. It was a group of session players who made music that was "played" by comic-book characters in a Saturday morning cartoon show. The lead singer was a guy named Ron Dante, who you've probably never heard of. His vocals came from the two-dimensional mouth of Archie Andrews, a "teenager" who'd really been born all the way back in 1941 on the pages of *Pep Comics* No. 22.

Archie Andrews had a band that was, predictably, called The Archies. Then again, it's probably no less original than Dokken or Van Halen.

Dante also lent his voice to a No. 9 hit called "Tracy" that same fall, this time with another studio group called The Cuff Links. At least they were three-dimensional.

He wasn't the only singer to make the rounds with different groups of studio musicians that cranked out radio-friendly "bubblegum" hits under various names. Tony Burrows sang lead vocals on top-40 singles with no fewer than *five* different groups, including the U.K. chart-topper "Love Grows (Where My Rosemary Grows)" with Edison Lighthouse and another U.K. top-10 entry, "My Baby Loves Lovin'," with The First Class — within the span of just a few weeks.

Long before Milli Vanilli made a splash with five straight top-5 hits in the late '80 — only to be unmasked as lip-synching front men for the real singers — studio groups were huge. The made-for-TV Monkees, derisively dubbed the Prefab Four, were the best-known and most successful. They didn't write their own songs and didn't play their own instruments when they hit the top of the charts in 1966. That didn't mean they *couldn't*, though. Davy Jones could play drums, but looked better out front, and Peter Tork was a guitarist... who played bass on the show. Gradually, they took a greater hand in songwriting and performing, but by then, their sales had started to wane.

Unlike Milli Vanilli, David Cassidy really *did* sing for another made-for-TV group, The Partridge Family, but he wasn't chosen to play Keith Partridge based on his voice. He'd already signed a contract to appear in the show (where he was supposed to have lip-synched to a studio singer's vocals), when he told the producers he really *was* a musician. So they gave him the chance to audition — and, ultimately, the right to sing in his own voice. But with the exception of Shirley Jones, a Broadway performer who also happened to be Cassidy's stepmom, no one else in the cast actually sang or played on the show or the group's records.

As for the Archies, they had another top-10 hit with "Jingle Jangle" in November of 1969, but never hit the upper reaches of the charts after that.

That was better than the band whose album topped the charts at the end of the year. That first single off its second album — the one that hit No. 4 — was the only one that broke into the top 10. But the band in question, whose guitarist had earned his reputation as a session musician himself in the early '60s, went on to far greater success than you might think. Six of their next seven records would hit No. 1 on the album charts, and the one that *didn't* became one of the 10 bestselling albums *of all time*.

The band, of course, was Led Zeppelin; the guitarist was Jimmy Page; and that No. 4 single was "Whole Lotta Love."

Zeppelin and The Archies would appear to have nothing in common, except that they both emerged in 1969, at the end of The Beatles' reign as the biggest band in the world. But what if you combined the two? What if you created an unholy mashup of bubblegum pop and heavy blues-based rock? What would you get?

You'd probably get something called pop metal.

Gates of Babylon

Labels can be confusing, especially when it comes to music, because they can be subjective. This is especially true for the musical acts covered in this book, which made their mark to varying degrees with their sound and/or their looks.

David Bowie

Some acts were so flamboyant and visually oriented that their music became almost secondary — in some cases, for the bands themselves, but more often for critics and detractors who scorned them as being all style, no substance. Their looks, in effect, overwhelmed their music. Bands like Twisted Sister, Kiss, Sweet, and Poison often fell into this category. Such bands were often dismissed as "glam" or, in the case of various '80s metal bands "hair," the latter term applied retroactively (and, usually, derisively) to bands whose look was defined in part by voluminous, heavily teased mounds of follicular growth.

Other bands focused on the music and didn't want anything to do with what they saw as the pretentiousness of the visually oriented bands. They might have a charismatic lead singer, or a flashy guitarist, but that flash and that charisma involved how they performed and how they carried themselves, not what they wore. Bands like these were often seen, by themselves and music critics, as more credible and less contrived than their makeup-wearing and colorfully clothed contemporaries.

A few acts managed to straddle both worlds: Their musical talent was considered so notable, experimental or artistically significant that it transcended their flamboyant appearance. Elton John was one of them: a musician and songwriter who was so gifted in both respects that he earned praise despite his garish outfits and outsize persona. In fact, his talent validated his looks, transforming gaudy pretense into an iconic, signature style.

David Bowie's theatrical look, meanwhile, was accepted because his Ziggy Stardust character was seen as experimental and cutting-edge — very much like his music. Bowie was the rare musician whose sound and look were both applauded as groundbreaking, independently from one another. This critical assessment endowed him with a unique place in the history of modern music.

Some labels encompassed aspects of an act's look, sound *and* attitude. Punk bands were raw and hard-edged in all three respects. "Grunge" referred to a stripped-down hard-rock sound that incorporated elements of punk, metal and, to a lesser extent, the blues. But it also referred to a fashion statement (or anti-fashion statement): Their ripped jeans and flannel shirts were seen as an understated backlash against the excesses of the "hair" look.

Still, any given act might incorporate one kind of look and another kind of sound.

All hair bands were glam, but not all glam bands were hair.

Poison was glam, hair and metal. Bowie was glam, but neither hair nor metal.

Alice Cooper's look started out as glam in the late 1960s, but morphed into gothic shock rock, while Kiss incorporated elements of both with comic-book overtones. They weren't the Archies, but they did have their own comic books. They even sang a song for a DVD movie in which they co-starred with that sleuthing hound Scooby-Doo, whose original show premiered on TV a year after *The Archie Show* did.

Jellyfish was a power pop band with a look that might have been described as retro-hippie-glam. Badfinger played power pop but wasn't glam; Sweet was glam, at least in the early '70s, and played a combination of power pop and heavy rock.

Metal could be divided into subgenres based on look (glam metal, hair metal) or sound (pop metal, speed metal, symphonic metal, etc.),

These definitions aren't always clear-cut. And with all these labels floating around, there's bound to be debate about what applied to whom.

The Who's guitarist and songwriter, Pete Townshend, actually coined the term "power pop" in 1967 to describe the band's then-current single, "Pictures of Lily," saying simply: "Power pop is what we play." Still, no one would consider hard-rock staples like "Won't Get Fooled Again" or "Who Are You?" to be power pop.

Despite the obvious influence of acclaimed bands like the Beatles, Beach Boys, the Kinks and the Hollies, power pop bands of the '70s and beyond were viewed less favorably than their forbears, often being dismissed as derivative by critics and ignored by record-buyers. Rock historian and commentator Ken Sharp described power pop as being "the Rodney Dangerfield of rock 'n' roll" (referring to the comedian known for his catchphrase, "I don't get no respect!").

Despite their talent, Queen struggled to gain respect from critics, as well. *Rolling Stone*'s Ken Barnes labeled the band's sophomore release "a floundering and sadly unoriginal affair." And the magazine's Bart Testa described the manic album cut "Sheer Heart Attack" off *News of the World* as the product of "warfare among equals in incompetent musicianship."

That was in 1978.

In 2015, the magazine would rank Queen guitarist Brian May as the 26th-best axeman of all time, and four years later, readers of *Guitar World* magazine would peg him as No. 2, behind only Eddie Van Halen and ahead of Jimi Hendrix, Jimmy Page and Stevie Ray Vaughan. Drummer Roger Taylor has made a number of all-time great lists, too. He's the guy who wrote "Sheer Heart Attack," which became a key inspiration for thrash or speed metal.

But Queen was either too glam or too derivative or too pretentious, the critics said. Maybe their real problem, though, was that they didn't fit neatly into any of the genre-boxes rock critics create to pigeonhole bands.

Queen's appearance, during the early to mid-'70s, fit in with — bit didn't epitomize — the glam style. Their long hair made them look androgynous, but with the exception of vocalist Freddie Mercury's eyeliner and the black nail polish on his right hand, they didn't go in much for makeup. Musically, they were impossible to define, incorporating elements of folk music, progressive rock, power pop, opera, funk, dance, vaudeville, and metal.

Cheap Trick's music was also hard to classify. It was clearly influenced by the Beatles and early power pop bands like the Raspberries, but their sound was heavier, beefed up by Rick Nielsen's electric guitar and Bun E. Carlos' thundering drums on tracks like "Just Got Back."

Enuff Z'nuff, which appeared on the scene in the late 1980s, was classified as a hair metal band based on their look, but their sound straddled the line between power pop and metal, with a dash of psychedelia thrown in for good measure,

Def Leppard started out as part of the New Wave of British Heavy Metal (NWOBHM), which included acts such as Judas Priest, Iron Maiden, and Saxon. But Def Leppard gradually refined its sound over its second, third, and fourth albums to emphasize its power pop influences, courtesy of bands like Queen, the Kinks, Sweet and Badfinger.

For purposes of this book, I've used the following definitions:

- *Glam* describes a visual style that can be applied to a broad spectrum of artists across a variety of musical genres. (John Lennon is said to have remarked: "Glam rock is just rock and roll with lipstick on.")
- *Glitter* is basically a synonym for glam, typically applying to acts from the early '70s.
- *Hair metal* refers to an approach that combines pop metal with a glam look, specifically built around big hair; it's typically applied to bands popular in the 1980s.
- *Hard rock* is a style that grew out of the blues via the British Invasion; it shares some characteristics with metal but is less aggressive and less reliant on power chords and blistering guitar solos.
- *Pop metal* features infectious hooks and choruses, leaning on electric guitar and heavy drums.
- *Power pop* grew out of the British Invasion era and is similar to pop metal in construction, but it tends

toward upbeat music and lyrics, while preferring jangling guitars to power chords.

- *Speed metal*, also known as thrash metal, focuses on driving guitar and emphasizes an accelerated beat over melody.
- *Shock rock* is typified by dark, sometimes grotesque stage shows and provocative lyrics, often drawing on satanic or other taboo themes.

These are my own definitions, and others may have slightly different takes. The intention here isn't to start a debate, but to set a framework for the discussion that follows. So, without further ado, in the words of Def Leppard, let's go.

STEPHEN H. PROVOST

1 Wanna Rock

Origins and Influence

The term "heavy metal" has been famously traced back to a lyric in the Steppenwolf hit "Born to be Wild," an ode to bikers written by Mars Bonfire, whose brother Jerry Edmonton was the band's drummer. It was used in the soundtrack to *Easy Rider* — a counterculture film featuring Peter Fonda and Dennis Hopper that centered on a drug-fueled bike trip from L.A. to New Orleans.

Bonfire got the idea for the lyric from a poster he saw on Hollywood Boulevard, which he described as "a picture of a motorcycle erupting out of the earth like a volcano with all this fire around it."

The "heavy metal thunder" in the lyrics was the revving of a motorcycle, not power chords from an electric guitar. And while the song was definitely heavy, Steppenwolf wasn't a metal band per se. No one was in 1968 when the song came out.

Another song by an American band released that year also contained the seeds of heavy metal. "In-a-Gadda-Da-Vida" was the biggest hit from a band that actually had metal in their name: Iron Butterfly. The lyric was supposed to be "In the Garden of Eden," but vocalist and songwriter Doug Ingle was so drunk he slurred the words, and drummer Ron Bushy heard them the way they came out. Somehow, the name stuck.

THEY'RE FROM BIRMINGHAM, ENGLAND.
IT'S A ROUGH TOWN.
THEIR FIRST ALBUM SHOWS IT--
TOUGH, STARK, UNCOMPROMISING ROCK.
AND ALREADY NO. SIX IN ENGLAND.

WS 1871
Black Sabbath is on Warner Bros. records and tapes

The track was the band's only glimpse of the top 30, and they broke up three years later.

By that time, something more sustainable was going on — not in the States, but overseas in Great Britain.

When Steppenwolf and Iron Butterfly were scoring with their landmark singles, two of the three British bands generally credited with giving birth to heavy metal — Black Sabbath and

POP GOES THE METAL

Led Zeppelin — hadn't even released their first albums yet. The third, Deep Purple, was still in its more progressive-psychedelic "Mark I" phase.

Despite being cited as the founders of heavy metal, none of the three bands liked the label. Deep Purple didn't care for it, although keyboardist Jon Lord allowed that the band might be godfathers of heavy metal... but not fathers. Despite their reluctance to claim the term, though, the opening riff from 1972's *Smoke on the Water* remains the archetypal heavy metal riff.

Sabbath bassist Geezer Butler said the Birmingham-based band "didn't like being called heavy metal" at first but "sort of got used to it."

As for Zeppelin, rock historian and media host Eddie Trunk said Zeppelin guitarist Jimmy Page once refused to appear on *That Metal Show* because it had the word "metal" in the title. Page, it seems, wanted nothing to do with the term. He preferred "riff music," which dates back to the electric blues that came out of Chicago in the 1950s.

Regardless of whether Zeppelin, Purple and Sabbath are considered metal or not, there's no doubt that each influenced the development of metal writ large, including melodic metal — where riffs are king. But they were far from the only ones. Almost everyone was influenced, to some extent, by the Beatles, who were as adept as anyone at shifting between pop tunes such as "Ob-La-Di, Ob-La-Da" and "Hello, Goodbye" on the one hand, and heavier rock like "Helter Skelter" (later covered by Mötley Crüe) and "Revolution" on the other.

Their rivals, the Rolling Stones, were also a huge influence, via singles like "Satisfaction" and "Paint It Black." Acts that covered Stones tunes include Guns N' Roses, who tackled "Jumpin' Jack Flash"; Scorpions, who recorded a version of

"Ruby Tuesday"; and Kiss, who covered "2000 Man." Poison and GN'R guitarist Gilby Clarke each covered "Dead Flowers."

Cover Me

The songs that bands choose to cover say a lot about where they came from.

And who inspired them.

A lot of modern groups start out as cover bands, playing bars or local parties, and they naturally perform the songs that motivated them to pick up their instruments in the first place. British Invasion bands were no different. They dipped into the American blues-rock songbook to re-record numbers by Chuck Berry, Bo Diddley and John Lee Hooker.

The Stones covered Howlin' Wolf's "Little Red Rooster," and the Beatles put their own stamp on Berry's "Roll Over Beethoven."

The Moody Blues, true to their name, started out as a blues band: Their first album featured "Bye Bye Bird" by Willie Dixon and Sonny Boy Williamson II. And they weren't the only ones who put the blues in their name. John Mayall & the Bluesbreakers served as an incubator for rock legends like Mick Fleetwood, Jack Bruce, John McVie, and Eric Clapton.

The Yardbirds, who started out as a blues band, produced hall-of-fame guitarists including Clapton, Jeff Beck, and Jimmy Page. When the group broke up in 1968, Page formed the New Yardbirds, who soon changed their name to Led Zeppelin. And Zeppelin itself would dig deep into the American Blues catalog, adapting Willie Dixon's "I Can't Quit You Baby," and Robert Johnson's "Travelling Riverside Blues," among others, to fit their distinctive style. "When the Levee Breaks," the last song on their fourth album, started out as a blues number about the

POP GOES THE METAL

Great Mississippi Flood written by Kansas Joe McCoy and Memphis Minnie way back in 1929.

The Beatles based their sound more on skiffle — a style of folk music based in part on banjos and jug bands — than they did on traditional blues, and that influenced their sound, as well. But like any other garage or club band that starts out playing cover tunes, it wasn't long before they began developing their own style.

They weren't alone.

Other British bands who'd cut their teeth on the blues in the early 1960s evolved, as well. As the decade wore on, they started playing music that was more melodic and experimental than the blues-rock roots from which it sprang. Fleetwood Mac started out as a blues band, but by the time they hit the mid-'70s, they'd become something else entirely. As they themselves would write: "Don't stop thinkin' about tomorrow."

As older styles like the blues and skiffle evolved into something else, it passed from one generation of bands to the next. The Beatles and the Yardbirds and the Stones passed the baton to a new crop of musicians who came after them, and who, in turn, covered *their* material.

So who did the next generation of bands choose to cover?

The list is too long to include here, but many of them are bands that had little in common with blues rockers like John Mayall or the early Stones.

The found their inspiration elsewhere, in British Invasion bands like the Kinks, the Hollies, the Turtles, Herman's Hermits and, of course, the Beatles. And they used that inspiration as the foundation for a new kind of music: power pop.

If you take melodic metal and dial back the guitars, you'll get something that sounds very much like it. Power pop sprang up simultaneously on both sides of the Atlantic, and hit its stride in the 1970s thanks to bands like the Raspberries, Big Star, Mud, Hello and the Arrows.

Perhaps the quintessential power pop song was a 1972 hit called "Go All the Way" by the Raspberries, a Cleveland band fronted by Eric Carmen, who was all of 21 years old when he wrote it for their debut album.

Carmen drew his inspiration from the Beach Boys to write "a bridge for (the) song that really had nothing to do with the verse or chorus," a technique that would later be used to maximum effect by the likes of Def Leppard.

As for the title, Carmen said it was inspired by an example of censorship: The Rolling Stones had planned to play a song called "Let's Spend the Night Together" on *The Ed Sullivan Show* back in 1967, but Sullivan wanted nothing to do with it. It was too suggestive, he said. Either the song had to go, or they did.

The Stones eventually compromised by singing a sanitized version of the lyric that went, "let's spend some time together," and the memory of that stuck with Carmen.

"I knew then that I wanted to write a song with an explicitly sexual lyric that the kids would instantly get but the powers that be couldn't pin me down for," he said.

It may have helped that Carmen sang the lyric in a lazy slur that made it sound, to some ears, like "go-o away" instead of "go all the way." That interpretation didn't make much sense in context, but a lot of people still heard it that way.

It also helped that the clean-cut Raspberries looked nothing like the sleazy, rebellious Stones: The song came out in the early '70s, but the band dressed in matching outfits that were a throwback to mid-'60s bands like Paul Revere and the Raiders or the Sir Douglas Quintet.

"Go All the Way" hit No. 5 on the charts, but it was the

POP GOES THE METAL

Raspberries' only appearance in Billboard's top 10. They would break up three years later, and Carmen go on to score solo hits with melancholy tear-jerkers like "All By Myself" and "Never Gonna Fall in Love Again" — songs that might seem like they have nothing to do with metal.

But listen closer, and you'll hear the germ of something familiar there. Add some electric guitar and a pump up the power a little on "All By Myself," and you've got the makings of the power ballad: a musical mainstay of metal bands in the latter half of the 1980s.

Few bands have covered "Go All the Way" — perhaps because the Raspberries themselves produced such a definitive version that it would have been hard to match. Other power pop bands, however, did produce singles that drew attention from later generations of melodic metal practitioners.

Kiss guitarist Ace Frehley took Hello's 1975 single *New York Groove* to No. 13 on the Billboard Hot 100 three years after the original hit No. 9 in the U.K.

Also in 1975, a band called the Arrows recorded a song by vocalist Alan Merrill and guitarist Jack Hooker, who wrote it in response to the Rolling Stones' "It's Only Rock 'n Roll (But I Like It)." The song failed to chart for the Arrows, but Joan Jett took "I Love Rock 'n' Roll" to No. 1 and kept it there for seven weeks in 1981.

Jett would become a master of the cover song. She has admitted that songwriting doesn't always come easy for her, which is probably why she's covered dozens of songs during her career — usually punching up the volume and cranking up the guitars to create a version that's heavier than the original. Her eclectic catalogue includes selections from Sly and the Family Stone, the Sex Pistols, and even a revved-up version of the theme from Mary Tyler Moore's 1970s TV show. But the list is heavy on glam and power pop, featuring numbers such as David Bowie's "Rebel, Rebel," Twisted Sister's "We're Not Gonna Take It," Sweet's "AC/DC" and several songs from Gary Glitter.

No Matter What

One of the biggest power-pop influencers in the early '70s was a band that started out calling itself the Iveys, a name borrowed from a street in their native Swansea on the coast of Wales.

There's no more tragic rags-to-riches-to-rags story in the annals of music than that of the band that would rename itself Badfinger.

The name change came about because they didn't want to be confused with The Ivy League, a pop trio who'd had a couple of U.K. top-10 hits back in 1965. "Badfinger" might have conjured up images of someone flipping the bird, but it was really based on a Beatles song John Lennon had written on the piano after he'd injured his finger, which he dubbed "Bad Finger Boogie."

The tune doesn't appear on any Beatles albums because *they* renamed *it* a couple of years before the Iveys renamed themselves: The song became "With a Little Help From My Friends," one of the few Lennon-McCartney tunes made more famous by another artist (in this case, Joe Cocker, who took it to No. 1 on the U.K. charts a year after the Beatles recorded it).

Badfinger, too, would take a McCartney song into the top 10 — this time on both sides of the Atlantic. A simple ditty called "Come and Get It" became the first of four singles to hit the Billboard top 20 for the band over the next three years. McCartney also produced two other tracks for them, and all three appeared on the soundtrack for a film titled *The Magic Christian* — which featured fellow Beatle Ringo Starr along with Peter Sellers and future Monty Python troupe members John Cleese and Graham Chapman.

All these Beatles connections made perfect sense because Badfinger was the first band to sign with the Fab Four's newly minted record label, Apple. When "Come and Get It" hit the charts, some fans mistook it for the Beatles themselves, and it's no wonder: Not only did McCartney produce it, he handed the band his own demo of the song with instructions to copy it "down to the letter."

Even those who knew Badfinger wasn't the Beatles were impressed, and the band was immediately anointed heir apparent to the Beatles' pop throne.

That was a lot of pressure, especially for a group whose only hit had been written by someone else. Fortunately, Badfinger had gifted songwriters of its own in Pete Ham, Tom Evans and Joey Molland. Ham and Evans combined bits of two different songs to create the lost-love masterpiece "Without You," which appeared on their third album, *No Dice*. It wasn't a hit. It wasn't even a single. But Harry Nilsson polished it up and made it famous, sending it all the way to the top of the Billboard Hot 100 in 1972, where it stayed for four consecutive weeks.

Like Eric Carmen's plaintiff solo ballads, "Without You" was a power ballad without the metallic sheen of the 1980s, but Nikki Sixx would recognize it for what it was and record a new version with his Sixx:A.M. project in 2016.

Ironically, Badfinger never had a chart-topper of their own, although they hit the upper reaches of the U.S. charts with "No Matter What" (No. 8 in 1970), "Day After Day" (No. 4 in 1971) and "Baby Blue" (No. 14 in 1972).

Creativity was never a problem for the band. It was the

commercial end of things that proved to be their undoing. When Apple Records fell apart after the Beatles' breakup, Badfinger had to go searching for another label. They found one in Warner Bros., which gave them a $3 million contract to crank out six albums over the next three years. But their last record for Apple came out just three months before their first Warner Bros. release, and they wound up competing with each other.

As a result, both flopped.

To make matters (far) worse, the band members never saw that $3 million. Their manager, Stan Polley had supposedly put the money in escrow, but he refused to tell them or the record label what he'd done with it. Despite being rich "on paper," the band members barely had enough money to live on.

It was worse for Pete Ham, who had a wife, a stepson, and an unborn daughter depending on him. He'd been the one who'd believed in Polley the most. But it was fast becoming clear that his trust had been misplaced.

One night, Ham sat down and talked with Tom Evans about their money woes.

"I know a way out," he said.

The next night, on April 24, 1975, a despondent Ham hanged himself, leaving behind a note to his wife and stepson that read: "Anne I love you. Blair I love you. I will not be allowed to love and trust everybody. This is better. Pete." Then, he added a postscript: "Stan Polley is a soulless bastard. I will take him with me."

Without Ham, the band disintegrated just two albums into its six-album deal. A third album, produced by Kenny Kerner and Richie Wise — who also helmed Kiss' self-titled debut — had been recorded but was shelved and didn't see the light of day until 2000.

Evans eventually formed a new version of Badfinger, which

also featured original member Molland, in 1979, but without much success. After signing another bad contract, Evans was hit with a $5 million lawsuit and had a falling out with Molland over royalties from "Without You."

In 1983, Evans went into the garden and, like Ham, hanged himself.

Years later, Polley pleaded no contest to swindling an aeronautics engineer out of $250,000. He died in 2009.

But despite all the death and heartache, the music lived on. Nilsson and Sixx:A.M. weren't the only ones to release versions of "Without You." In fact, it's been covered nearly 200 times, by acts as diverse as Mariah Carey, Johnny Mathis, and Air Supply.

In addition, metal and hard rock acts have recorded at least two other Badfinger hits. Savatage released a version of "Day After Day" in 1986, while "No Matter What" received new treatments from Lillian Axe, Def Leppard and the duo of Tommy Shaw (Styx) and Jack Blades (Night Ranger).

Cum On Feel the Noize

A couple of other British bands had even more influence on modern melodic metal than Badfinger: And one of them did it with just one song.

At least, that's how it appeared on the surface. Slade was actually a huge success in Britain for much of the 1970s. It's just that few people in America had ever heard of them. For all their fame in the U.K. — 17 top-20 singles in the first half of the '70s — Slade had barely cracked the Hot 100 across the pond.

The story was similar for a lot of other British bands.

For one reason or another, things had changed a lot in the course of a decade. After the Beatles ushered in the British

Invasion, American record companies had rushed to sign just about any band that came across the Atlantic from England. The Who, the Stones, the Kinks, and the Animals led the charge, along with the Yardbirds and the Hollies, but dozens of lesser bands like as the Swinging Blue Jeans and Unit 4+2 tagged along for the ride.

The trend also brought copycat U.S. bands out of the woodwork, such as San Francisco's Beau Brummels, who appeared in cartoon form on an episode of *The Flintstones*, and the Sir Douglas Quintet, whose British-sounding name belied the fact that they'd come from Texas, of all places. Then, of course, there were the made-for-TV Monkees: Yes, they were fronted by diminutive Brit Davy Jones, but the other three members were all Americans — including another Texan, Michael Nesmith.

By the 1970s, however, the American appetite for British acts seemed to have all but dried up. In England, Beatlemania gave way in 1971 to T. Rexstasy, a phenomenon surrounding Marc Bolan and his band, T. Rex, that was kickstarted by a performance of "Hot Love" on the popular British music show *Top of the Pops*. The song went to No. 1 and stayed there for six weeks.

"Hot Love" followed a No. 2 showing by Bolan's previous single, "Ride a White Swan," which began an impressive string of eight straight hits that reached No. 1 or No. 2 in Britain. Only one of these, however, made any impact at all in the United States: the infectious "Get It On," which only reached No. 10 and had to endure the added indignity of being retitled "Bang a Gong (Get It On)" here, so it wouldn't be confused with another song by the same title that far fewer people remember.

The lack of a major U.S. breakthrough doubtless explains why T. Rex had to wait until 2020 to join the Cleveland-based

POP GOES THE METAL

Marc Bolan

Rock and Roll Hall of Fame, despite their dominance of the British charts in the early '70s and Bolan's role ushering in the glam rock movement.

But T. Rex wasn't the only British band to find itself all but ignored in America. Status Quo hit No. 12 on the Billboard chart with the psychedelic single "Pictures of Matchstick Men" in 1968, but it was their only American hit. When they changed their style to focus on good-time boogie rock in the '70s, they exploded in Britain, kicking off a string of 22 entries in the

British top 10.

America simply ignored them.

It didn't help that Americans couldn't tune in to *Top of the Pops*, which not only launched T. Rex but featured Status Quo a whopping 106 times — more than any other band.

Slade, a band from Wolverhampton, also benefited from exposure on the show, scoring its first of six U.K. chart-toppers with "Coz I Love You" after an appearance in 1971. The band's biggest hit in its native country was "Merry Xmas Everybody," which sold a million copies two years later. But it's not the Slade song that's most familiar to U.S. listeners. That honor belongs to "Cum on Feel the Noize" (The band intentionally misspelled the names of its songs to promote its rebellious image.) The song was the band's fourth chart-topper at home but, like everything else it had released to that point, it failed to make a dent on this side of the pond.

At least in 1973.

A decade years later, a cover version of the song became a monster hit for a Los Angeles-based band called Quiet Riot, making it all the way up to No. 5 — rarified air for a metal song in the U.S. at that time — and propelling the band's album *Metal Health* to the top of the Billboard charts. It was, in fact, the first LP by a metal band to hit No. 1.

Ironically, Quiet Riot recorded the song over the objections of lead singer Kevin DuBrow, who, according to drummer Frankie Banali, didn't care for Slade and wanted all the songs on the record to be originals. But DuBrow sounded a lot like Slade vocalist Noddy Holder, and the producer, Spencer Proffer, insisted that they give it a go.

The band grudgingly went along, but they were so annoyed at the idea that they didn't even bother to rehearse the song. When they got to the studio, Banali told the engineer to start recording a dry run of the instrumentals, without his bandmates' knowledge. They started playing — with DuBrow sitting in a corner of the studio, making fun of it all — and got part of the arrangement wrong. It wasn't, however, the "train wreck" DuBrow had expected. Just the opposite: Even though it didn't follow the original faithfully, it sounded so good that a reluctant DuBrow ended up adding his vocals, and the song made it onto the album.

Not only that, it was a huge hit. And that hit status prompted the band to record another Slade tune, "Mama Weer All Crazee Now" for its follow-up album. It didn't perform nearly as well, but it still reached No. 51, the last time Quiet Riot would hit the Billboard Hot 100 singles chart. In fact, it meant two of the band's three charting singles were covers of Slade songs.

Slade itself, however, found it almost impossible to break through in the States. The band actually moved to the U.S. full-time in 1975, taking 12 tons of equipment with them, and toured with the likes of Aerosmith and ZZ Top, but they still couldn't connect with their records.

It wasn't until Quiet Riot broke through with its cover of "Noize" that Slade finally found the path to recognition in the U.S. Encouraged by the success of Quiet Riot's cover in 1983, CBS Records signed Slade the following year. The band's 1984 album, *Keep Your Hands Off My Power Supply*, contained their first two charting U.S. singles: "Run Runaway" (No. 20) and "My Oh My" (No. 37).

But they still never came close to matching their homeland success. A third American single, "Little Sheila," managed to claw its way onto the lower reaches of the chart in 1985, but it was the band's last Billboard hurrah. Still, that didn't change the fact that Slade was among the most influential bands when it

Slade

came to defining the shape of pop metal, both with its own recordings and via later covers.

Quiet Riot wasn't the only band to feel their influence. Cheap Trick would cover "When the Lights Go Out" for their 2009 album, *The Latest*. And while Kiss didn't cover any of their songs, the title of their 1975 breakthrough double-disc, *Alive!*, was a tribute to *Slade Alive!* from three years earlier.

Despite all this, though, one of Slade's contemporaries from the early 1970s was just as influential, and better remembered, at least in the United States.

POP GOES THE METAL

Sweet F.A.

The band that may have best epitomized British melodic hard rock to U.S. audiences in the '70s started off calling itself Sweetshop in 1968. But it wasn't long before they shortened the name to The Sweet (and, eventually, just Sweet).

The band was an offshoot of a group called Wainwright's Gentlemen, which found its earliest success by beating out a group called the Detours in a regional battle of the bands at the beginning of 1964. If you've never heard of the Detours, it's understandable; they later changed their name to The Who.

Wainwright's Gentlemen, like other bands such as John Mayall's Bluesbreakers, became a bit of a revolving door for various musicians in the 1960s. Its third incarnation, in 1965, featured future Deep Purple vocalist Ian Gillan and introduced Mick Tucker, later of Sweet, on drums. Gillan left later that year, and another future Sweet member, vocalist Brian Connolly joined in 1966. Then Frank Torpey, who'd been in the band at its inception, rejoined briefly on guitar — only to be ousted after a few gigs.

Connolly and Tucker weren't happy about this, so they quit the band and joined Torpey in a new outfit, along with bassist Steve Priest. But Torpey himself soon left the newly constituted band, which by this time was calling itself The Sweet.

Their first single, the jangly "Slow Motion," was released in 1968 and incorporated elements of sunny pop, psychedelia and a neo-vaudevillian style popular in the mid-'60s. Singer Brian Connolly's slightly quavering voice was somewhat reminiscent of Bobby Goldsboro and the Monkees' Davy Jones.

The song didn't chart, and it was two years before the band recorded an album — well, half an album. Six of their songs appeared on Side One, but the album was named "Gimme Dat

Ding" after a song by the Pipkins, who had six songs on Side Two and featured Tony Burrows from Edison Lighthouse on vocals.

Three of The Sweet's songs were lightweight, silly tunes that were quintessential bubblegum pop. In fact, they were so juvenile that they sounded like something *Sesame Street* residents might enjoy. ("Lollipop Man?" Really?) One of them was even a cover of an Archies song. But the tunes penned by the band itself, especially one called "The Juicer," were far heavier and more complex. Two of these were written by Torpey's replacement, guitarist Mick Stewart, who was only with the band for a year before leaving. But they helped establish a pattern that would continue for the next few years: The band would rely on outside writers to provide lighter, bubblegum-pop tunes as singles, while indulging themselves with self-penned heavy rockers as B-sides and album cuts.

Two important developments occurred for the band in 1970. First off, guitarist Andy Scott replaced Stewart. Prior to joining The Sweet, he'd backed a comedy-musical trio called The Scaffold that included Paul McCartney's brother (stage name Mike McGear). Second, the band recorded a song called "Funny Funny," written by the composing team of Nicky Chinn and Mike Chapman. It was another example of bubblegum pop, with its repetitive title and bouncy melody unapologetically modeled after the Archies' "Sugar, Sugar."

The song didn't chart in the U.S. but hit No. 13 in Britain and made it all the way to No. 1 in four other countries. Chinn and Chapman signed a deal to write more singles for The Sweet, which produced one of the most successful writing-performing partnerships of that or any other era.

Chinn and Chapman worked with other artists, too, whipping up No. 1 U.K. hits for Mud (another band ignored in

POP GOES THE METAL

the U.S.) and Suzi Quatro. Later, as bubblegum pop gradually fell out of style, they adapted by writing U.S. hits such as Exile's chart-topper "Kiss You All Over," Huey Lewis's "Heart and Soul" and Tina Turner's "Better Be Good to Me." They also came up with "Mickey" for choreographer-turned-pop star Toni Basil, a tune with hints of leftover bubblegum that shot to No. 1 with the help of repeated airplay on MTV.

But it was with Sweet that they found their greatest success, creating a template for power pop hits that included the band's U.S. breakthrough, No. 3 "Little Willy" — later covered by Poison — in 1972. Their output also included an impressive string of seven U.K. top-5 hits, four of which reached No. 2 while the siren-driven "Block Buster!" made it all the way to the top. (The title really *is* two words, even though some writers insist on rendering it incorrectly as "Blockbuster," like the defunct video rental store. All you have to do is listen to the lyrics to learn that the song describes an annoying fellow named Buster can't be blocked.)

The Sweet was less successful in the States, where "Block Buster!" only managed to climb as high as No. 73 despite going to No. 1 in seven countries. Still, they managed to nearly duplicate the success of "Little Willy" with "Ballroom Blitz," which hit No. 5 and proved to be the band's most-covered track. Switzerland's Krokus and the Norwegian pop metal band Wig Wam are among more than 30 artists who have recorded versions of the song.

The Sweet backed Chinn-Chapman singles with their own hard-rock compositions on the B-sides, which sounded more like The Who than the Archies. (They even covered The Who's "My Generation" on the U.K. release of *Desolation Boulevard*, although it doesn't appear on the U.S. version of the record.) The band cut ties with Chinn and Chapman around 1975 and released the first single written by the band itself. "Fox on the Run," credited to all four members, was originally produced by Chapman and Chinn as an album cut for *Desolation Boulevard*. But the band reworked it, adding a spacy synth intro and fuller sound before releasing it as a single and including it on the U.S. version of the album.

Their instincts were spot-on.

The band's version of the song hit No. 5 in the U.S. and represented a successful synthesis of Chinn and Chapman's power pop with Sweet's own heavier leanings. The follow-up single, "Action," was an even more seamless blend of the band's two sides, although it didn't climb quite as high on the Billboard chart (No. 20). Together with "Ballroom Blitz," these two songs represented what was possible when pop sensibilities and hard rock worked together.

"We all loved heavy metal bands like Led Zeppelin and Deep Purple," Andy Scott explained in a 1978 interview. "We wanted to try and get some of their sound into our music. The fans who had enjoyed our early records had grown up a little, and they seemed happy to accept our hard rock sound."

Other artists recognized this, too. "Fox on the Run" has been covered by the likes of Girlschool and former Kiss axeman Ace Frehley, while "Action" has been recorded by Def Leppard, Nelson, Rikki Rockett of Poison, and Black 'n Blue (featuring another Kiss guitarist, Tommy Thayer).

Both songs were huge hits in Germany, with "Fox" topping the charts and "Action" checking in at No. 2, which helps explain the most interesting covers of all: musically faithful German-language renditions by a band known as the Hunters. If the singer's voice sounds familiar, it should: It belongs to Klaus Meine, lead singer of Scorpions. The Hunters, it turns out, were really just Scorpions recording under an assumed name.

POP GOES THE METAL

But Sweet, like Kiss after them, never quite reconciled their hard-rock instincts with their appeal to younger fans. The split personality manifested itself during their shows.

This was illustrated in starkly surreal terms during the final show of their 1975 tour. The evening began with news that the supporting act, Back Street Crawler, was a no-show: English guitarist Paul Kossoff — who had formed the band after the breakup of his previous group, Free — had just died.

Rainbow guitarist Ritchie Blackmore helped fill the void by joining Sweet onstage. But the band's finale doubtless horrified parents who'd brought young teens to the show: A lifelike but oversized stage prop shaped like a penis swung down from the ceiling and spewed confetti out over the audience.

Talk about overcompensating for their bubblegum image.

It was mostly downhill from there. After "Action," Sweet had just one more charting single, "Love is Like Oxygen," which retained some elements of their early style — including a heavy guitar riff — but on the whole, mined more ethereal and progressive waters.

Connolly left the band shortly before the next album could be completed. His voice hadn't been the same since he'd been kicked in the throat during a pub fight back in 1974; smoking had only made it worse, and other members of the band said he'd been drinking heavily, too. Connolly denied it, but confessed he did start abusing alcohol after being kicked out of the band. "I was just thinking, 'What they're going to say about me if they see me, they've already said,'" he later recalled.

Connolly got the heave-ho on Sweet's 1978 tour after he showed up so wasted on downers that, according to bassist Steve Priest, he didn't even know where he was. The band had some discussions with Ronnie James Dio, who'd recently left Ritchie Blackmore's Rainbow, about replacing Connolly behind the mic, but ultimately chose to continue as a trio.

Neither Connolly nor Sweet would ever be the same again. Connolly suffered a series of heart attacks, developed the shakes and died of renal failure in 1997 at the age of 51. He looked about 20 years older than that.

Two versions of Sweet continued, one fronted by Scott and the other by Priest; Scott's version of the band produced several new recordings, featuring some strong material, but no hits and scant exposure. Their best recordings were *Sweetlife* in 2002 and an album of covers titled *New York Connection* in 2012.

High Priests of Rhythmic Noise

After looking at the cover of Cheap Trick's second album, *In Color*, you might be forgiven for thinking you were in for a metal album. It showed lead vocalist Robin Zander and bassist Tom Petersson, a couple of prototypical long-haired rockers on motorcycles, staring you down with plenty of attitude. It would be easy to imagine Vince Neil and Nikki Sixx striking a similar pose for the cover of Mötley Crüe's 1989 hit single "Kickstart My Heart."

If you think David Lee Roth created the American template for the blond, long-haired sex symbol of a frontman that took over the planet in the 1980s, think again: Zander got there first. When you looked at the front cover of that album, and you knew what you were getting.

Or did you?

Because when you turned the cover over, you might have said to yourself, "Now *that's* a cheap trick!"

There on the back were two other guys astride two-wheelers, like the guys on the front. But these were *bicycles*, not motorbikes. And the guys riding them looked like anything but rock stars. The one on the left might have been a refugee from a tedious 9-to-5 desk job on his way out for drinks after work: He wore glasses, a loosened tie, and a short-sleeved dress shirt, had a moustache and a slightly receding hairline, and a cigarette dangled from his mouth. Oh yeah, and he looked a few pounds overweight.

Definite nerd.

If possible, the guy on the right looked like even more of a dork in his too-small half-buttoned sweater, Chicago Cubs baseball cap and... was that a bowtie? His wide-eyed expression was the kind of look an alien stoner might use if he wanted to hypnotize you into taking him to your leader.

The front of the album was, as advertised, "in color," while the back was in black and white. (In case there was any doubt about this, it even said so.)

Perhaps no album cover in history managed to capture the intersection of power pop and heavy metal so perfectly. It's that weird, elusive nexus where it's possible to be cool and nerdy at the same time. Somehow, Cheap Trick pulled it off, not just on *In Color*, but on album after album. This was thanks in no small measure to the guy in the baseball cap, Rick Nielsen, who was the guitarist and main songwriter.

Nielsen, Petersson, and drummer Brad M. Carlson (the guy with the glasses and the receding hairline, who went by the stage name Bun E. Carlos) originally got together in a band called Fuse. They cut an album in 1970 before changing their name to Sick Man of Europe — later the title of a Cheap Trick song — and, after recruiting Zander, to Cheap Trick.

Cheap Trick was always in its own category, somewhere between power pop and metal, but that didn't stop people from trying to describe them. *Rolling Stone* called them "humorous, hook-filled, bracingly loud, and subtly sensitive," a band that played "Beatlesque melodies with the might of Kiss or (Ted) Nugent." A radio DJ once said they were a cross between ELO and Kiss, which was an apt description: Cheap Trick not only toured with Kiss, they famously name-checked the band in the lyrics to their seminal hit "Surrender." On the same album (*Heaven Tonight,* their third), they covered "California Man," a song by The Move, which featured Jeff Lynne before he went on to form ELO. And they would cover another Move track, "Brontosaurus," two decades later.

Cheap Trick, like a number of other acts, found their first big success in Japan, which had a history of treating even little-known bands like conquering heroes. The all-girl Runaways never made it beyond cult status in the U.S., but they were Japan's fourth-most-popular band in 1977 (the Beatles and Led Zeppelin still outranked them).

Cheap Trick booked some concerts there in April of 1978 and didn't even fly first class on their way in. When they got there, though, something like 5,000 people were waiting at the airport. Nielsen figured the crowd was there to greet some visiting dignitaries, but he found out otherwise when they started screaming as the band got off the plane. It was like Beatlemania all over again, with girls in taxis chasing them at 70 mph and another mob of fans waiting for them at their hotel.

They recorded a concert album as a thank-you to their fans in Japan, and it was released there in early October. Epic Records waited four months before apparently deciding they were on to something and shipping the album to U.S. record stores, too. *Cheap Trick at Budokan*, named for the Tokyo arena where it was recorded, proved to be a massive hit, going triple-platinum. Its sales even topped Kiss' *Alive*.

Not bad for some nerdy kids from Rockford, Ill.

POP GOES THE METAL

Fallen Angels

Another, far less famous band to straddle the line between metal and power pop was Starz, a near-supergroup which, for some reason, never managed to make it big despite a killer logo and a knack for writing hard but catchy tunes.

The band would never be as well known as its predecessor, Looking Glass, which had scored a No. 1 hit with "Brandy (You're a Fine Girl)" in 1972. But the pop sensibilities they'd shown in that song would translate into a new, harder-rocking context.

With the exception of a modest hit called "Jimmy Loves Mary-Anne," which made it to No. 33 in 1973, Looking Glass hadn't found much success post-"Brandy." They replaced their singer, then changed their name to Fallen Angels and caught the attention of Bill Aucoin, who would soon help put Kiss on the musical map. Then they added Richie Ranno as a second guitarist in '75 before changing their name yet again — to Starz.

The name was the brainchild of Sean Delaney, a musician and songwriter who was, like Aucoin, part of the Kiss team: He would go on to co-write songs with all four members that band, including three on their *Rock and Roll Over* album the following year. Delaney pointed out that the name Fallen Angels might invite confusion with Kiss' Casablanca labelmates, Angel, so he pitched "Starz" as an alternative.

According to Ranno, the band wasn't thrilled with the idea. But when they saw the sketch for their proposed new logo by artist Michael Doret (who designed the covers for Kiss' *Rock and Roll Over* and *Sonic Boom* albums), they loved it and decided to go with it.

Ranno had been in a band called Stories, which topped the charts with a hit of their own called "Brother Louie" in the summer of '73. Not many bands start off with *two* No. 1 singles in their back pocket before they even cut their first record. But Starz did.

They also had a top-flight lead singer in Michael Lee Smith, who had a name that sounded like David Lee Roth (before anyone knew who Roth was), and a look that channeled John Bon Jovi (before anyone knew who he was, either) and Steven Tyler. Ranno would call him "quite possibly the best frontman in rock 'n' roll history."

Drummer Jeff Grob adopted the stage name Joe X. Dubé and wore a Van Dyke moustache that made him look like one of the Three Musketeers. Guitarist Brendan Harkin and bassist Pete Sweval rounded out the lineup.

Starz got plenty of exposure on tour, supporting the likes of Kiss, Aerosmith, and Ted Nugent. But like Cheap Trick, the band didn't fit neatly into any category, so it was a challenge to market them: Dubé would describe them as a hard-rock version of Supertramp, and their style sounded a little like Kiss-meets-Montrose. Ranno, in fact, was a fan of Kiss' debut album, and would go on to play on Gene Simmons' 1978 solo release.

The band played radio-ready hard rock that, somehow, didn't make it on the radio much. Their record company, Capitol, dealt mostly with pop acts and didn't know what to do with them; Aucoin, meanwhile, got distracted when Kiss turned into the biggest act in America and had little time for Starz after that.

The first Starz album, released in 1976, was packed with riffs and power chords, and their '77 follow-up, *Violation*, was a loose concept album about a future when rock music is banned. The album's hero is a kid who finds an old 45 of Aerosmith's "Walk This Way" in a thrift store and defies the ban. For his trouble, he's locked away in an institution called S.T.E.A.D.Y.

POP GOES THE METAL

— an acronym for Steps Toward Eventual Acceptance of a Disciplined Youth. When he finally gets out, he can't tell the difference between a streetlight and the moon.

The album's opening cut, "Cherry Baby," turned out to be the band's biggest hit, even though it only got to No. 33.

The album fared even worse, stalling out at No. 89.

Starz released not one but two albums in '78, turning down the guitars on the more power-pop *Attention Shoppers* before reverting to form with *Coliseum Rock*. The latter album made a minor impact on AOR radio with "So Young, So Bad" and "Last Night I Wrote a Letter." But neither those songs nor the album went anywhere on the charts, and the band refused to stick with Capitol after that. Unfortunately, acts like the Cars and the Clash were all the rage, and no other label wanted them. Punk and New Wave were in. Hard rock was out.

"You could almost count those bands on one hand," Ranno said. "They were Aerosmith, Kiss, Queen, Ted Nugent, Starz, and Angel. We kept the flame alive between the original hard rock groups and heavy metal today."

Starz disbanded after *Coliseum Rock*, but the likes of Jon Bon Jovi, Tom Kiefer of Cinderella, Nikki Sixx of Mötley Crüe, and even Lars Ulrich of Metallica would cite them as a major influence in the years ahead.

The band's website quoted Bon Jovi as saying, "Whatever your dreams may be, always shoot for the Starz!"

STEPHEN H. PROVOST

Dude Looks Like a Lady

Glam and Glitter

"Before the Riot was Quiet, the metal was glitter."

So proclaimed a headline in the October 1985 edition of *Creem* magazine's *Metal Rock 'n' Roll*.

That said it all.

Sweet weren't just pioneers in the sound that would shape melodic metal, they were trailblazers in establishing the look that would dominate much of the 1980s. Their long, flowing hair, eyeshadow and the sparkling glitter on their faces were all flamboyant, to say the least. In one photo from 1972, Steve Priest appears wearing bright red lipstick, with a black heart on his cheek and black face paint descending in spikes from both of his eyes.

Did Gene Simmons of Kiss see that photo and use it as inspiration for an early incarnation of his "demon" makeup? Who knows? Alice Cooper was doing the same thing. But regardless, the trend was clear.

Androgyny was in.

Bowie's Ziggy Stardust was doing it. So were the New York Dolls, and, during their earliest period, Kiss. It was all lumped together as "glam rock," but the sounds couldn't have been more different. Bowie and Roxy Music were more experimental, and the Roxy's sound quickly became lush and

New York Dolls

minimalist. The Dolls were proto-punk Stones clones in drag. Slade's pub rock sounded like soccer stadium chants set to heavy music. Sweet was a bubblegum singles act with hard-rock sensibilities that were constrained by packaging and marketing. T. Rex had started it all, and Kiss was, well, Kiss.

"Glam rock" is, in the end, a label that has everything to do with fashion and almost nothing to do with musical genres — even now. Adam Lambert calls himself glam and dresses the part. But his solo recordings are contemporary dance-pop, and his tours fronting the post-Freddie Mercury version of Queen offer a smorgasbord of rock styles. Either way, he's glam. It has zero to do with the music.

Mercury was glam, too, at least in the beginning. When one

DJ introduced "Killer Queen" to L.A. radio audiences back in the day, he didn't comment on Freddie's voice or the music; he zeroed in on the fact that he wore black fingernail polish. (You can see it clearly on the cover of *Sheer Heart Attack*.)

Queen's music was so diverse that it would be impossible to label the band's entire catalog as glam. Or anything else.

But there was a time during the 1980s when glam came to be associated almost exclusively with pop metal, and Sweet provided the template. Anyone who looks at Sweet circa 1972 and Poison circa 1986 can't help but notice the similarities. Yes, Sweet wore their hair long and flowing, while Poison teased theirs up as high as it could go. But the overall look was the same: Androgynous bordering on (and sometimes crossing over into) feminine.

Rock and Roll Part 2

The glam sensibility started in Britain with Marc Bolan, who had founded a psychedelic folk group called Tyrannosaurus Rex in 1967. A couple of years later, he punched up the sound and shortened the act's name to T. Rex. He began wearing flamboyant outfits and applying dark eyeliner. He put glitter on his face and donned a top hat on stage (a fashion statement later employed by Noddy Holder of Slade and Slash of Guns N' Roses). The look became known as "glam," and because Bolan was the first to do it, the music did, too.

But it's actually hard to categorize Bolan's music at all. His song structures were normally pretty simple. Sometimes the sound was heavy, and sometimes it wasn't, but his voice was light and airy. The closest he probably came to proto-pop metal was "Get It On" and "20th Century Boy," which was later covered by Def Leppard.

He did put out a song called "Metal Guru," but it wasn't metal in any sense of the word. Another song title might be more apt in describing his style: "Electric Boogie."

But acts didn't have to play that kind of music, or any other specifically, to be classified as glam. The common threads (pun intended) were in the clothes and the makeup. Even those, however, were diverse. The point of glam was to emphasize individuality, then take it to an outrageous extreme. Artists wanted to stand out — not just from more mundane acts, but from one another.

Bowie probably stood out more than anyone else. Riding on Bolan's coattails, he dyed his hair red and cut it in a style similar to tennis player Billie Jean King's. His pale makeup, accentuated with light rouge on his cheeks, made him like a mime or a kabuki performer. Or an alien, which his Ziggy Stardust character was intended to be.

Freddie Mercury showcased a variety of flashy outfits, from a jumpsuit fashioned entirely of silver sequins to a yellow leather vest. Sometimes he wore a royal crown, sometimes he wore fur, and sometimes he wore feathers.

"I have fun with my clothes on stage," he told *Circus* magazine in 1977. "It's not a concert your watching, it's a fashion show."

That was Sweet's attitude, too. Their first shirts were made of curtains, but by 1974, band members had enlisted a designer to custom-tailor the outfits they wore on stage. Each cost somewhere between about $160 and $230 and was worn just once. Some were more outrageous than others: In one TV appearance, Steve Priest wore a Nazi outfit with a spiked helmet and a painted-on Hitleresque mustache.

The idea was to attract attention. In a 1974 documentary, the narrator explained: "The Sweet have often come in for a lot of criticism about their stage clothes, but they've always been deliberately outrageous. They set out to shock. It's part of their plan, part of their image."

One of the band members elaborated: "Everybody thought we were queer, and so I thought, let's go to extremes."

They weren't alone.

Queen's very name suggested that its members might be gay, even though only Mercury was — and he didn't explicitly claim to be. The idea wasn't to admit to anything, but to tease fans with different possibilities and keep them guessing. That kept them interested.

Bowie was a master of this cat-and-mouse game with fans. In 1972, he proclaimed, "I'm gay and always have been, even when I was (known as) David Jones." Then, in 1974, he said he was bisexual, and, in the '80s, said he'd been a "closet heterosexual" the whole time. Appropriately, he wed a fashion model in 1992. Also appropriately, she went by the name Iman.

Bowie was ever the chameleon, always interested in exploring new personas and creating new characters, so he moved on from Ziggy after a couple of years to become the Thin White Duke, shedding the glam label in the process.

If Bowie kept people talking about his sexuality the same could be said for Elton John, who wore some of the most flamboyant clothes of all. His array of outfits, including the sequined baseball uniform he donned for a concert at Dodger Stadium, were — and remained — a major part of his image, along with his many pairs of outrageous and oversized eyeglasses.

Elton celebrated the glam movement in his No. 1 hit "Bennie and the Jets," the story of a fictional band whose lead singer wears "electric boots" and "a mohair suit." Sexual ambiguity makes its way into the song, as well: Although the singer is referred to as "she" in the lyrics, her name is more typically male. Adding to the air of mystery, it's even spelled "Bennie" on some versions of the album and single, and "Benny" on others.

John himself is openly gay and happily married to a man named David Furnish, with whom he's been in a relationship for nearly three decades. But his public sexuality wasn't always so clear-cut. He declared himself bisexual in a famous *Rolling Stone* interview in 1976, but he was engaged to one woman in the 1960s and married to another for four years in the 1980s.

John was the world's best-selling artist in the early '70s, racking up six straight No. 1 albums, all of which went platinum or better, and a series of chart-topping singles that would extend all the way into the 1990s. But despite his wild outfits, which he continued to wear long after most "glam" acts had abandoned theirs, John isn't often considered to have been at the heart of the glam movement.

The reason isn't entirely clear. Is it because his music was just too critically acclaimed to be mentioned in the same breath with bands like Sweet that grew out of the bubblegum craze? Of course, others once associated with glam, such as Bowie and Queen, also achieved a high level of acclaim. Is it because he played a more "serious" instrument, the piano? But then, there's always Liberace, too, who wasn't a rocker but was about as glam as you could get. So, in the end, it's hard to say.

Other British acts labeled as glam or glitter had an impact, as well, even though they never made it big on this side of the Atlantic.

Gary Glitter's "Rock and Roll Part 2" hit No. 7 on the U.S. charts and entrenched itself in popular culture as an anthem that's played at high school and college athletic events even today. Beyond that, it served as the basis for a 1988 No. 1 hit on

Suzi Quatro

the British charts called "Doctorin' the Tardis." Created by a group called the Timelords, an alter ego for techno-rockers KLF, it also sampled Sweet's "Block Buster!" And Sammy Hagar's "Mas Tequila" owes something to the song, as well.

"Rock and Roll Part 2" has certainly outlasted Glitter's own fame, which faded long before he was convicted repeatedly in child porn and child sex cases. In 2015, he was sentenced to 16 years in prison for, among other charges, having sex with a girl younger than 13.

Stumblin' In

Suzi Quatro, meanwhile, rode the Chinn-Chapman train of hits to stardom, becoming the first female bass player to hit it big with nine U.K. top-20 hits in the 1970s, including seven in

1973 and '74 alone. Oddly enough, though, she wasn't British: Quatro was born in Detroit, but moved to England in 1971 at the suggestion of Mickie Most, who had produced hit singles for Donovan, the Animals and Herman's Hermits.

Quatro reached the top of the U.K. charts twice with Chinn-Chapman compositions: in 1973 with "48 Crash" and again the following year with "Devil Gate Drive," but like other British success stories, she failed to make much of a dent in the States. Her only top-40 single here was a duet with Chris Norman of Smokie on another Chinn-Chapman offering, "Stumblin' In," which reached No. 4 in 1978.

While male artists like Bowie and Sweet were exploring onstage androgyny from the masculine side, Quatro crafted her image from the opposite direction. She was an Elvis Presley fan, so when Most asked her what she wanted to wear for her first photo shoot, she told him: "Leather." He tried to talk her out of it, but when he couldn't, he suggested that she wear a leather jumpsuit. It became part of her tough-girl image, which wasn't just an act.

"I don't look at gender," she said in a 2012 interview. "I never have. It doesn't occur to me if a 6-foot-tall guy has pissed me off not to square up to him. That's just the way I am."

The leather-clad Quatro caught the eye of Garry Marshall, producer of the hit ABC comedy *Happy Days*, when he saw her in a poster on his daughter's bedroom wall. The show mined the same appetite for '50s-era nostalgia that had made *Grease* a Broadway sensation and George Lucas' *American Graffiti* a hit in theaters. Musically speaking, wistful memories of the sock-hop-and-malt-shop era had inspired bands like New York doo-wop revival group Sha Na Na, along with British rock acts like Mud and Roy Wood's uber-glam project, Wizzard, to revisit that era's sound.

POP GOES THE METAL

Happy Days topped the Nielsen TV ratings in the mid-'70s thanks in large part to the emergence of leather-clad tough guy Arthur Fonzarelli — aka "Fonzie" — played by Henry Winkler. Originally a minor supporting character, Fonzie was so popular with viewers that Winkler became the virtual star of the show.

So, Marshall thought, why not have a leather-clad *female* character, too? The poster of Quatro got his wheels spinning, and he contacted her about playing a new character in the show: the aptly named Leather Tuscadero, younger sister of Fonzie's girlfriend.

Quatro wound up appearing in several episodes of the series over a three-year period, portraying (naturally) a bass player in a band who wore leather on stage, just like her real-life alter ego. Marshall's instinct had been right on the money: Quatro got more fan mail than any other cast member except for Winkler, and Marshall even offered her a spinoff show of her own. She declined, fearful of being typecast: "It was enough. Time to move on."

Quatro's take-no-prisoners attitude would inspire another leather-clad rocker who went on to make an even bigger name for herself: Joan Larkin, an aspiring teenage guitarist who began pursuing music in earnest around the same time Quatro was hitting the charts in Britain.

Larkin had moved from Philadelphia to Southern California with her parents at the age of 12, and got her first guitar a year later.

She enrolled in a guitar class, saying she wanted to learn rock 'n' roll, but dropped out after the instructor tried to teach her "On Top of Old Smokey" instead. Her parents had told her she could be anything she wanted to be, and she'd taken it to heart: She wanted to play rock music.

"Tell me I can't do something," she would later say, "and

you'll make sure I'm gonna be doing it."

Determined to learn on her own, Larkin retreated to her room and taught herself to play chords while listening to Zeppelin and T. Rex.

"I'd been screwing around with the guitar, and I think the fact that I was able to hear people like Suzi Quatro having success playing rock 'n' roll made me think, 'Well, if she's doing it, why can't I?' " she said in a 2007 interview with *The Guardian*.

She'd heard some of Quatro's music while hanging out at a nightclub called Rodney Bingenheimer's English Disco on the Sunset Strip in West Hollywood. It wasn't your typical American nightclub. They didn't play the kind of music you heard on the radio; they showcased acts like Sweet, Bowie, and Alvin Stardust.

Larkin had read about the place in a music magazine when she was still in Philadelphia and, when her family moved west, she decided to check it out for herself. She'd also heard Gary Glitter's "Rock and Roll Part 2" on the radio.

Obviously, that wasn't Glitter's real name. Born Paul Francis Gadd, he tried out a variety of stage names, including Paul Russell and Paul Raven. Then, when the glam craze took hold, he opted for Gary Glitter after considering various other alliterative options such as Terry Tinsel and the androgynous if repulsive Vicky Vomit.

The idea struck Larkin as a good one, so after her parents divorced, she adopted an alliterative name of her own.

Joan Jett.

She loved the campy style of the movie "Cabaret," and Bowie was another influence. She cut her hair short to match his style, and her sexuality would ultimately become the object of public curiosity, just as it was for him.

POP GOES THE METAL

As with Bowie tunes like "Queen Bitch," the lyrics to some of Jett's songs would invite listeners to speculate: She cowrote "Everyone Knows," an in-your-face rebuke of gawkers and relationship critics, in 2004, the same year she covered a tune called "Androgynous" by the Replacements. Two years later, she recorded a cover of Sweet's rollicking tribute to bisexuality, "AC/DC." But she didn't come out and announce her sexual orientation or address it directly in an interview, saying she preferred to let her music do the talking and keep her private life private.

Cherry Bomb

The seeds for Jett's distinctive public persona and musical style were sewn at Rodney's on the Sunset Strip, a stretch of road that would become the epicenter of the 1980s hair metal movement a few years later.

Bingenheimer, a DJ and former Mercury Records publicist known as the "Mayor of the Sunset Strip," opened the club in late 1972, and operated it until 1975, during the height of the glitter trend. His club attracted big names ranging from Led Zeppelin to Iggy Pop to Shaun Cassidy (who was in a band called Longfellow then, before following in the footsteps of half-brother David and hitting it big as a teen idol). Elvis even showed up one night, and Bingenheimer played Suzi Quatro's version of "All Shook Up" for him.

It was also a hangout for teenage girls, including Mackenzie Phillips, daughter of John Phillips from The Mamas & the Papas, who appeared in *American Graffiti* and, from 1975 to 1980, in the sitcom *One Day at a Time*. (Her younger sister on the show was played by Valerie Bertinelli, who would later marry the guitarist in a band that got its first break at another

Sunset Strip club — Gazzarri's — in '75. The guitarist, of course, was Eddie Van Halen.)

Other girls who showed up at Rodney's included Kari Krome and Cherie Currie, both of whom would play a role in Jett's future.

In an essay years later, Krome would describe her first visit to the club, at age 12, with a guy with orange rooster hair, green glitter eye shadow and nail polish to match. His look turned plenty of heads, but according to Krome, he wasn't alone: "Some of the dudes were more made up than any woman I'd ever seen."

Inside, a long, wooden bar ran the length of the place, and the walls were covered with posters of English glam rockers. A poster of a Suzi Quatro album cover caught Krome's attention: It showed Quatro surrounded by three guys in tank tops, one of them chugging a bottle of beer, a look on her face that said, "Bring it on." Her pose and attitude made an impression on Krome, as it did on Jett. (Coincidentally, Bingenheimer recalled that Jett once *stole* a poster of Quatro from the club; it's not clear whether it was the same poster.)

For Krome, Rodney's was a revelation, like being on a different planet, filled with guys who looked like girls and girls who looked like guys. "The minute I entered," she recalled, "I heard this strange music I had never experienced before, saw the fabulous creatures gliding about, (and) my life was forever changed."

One of the creatures who hung out at Rodney's was Kim Fowley, a record producer, singer and songwriter who'd had an up-and-down career working with and promoting a variety of acts. Sometimes successfully, sometimes not so much.

Fowley glammed himself up like a wannabe Bowie — although, at 6-foot-5, he looked more like Lurch with makeup

— and he'd made several albums of his own, all of them flops. But he'd also worked with some big names, like Frank Zappa and Alice Cooper.

Fowley had first made his mark by producing novelty tunes like "Alley Oop," a No. 1 hit for a band called the Hollywood Argyles — which wasn't really a band at all: They were just a collection of musicians brought together by Fowley and fellow producer Gary Paxton for the occasion. Sure, it was a gimmick, but it sold, and that's what mattered to Fowley.

Looking for gimmicks that would sell and creating bands from scratch: That's just what he did. He once reportedly asked Bob Dylan what *his* gimmick was.

Shortly after he met Krome, Fowley was called upon to contribute some songwriting for *Destroyer*, the signature album by the best-selling gimmick band in history: Kiss. In response, he co-wrote a rock star's pouty, almost plaintive groupie serenade: "Do You Love Me?" On an album of great material, it more than held its own. He also contributed a song called "King of the Night Time World," which he'd penned for a band called the Hollywood Stars a couple of years earlier.

Alice Cooper, maybe the *second*-best-selling gimmick rock act of all time, recorded another song Fowley had written for the Stars, "Escape," on his blockbuster debut as a solo artist, *Welcome to My Nightmare*. With the line "Just put on my makeup and get me to the show," it was perfect for Cooper — as it would have been for Kiss. But the Hollywood Stars did it first.

The Stars had been another of Fowley's manufactured gimmick groups, although they actually did play live. Fowley envisioned them as L.A.'s answer to the New York Dolls and got them several gigs at the Whisky a Go Go and Troubadour in West Hollywood. They got so far as signing with Columbia

Records, but management changed at the company, and the record was shelved. (Although a new lineup issued an album four years later, that would be the sum total of their output until the unreleased record finally saw the light of day in 2013.)

With the Stars comatose in 1975, Fowley hit on another idea. Who actually thought of it first depends on who you talk to. Fowley insisted the idea of starting an all-girl group was his, and that the band members were just "guests in my concept," but Jett already had the same concept in her mind. Krome, meanwhile, had met Fowley at a birthday party for Alice Cooper; she'd signed a contract to write songs for him on her own 14th birthday.

At some point after that, Jett met Krome at Rodney's and suggested forming an all-girl band; Krome, however, said she was a songwriter, not a musician, and referred her to Fowley. Then, that summer, Fowley ran into a 16-year-old drummer named Sandy West in the parking lot of another Sunset Strip gathering spot, the Rainbow Bar & Grill. West, who had already played with guys in various bands, introduced herself, and Fowley called the next day to give her Jett's number. The two teens got together and jammed, and the first two pieces of the band that would become the Runaways were in place.

The group added singer/bassist Micki Steele, but she soon quit and was replaced on bass by Jackie Fox and on vocals by Cherie Currie — who became the face of the group, and the only member to appear on the cover of their debut album. Lita Ford rounded out the group as the lead guitarist, with Jett switching to rhythm guitar.

According to the documentary *Edgeplay: A Film About the Runways*, each of the five classic lineup members based her persona on a different rock star: Currie patterned herself after Bowie; Jett's choice (of course) was Quatro; Fox modeled

POP GOES THE METAL

herself on Gene Simmons of Kiss; West chose Queen drummer Roger Taylor; and Ford was a mix of Jeff Beck and original Deep Purple axeman Ritchie Blackmore.

The Runaways released their self-titled debut album in 1976, with Bingenheimer providing the orchestration, and followed it up with two more studio albums in 1977 and their final record in '78. Their debut single, "Cherry Bomb," became their signature song and topped the charts in Japan, but couldn't crack Billboard's top 100 in the U.S. In fact, none of their singles did.

Even if they didn't sell a lot of records here, they quickly became a huge cultural phenomenon. In the winter of '77, *Creem* magazine ran a piece titled "California is Quaking" with the subtitle "Runaways, Weirdos and Screamers on the Strip." What they didn't know is that, a decade later, there would be a whole lot more weirdos and screamers on Sunset Boulevard and the surrounding environs.

The Runaways, however, would be ancient history by then. The band broke up after four studio albums, the last two of which were made without Currie and Fox, with Jett handling lead vocals. Vicki Blue replaced Fox on bass, then left after a single album. At the end, the band fell apart due to what Ford called musical differences, with Jett, Ford, and West going their separate ways.

"The Runaways," she said, "had been through hell."

At least some of that hell can be attributed to Fowley, who stoked internal divisions by pitting the band members against one another, seemingly for his own amusement. In recruiting Fox, he declared it would be a "battle" between her and West as to who would lead the band (in the end, neither one did). There were accusations of financial improprieties, too, with West later declaring: "I owe him my introduction to the music business,

ROCK & ROLL JUST HAD A MINOR REVOLUTION

Lita, Joan, Jackie, Sandy and Cherie are high-school minors. Together they form a rock 'n roll band called the Runaways. They sing good. They play good. They compose good. But what they do best of all is communicate what it's like to be a teen-ager.

THE RUNAWAYS

If you're in your teen years (or can remember what your head was like then), you'll relate to their message. Because it's all happening to them right now.

Mercury SRM-1-1090 8-Track MC8-1-1090
Musicassette MCR4-1-1090

mercury

products of phonogram, inc., one IBM plaza, chicago, ill. a polygram company

but he's also the reason I'm broke now."

Fowley made things worse by promoting the band as sex objects rather than musicians, to the point that Jett later said, "everyone thought we were sluts." The band was certainly a hot topic among sex-crazed high school boys in the San Fernando Valley around 1977. And it was no surprise that fans came to their concerts, according to Jett "expecting to see some sort of sex show."

Keep in mind, these were 15- and 16-year-old girls.

But Fowley didn't care, and even exploited their youth, claiming he'd envisioned the band as what he called "jailbait rock" from the outset. If there was any doubt, the cover to their second album, *Queens of Noise*, featured the band members standing in a cloud of smoke that rose to their waists, each of them holding what looked like a stripper's pole. The cover's reddish hue evoked images of hell's forbidden fruit and the archetypal red-light district, both in one.

Perhaps none of this should be too surprising, considering the band was birthed on the Sunset Strip, which had a reputation for debauchery that preceded them and would be cemented further when it became ground zero for the sex-saturated hair metal scene in the 1980s. But it was even worse than that. Shortly after Fowley's death in 2015, Fox — a straight-A student who had aced the SAT but quit school to join the band — disclosed that she had been drugged with Quaaludes and raped by Fowley at a New Year's Eve party in 1975.

Krome said he sexually assaulted her, as well, on several occasions.

"He could be really scary," she said.

In various interviews, different band members have described Fowley as heavy-handed and verbally abusive. He threatened to kick them out of the band if they didn't go along with his demands, claimed credit for their success and mocked their supposed lack of talent.

"I am a con artist who wanted to pull the ultimate scam," he said in 1976.

But if he thought the Runaways being a scam, he was wrong: There was plenty of talent there.

After the band split up, Cherie Currie went into acting, landing a part in the major motion picture *Foxes* alongside Jodie Foster and Scott Baio.

Founding member Micki Steele went on to join the Bangles, another all-girl group that became more successful than the Runaways had ever been. In 1986, they scored with the No. 2 single "Manic Monday," followed by the chart-topping "Walk Like an Egyptian." The Bangles thrived on the kind of catchy pop-rock that had powered bands like Badfinger and Sweet. Steele even sang lead on a cover of "September Gurls" by Big Star, one of godfathers of power pop.

(Later, Bangles singer Susanna Hoffs would team up with Matthew Sweet on a series of cover songs, becoming one of the few artists to record the Raspberries' "Go All the Way" and also revisiting another Big Star tune, "Back of My Car.")

Lita Ford, meanwhile, went on to become the first lady of metal in the '80s, charting at No. 12 with a catchy piece of pop metal called "Kiss Me Deadly" in 1988 and reaching No. 8 with "Close My Eyes Forever" — a duet with Ozzy Osbourne — the following year.

But the most successful Runaway turned out to be Jett. After the band split up, she went on to huge success as a solo artist, recording the blockbuster No. 1 hit "I Love Rock and Roll" and following that up with eight other top-40 singles.

She was inducted into the Rock and Roll Hall of Fame in 2015.

Shock Me

Larger Than Life

The glam vibe was a natural outgrowth of flower power and the free-spirited attitude of the late '60s. Before the likes of Sweet and Bowie got glammed up on stage, squares and old fogeys were complaining that they couldn't tell whether "longhairs" were guys or girls — at least from the back. (Check out the cover of Alice Cooper's second album, *Easy Action*, for an example.)

If clueless parents and uptight preachers were determined to judge them anyway, the thinking went, why not give them something to *really* talk about?

Alice Cooper did just that, but went even further, juxtaposing the appearance of innocence against a deeper, more sinister reality. The name "Alice Cooper" itself was "a spit in the face of society," lead singer Vincent Furnier explained to *Rolling Stone*. According to Furnier, it "conjured up an image of a little girl with a lollipop in one hand and a butcher knife in the other."

"There was something axe-murderish about Alice Cooper," he said. "It reminded me of Lizzy Borden."

An '80s-era melodic metal band from New Orleans would use a similar rationale in adopting the moniker Lillian Axe:

Guitarist and horror fan Steve Blaze was inspired by a scene from the Stephen King movie *Creepshow*, which showed a skeleton in a bridesmaid's dress floating in a window. Blaze came up with the name Lillian as a "creepy old lady name" and added the word axe to create a Lizzy Borden feel. (Speaking of Lizzy Borden, there was metal band with that name, too.)

But back to Alice Cooper, a name that applied to the entire band — but which Furnier made his own, and retained when he went solo in 1975. He was already pretty much synonymous with the name by that point, anyway.

The band's satiric sensibility had been there right from the outset. Members of the Cortez High School track team in Phoenix went out and bought some wigs at Woolworth's, then got up on stage and started playing parodies of Beatles songs. Ear*wigs*. Beatles. Get it?

The opening words to the Beatles' "Please Please Me" were transformed from "Last night I said these words to my girl" to "Last night I ran four laps for my coach." They'd been singing songs like that as they ran around the track to maintain their rhythm, so they decided to form a band, taking the stage in black turtlenecks and bright yellow jackets that reflected another name they'd considered: Joe Banana and the Bunch. Their motto? "Music with a-peal."

(Eat your heart out, Stryper.)

The Earwigs' first gig also foreshadowed the band's future goth overtones: When they played the school's Halloween Dance, they used a guillotine from their journalism class as a prop, built cardboard coffins and turned clotheslines into giant spiderwebs.

They kept the spiderwebs as a backdrop and changed their name to the Spiders, then moved to L.A. and rechristened themselves the Nazz. But when they realized Todd Rundgren was already using that name for *his* band, they underwent one final change, becoming Alice Cooper.

The name had "a 'Whatever Happened to Baby Jane?' feeling to it," Furnier said. "It was like feminine, but it wasn't feminine. It had some sort of ring to it, something disturbing."

That's the look that Furnier adopted, sporting long, flowing blond hair, eyeliner and trashy, thrift-shoppy women's clothes. It caught the attention of Frank Zappa, who signed the band to his new facetiously named label, Straight Records. The first album, *Pretties for You*, sounded more like Syd Barrett-era Pink Floyd or a distorted version of the Kinks-meet-Zappa than the harder-edged music the band would eventually produce.

It wasn't particularly commercial. Or popular. *Rolling Stone*'s Lester Bangs deemed it listenable, but "lacking in "any hint of life, spontaneity, joy, rage, or any kind of authentic passion and conviction." It was, he wrote, "totally dispensable." It barely made the Billboard 200 albums chart, sneaking in at 193 before disappearing without a trace.

Alice Cooper's musical style would come into better focus on their Bob Ezrin-produced third album, *Love It to Death*, which featured their breakout single, "I'm Eighteen" (No. 21 on the singles charts in 1971.) The proto-pop-metal classic set the stage for the band's future success and helped create the template for the anthem in heavy metal. Its enduring influence would be demonstrated 27 years later, when the publisher sued Kiss for recording a strikingly similar track called "Dreamin'" for their *Psycho Circus* comeback album.

Kiss settled out of court.

Ezrin, who would later produce three Kiss albums, would helm a total of 11 albums for Alice Cooper. The band continued its success with the singles "Under My Wheels," which charted modestly in 1971, and its highest-charting cut, "School's Out," which hit No. 7 the following year and topped the charts in the U.K. It was a youthful middle finger at the school system seven years before Pink Floyd sang, "We don't need no education."

Aside from "Dreamin'," the extent of Alice Cooper's musical influence on 1980s melodic metal is further reflected in the personnel who played on an all-star cover of "Under My Wheels": Joe Elliott and Phil Collen (Def Leppard), Chuck Wright (Quiet Riot), Pat Torpey (Mr. Big), and Bob Kulick (uncredited guitar work for Kiss). "School's Out," meanwhile, became a perennial favorite of classroom-weary students every June, in much the same way Queen's "We Are the Champions" became a fixture at high school football games.

After going solo, Furnier/Cooper would join the pop metal movement himself with songs such as his No. 7 hit "Poison" in 1989 and the title track to his album "Hey Stoopid" two years later.

Welcome to My Nightmare

Cooper's image evolved, as well, with his stage antics becoming more and more extreme — even if they were sometimes exaggerated or invented out of whole cloth. His theatrics owed something to the British scene, and Cooper even admitted that "most people thought we were British at first" because of it.

"We were into fun, sex, death and money when everyone else was into peace and love," Cooper said. "We wanted to see what was next. It turned out we were next, and we drove a stake through the heart of the Love Generation."

The band's foray deeper into the macabre began by accident at the 1969 Toronto Rock and Roll Revival Festival, where Alice Cooper preceded headlining act John Lennon on the bill.

POP GOES THE METAL

During their set, someone in the audience threw a chicken onto the stage.

"I'm from Detroit," Cooper said. "I'm not a farm kid. I figured the chicken had wings; it'll fly away. So I took the chicken and threw it, and it didn't fly. It went into the audience. (There was) blood everywhere. The next day, everybody's reading 'Alice Cooper rips chicken's head off, drinks blood.' Zappa called me. He said, 'Whatever you did, keep doing it.'"

So, he did.

"It seemed to upset the whole world," Cooper said in an interview with *The Guardian*. "That's when I realized rock was looking for a villain, somebody that would have done that on purpose. That spurred me to create the Alice character to be darker."

At a concert in Knoxville, he took a 15-foot boa constrictor on stage and sang with it wrapped around his arm. Afterward, he left the snake in a hotel bathtub, but it got out and escaped down the toilet. Later on, Cooper heard that the snake had climbed back up through the pipes and appeared in the bathroom of country singer Charley Pride.

"He must have turned white," Cooper said.

The snake and the chicken aside, most of Cooper's antics involved stage props, not living creatures. He stuck with the guillotine from way back in his Earwig days, using it in an act where it appeared to slice off his head. And, during the 1973 tour promoting his band's album *Billion Dollar Babies*, he impaled baby dolls with a sword. But he never stomped baby chicks on stage, and he never bit the head off a dove or a bat — that was Ozzy Osbourne, who knew what he was doing with the dove but thought the bat was a rubber prop.

Nor did Cooper ever engage in a "gross-out contest" with David Bowie during which one of them defecated on stage and

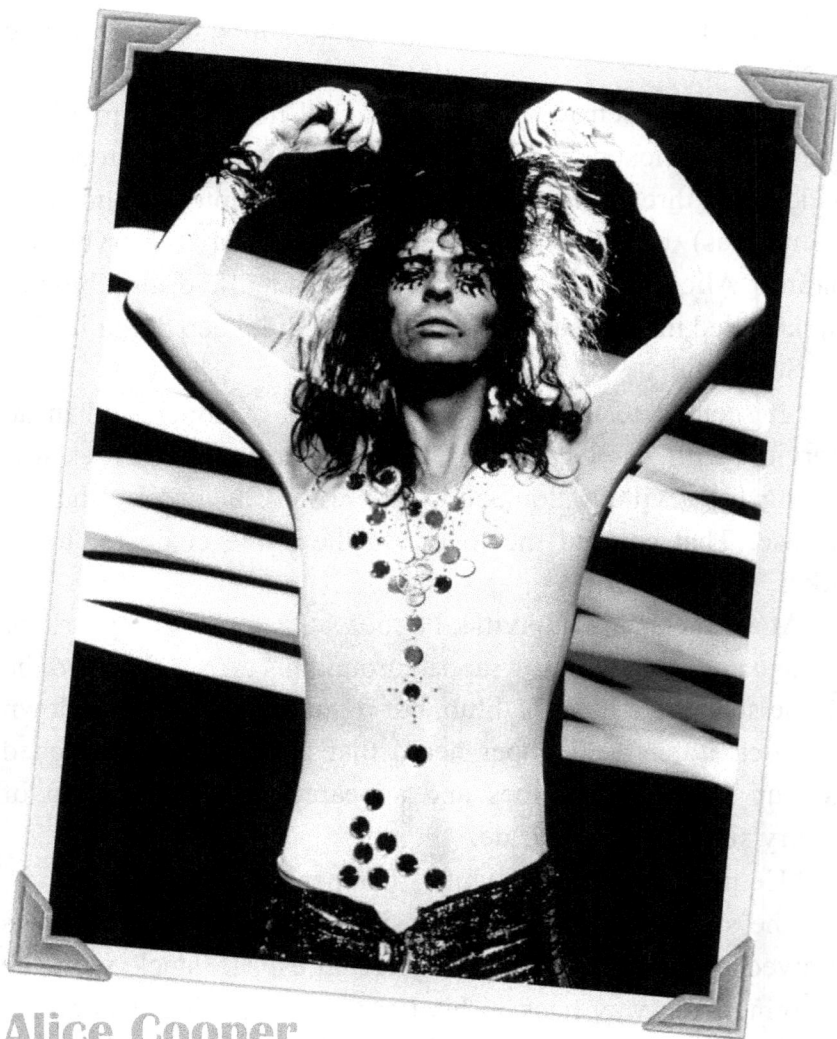

Alice Cooper

the other ate it. That rumor was making the rounds in the San Fernando Valley during the mid-'70s, probably based on an older rumor involving Cooper and Zappa, and a still older one involving Zappa and Captain Beefheart.

None of them was true.

Zappa put the original version to rest, recalling: "I was in a London club called the Speak Easy in 1967 or '68. A member of a group called the Flock, recording for Columbia at the time, came over to me and said: 'You're fantastic. When I heard about you eating that shit on stage, I thought, 'That guy is way, way out there.'

"I said, 'I never ate shit on stage.' He looked really depressed — like I had just broken his heart. For the record, folks: I never took a shit on stage, and the closest I ever came to eating shit anywhere was at a Holiday Inn buffet in Fayetteville, North Carolina, in 1973."

How do these things get started?

Well, once Cooper's *snake* defecated down the side of his outfit onstage, and Bowie did record a *song* with lyrics that referred to "dancing where the dogs decay, defecating ecstasy." The legend is probably the product of stories told and told and told again — and twisted like a pretzel in the retelling. Middle school students in Southern California had a keen imagination. But whatever the story's origins, it never happened.

What did happen is Cooper got bigger, and so did his stage shows.

Meanwhile, his personal look evolved as well. As time went on, he became less and less androgynous, and more menacing, exchanging the thrift-store look for dark material and leather, while expanding the eyeliner until it became a ghoulish sort of clown makeup that paved the way for...

Kiss.

New York Groove

Four musicians from New York City would develop one of the most distinctive looks and stage shows in the history of rock, which tends to obscure the fact that — despite their talent and success — they've been copycats as much as trendsetters.

"Originality," Kiss co-founder Gene Simmons would later opine, "is highly overrated."

After disco got big, Kiss recorded a disco-rock song in 1979: "I Was Made For Lovin' You." It would become their third-highest-charting single, but it also convinced half their fans they'd sold out. More tuned out when they reinvented themselves as a power-pop band in 1980, then tried to reinvent themselves again with a failed concept album the year after that. They took off their makeup and jumped on the hair metal bandwagon in the '80s, and when grunge destroyed that gravy train in the blink of an eye, they tried to sound like Alice in Chains. In the end, they decided to copy *themselves*, putting the makeup back on and climbing back into the same costumes they'd worn two decades earlier.

The band had even *started off* trying to copy someone else: the New York Dolls, who themselves invited comparisons to others. A 1972 story in the *New York Daily News* began by comparing three members of the band to known quantities:

"David, lead singer of the Dolls... looks like Mick Jagger, sort of, only thinner and younger and punkier. One guy in the band looks like Rod Stewart, or Ron Wood maybe, or a little of both. There is also a pale Edgar Winter type wearing Mary Quant lipstick and yet another guy with the ringlets and thin petulant dark mouth of Marc Bolan."

Most of the piece focused on the Dolls' look, rather than their music, only describing it as "the kind that makes parents crazy" — which could have meant almost anything.

The frontman, David Johansen, downplayed the Dolls' look in an interview that same year: "We wore high-heeled shoes six years ago," he said. "We're not into theatricals or costumes, either. It's just clothes. Basically, we just have a fabulous rock and roll band."

POP GOES THE METAL

Johansen's charisma was undeniable, and the comparisons to Jagger were apt. His high-energy performances, his sneering and strutting, made him seem like a younger, rawer version of the Rolling Stones' singer. But it was the Dolls' look, not their music, that made headlines. They landed a deal with Mercury Records, but they didn't sell a lot of albums and never had a hit.

The band broke up after just two albums, the second of which bore the prescient title "Too Much Too Soon." Johansen went solo and had some success in 1982 with a medley of three hits by the British Invasion blues band the Animals: "We Gotta Get Out of This Place," "Don't Bring Me Down" and "It's My Life." The video received significant exposure on MTV. Five years later, he created a lounge-singer alter ego called Buster Poindexter and recorded a cover of the dance single "Hot Hot Hot," which hit No. 45 on the Billboard Hot 100 and No. 11 on the dance club chart.

The song was released at the height of the glam metal craze, but Johansen had gone in the opposite direction. The video for the song begins with "Poindexter" — dressed in black-tie formalwear — referring to his time in the New York Dolls as he holds up some of their records and casually tosses them aside.

"Now, look at some of these outfits," he says. "I mean, we used to wear some really outrageous clothes. You know these heavy metal bands in L.A. don't have the market cornered on wearing their mothers' clothes."

The artist's casual, tongue-in-cheek disdain for his former persona only highlighted how influential it had been, not just to '80s bands on the Sunset Strip, but to their predecessors in the mid- to late '70s.

Steven Tyler of Aerosmith, interviewed in the late '80s for a documentary called *The Decline of Western Civilization Part II: The Metal Years*, admitted that he was "in awe" of the Dolls.

"They used to say I was a Mick Jagger lookalike," Tyler said. "Man, he (Johansen) had lips for miles. I mean, that guy could swallow the Earth. And has."

Johansen's wife, Cyrinda Foxe left him after a year and married... Tyler.

They, too, ultimately divorced, after nine years.

Foremost among the bands influenced by the Dolls was Kiss, which rose from the ashes of a soft-rock band called Wicked Lester that had recorded one (unreleased) album. That LP included a hodgepodge of styles that ranged from pop to folk and also featured a cover of the Hollies' "We Want to Shout it Out Loud."

In *Billboard*, rhythm guitarist Paul Stanley compared Wicked Lester to "Jethro Tull meets the Four Seasons." Simmons told *Rolling Stone* they sounded like "a cross between Three Dog Night and the Doobie Brothers."

Talk about an identity crisis.

After the band's inevitable demise, Simmons and Stanley decided to start from scratch with a completely different look and sound. They wanted the music to be heavier, but they also needed an image. Being from New York, it was only natural that they should check out the Big Apple's hottest band, the Dolls, who were playing at the Hotel Diplomat.

They were impressed with what they saw.

"They looked amazing," Stanley would later admit.

And their look would serve as the blueprint for Kiss' first experiment with makeup. Stanley and Simmons added a drummer named Peter Criss, whose previous band, Lips, had broken up, and who had taken out this ad in *Rolling Stone*:

EXPD. ROCK & roll drummer looking for orig. grp. doing soft & hard music. Peter, Brooklyn.

POP GOES THE METAL

In his memoir *Kiss and Make-Up*, Simmons wrote that he called Criss and said he was starting a new band that was looking for a drummer, "and was he willing to do anything to make it? He said he was, right away."

The band later added guitarist Ace Frehley — whose real first name was Paul. Stanley's given name, meanwhile was *not* Paul. It was Stanley, which he used as his last name in place of his birth name, Eisen. In fact, all four members of the band went by different names than the ones they were born with, which seems fitting for a band that became known for hiding their identities behind makeup. Criss was short for Criscuola, and Simmons had been born Chaim Witz before changing his name first to Gene Klein, then to Simmons.

The four quickly set to the task of establishing their image, which Simmons emphasized in that initial call to Criss: He couldn't be overweight, should be willing to wear lipstick and women's makeup, and would have to shave any facial hair he had because Simmons didn't want to be "a San Francisco hippie band."

Simmons wasn't kidding about the lipstick and makeup. When the band made its live debut in the spring of 1972, their image didn't look anything like the goth-kabuki superhero concept that would make them famous. They looked like, well, a bad imitation of the New York Dolls.

A black-and-white photo from the period shows Frehley (appearing completely disinterested), with a cigarette hanging out of his mouth and wearing a hat with a bow and feminine clothes. Stanley appears to be wearing rouge and lipstick, a la the Dolls. Criss is in whiteface, with exaggerated painted eyelashes and a false cheek mole. Simmons, in the background, is in full drag-queen mode, sporting lighter hair, heavy lipstick and eye makeup, and a sneer out of David Johansen's playbook.

"We put on makeup, but it wasn't Kiss makeup," lead guitarist Frehley said in a 1976 interview. "It was feminine makeup, like the New York Dolls. Back then, the Dolls were the hottest thing, and we always wished we could be the Dolls, 'cause we were nobody at the time. But we weren't physically like the Dolls, who were small, skinny guys..."

Stanley put it more bluntly, saying the band "looked like linebackers in drag." The Dolls, who were physically smaller, could make it work. Kiss could not. So instead of trying to squeeze into the Dolls' shoes, Kiss went the opposite direction, adopting larger-than-life personas.

Simmons, at 6-foot-2, and Stanley and Frehley, each just an inch shorter, would don platform boots as part of their costumes that would help elevate their image (literally) by 7 more inches. The band would wear black outfits onstage, Frehley's adorned with a lightning bold, and Simmons' with a skull and crossbones. Most importantly, all four members would start wearing whiteface, each with distinctly shaped black — or, in Frehley's case, silver — outlines around the eyes:

- Simmons' eye makeup would mimic the wings of a bat. Together with a painted-on widow's peak, they made him look like a child of Transylvania.
- Stanley would wear a single black star over his right eye, although he experimented very briefly with a bandit's mask.
- Criss, inspired by his wife's cat, would draw whiskers beside his mouth (and would also eventually accentuate his black eye makeup with green highlights).
- Frehley, who fancied himself an alien from a planet called Jandel, created jagged silver starbursts outlined in black.

POP GOES THE METAL

The makeup would evolve slightly over time, and the costumes would grow more elaborate, but the template was in place to make Kiss something entirely different than a New York Dolls knockoff.

The music was different from the Dolls', too. It had a lot more in common with what Sweet and Slade were doing over in England than with the Dolls' proto-punk. Simmons drew on his love of horror movies to help create Kiss' menacing look, but his biggest musical inspiration was the Beatles, the godfathers of power pop whose success Simmons aspired to replicate.

Many of the songs were heavy, as early songs like Frehley's "Parasite" and Simmons' "Deuce" illustrated with their killer riffs. But that hard edge belied the fact that they were also catchy. Stanley knew how to craft a hook with the best of them, as songs like "Let Me Know" off the band's self-titled debut album demonstrated.

Rock and Roll All Nite

One result of this blend would be a style of song that helped launch and define rock 'n' roll in the first place — often by mentioning rock 'n' roll in the title.

The anthem.

Kiss would become masters of the anthem, but they were far from the first band to write one.

The song may historians consider the record that catapulted rock into the mainstream was just such a tune: "Rock Around the Clock" by Bill Haley and His Comets. Just over 2 minutes long, it was used in the opening credits of the 1955 movie *Blackboard* Jungle, about an English teacher (Glenn Ford) facing a challenging assignment at a violent inner-city school.

The movie captured the kind of teen rebellion that would come to be associated with rock music in the years ahead, and Haley's song provided the first soundtrack to that rebellion.

"We're gonna rock around the clock tonight," the lyrics defiantly declare. The implication being: "and you can't stop us!"

Haley's song became the first rock record to top the Billboard charts — and stayed there for eight weeks. It created a template for later rock anthems, which, as the name indicates, plant a metaphorical flag in the service of loud music and the glory of youth. Rock anthems, like national anthems, were meant to generate feelings of pride and celebration. They were at once exultant and defiant.

The Who followed in Haley's footsteps with perhaps one of the first anthems of the British Invasion era, 1965s "My Generation," a declaration of teenage independence that called for the older set to "f-f-fade away" and brazenly declared, "Hope I die before I get old."

Ironically, songwriter and guitarist Pete Townshend was still writing and performing songs at the age of 75, having released The Who's 12th studio album with founding vocalist Roger Daltrey in 2019. In the interim, he's been as successful as anyone at churning out memorable rock anthems, including "Won't Get Fooled Again" in 1971, "Baba O'Riley" the next year, and "Long Live Rock" in 1974 — the year Kiss released their self-titled debut album.

That was the kind of success to which Kiss aspired, and they thought they'd hit on the right formula when Stanley and Simmons wrote "Let Me Go, Rock and Roll," released as the first single off their second album, *Hotter Than Hell*.

Disappointingly, it failed to chart.

Undaunted, Simmons and Stanley tried again, penning

another anthem for their next album, *Dressed to Kill*. The song became Kiss' highest-charting single to that point — but that wasn't saying much: It topped out at No. 69, which was 20 slots higher than the band had reached with its first single, a cover of Bobby Rydell's "Kissin' Time."

At this point, Kiss found itself on the ropes, financially speaking. They'd built a cult following and a devoted concert fan base, but they hadn't broken through on the radio or with their album sales. In an attempt to capture the energy of a Kiss concert on vinyl, Casablanca Records decided to record the band on stage, clean up that recording in the studio, and release the result as a double album. It would be cheaper than another studio album, but even then, Casablanca couldn't afford it, having just blown a ton of money on another double album: a series of highlights from *The Tonight Show* with Johnny Carson.

Casablanca had shipped out 750,000 copies of the Carson album, but it had flopped spectacularly: so badly, in fact, that distributors even returned promotional copies they'd received for free.

So Kiss manager Bill Aucoin stepped in and fronted $300,000 of his own money for the project, which would be produced by Eddie Kramer, who had previously worked with Led Zeppelin and Jimi Hendrix, and had worked on Kiss' original demo tape.

The result, a collection of 16 songs from Kiss' first three studio albums, recorded live at four different venues, performed better than anyone's wildest dreams. Released in 1975, *Alive!* hit No. 9 on the Billboard album chart and spawned a single that went to No. 12 on the Hot 100: a live version of the anthem off *Dressed to Kill* that had barely registered six months earlier.

That song was "Rock and Roll All Nite," the title of which sounds a lot like "Rock Around the Clock."

The success of *Alive!* paved the way for other career-defining live albums, such as Peter Frampton's *Frampton Comes Alive* in 1976, and Cheap Trick's *At Budokan* in '78. Led Zeppelin, which had released a concert film titled *The Song Remains the Same* in 1973, didn't release a soundtrack for the film until three years later — in the wake of Kiss' *Alive!*

"Rock and Roll All Nite," meanwhile, channeled the spirit of teenage rebellion so successfully that Kiss topped a Gallup poll as the most popular band among American teens in 1977. By then, Kiss had recorded two more anthems for their next studio album: "Flaming Youth" and "Shout it Out Loud," the title of which owed something to Wicked Lester's cover of the Hollies' song a few years earlier.

Other anthems followed throughout the band's career, but none would ever match the popularity or impact of "Rock and Roll All Nite," essentially a power-pop masterpiece amplified by attitude and electric guitar. Along with Alice Cooper's "School's Out," it provided the blueprint for the pop-metal anthems of the 1980s that became standard fare for acts like Twisted Sister and Def Leppard.

But that wasn't the only element of '80s pop-metal that could be traced to Kiss. The band was also one of the first hard rock acts to include a ballad among their more heavy hooks and driving riffs.

The power ballad, while closely associated with the 1980s, can be traced back to the likes of Lynyrd Skynyrd's "Freebird" and Aerosmith's "Dream On" in 1973, the Led Zeppelin classic "Stairway to Heaven" in 1971, and, a year earlier, to "Layla" by Derek and the Dominoes.

The power generally comes from an emotive electric guitar, with the ballad consisting of restrained, often melancholy verses that build to wave-of-emotion chorus.

POP GOES THE METAL

By that definition, Kiss' "Beth" wasn't really a power ballad.

It was just a ballad.

There wasn't any guitar on the track, which consisted of Peter Criss singing, accompanied by piano. But it did mark a watershed moment. Before "Beth," hard rock bands hardly ever included ballads on their albums, and they didn't score hits with them. (Zeppelin had never even released "Stairway to Heaven" as a single.)

Criss had written the song with Stan Penridge before Kiss even formed, under the title "Beck" (short for Becky, the wife a former bandmate). It sounded so different from Kiss' typical sound that Stanley and Simmons didn't want it on the album *Destroyer*, the band's follow-up to *Alive!*

But manager Bill Aucoin and producer Bob Ezrin liked the song. Ezrin, had earned his reputation producing Alice Cooper albums, including the singer's solo debut, a concept album called *Welcome to My Nightmare*, a year earlier. That album had included a ballad called "Only Women Bleed," which made it to No. 12 on the Billboard chart, setting the stage for "Beth."

Although it wasn't a power ballad, "Beth" did for Kiss what power ballads like Mötley Crüe's "Home Sweet Home" and Poison's "Every Rose Has Its Thorn" did for pop metal in the '80s: It expanded hard rock's audience to include female fans. Unlike "Dream On" or "Stairway," the lyrics to Criss' ballad addressed a woman (and women) directly.

In concert, the Catman would come out from behind the drums, sit on a stool at center stage, and serenade the fans. Sometimes, he'd even hand out roses to women in the audience after the song concluded.

KISS

"Beth" wasn't supposed to a single; it was released as the B-side of "Detroit Rock City," the first cut on the album, but a DJ in Windsor, Ontario, started playing "Beth" instead, and it became so popular Casablanca reissued it as the A-side. It rose all the way to No. 7, becoming the biggest hit of the band's career — one spot higher than a true power ballad, "Forever," which the band released 14 years later.

By that time, Kiss had found new life without makeup, and had, ironically, adopted the kind of feminine look they'd discarded a decade earlier when they stopped trying to compete with the Dolls. Lipstick, rouge, eyeliner and colorful clothes were back in. The Dolls were long gone by that time, and Kiss found itself competing with the likes of Poison and Twisted Sister.

Everything old was new again.

PART II:
CHORUS
Raising the Curtain

STEPHEN H. PROVOST

Eruption

Evolution and Transition

In the '70s, rock became big business. Major acts were packing arenas and stadiums. Zeppelin demanded 90 percent of the take from their concerts because they could: They were earning so much that 10 percent of a Led Zeppelin concert was better than the traditional 50 percent promoters got from lesser bands.

Elton John drew 100,000 fans to a pair of sold-out concerts at Dodger Stadium in October of 1975. Two years earlier, Zeppelin had obliterated the Beatles' U.S. attendance record of 55,000, set at Shea Stadium in 1965, by drawing 56,800 to a show on May 5, 1973, in Tampa. The event grossed a record $309,000.

Still, for most bands, concerts were a means to an end: The big money was in selling records. You might have a great live band with a rabid following, but if your albums didn't sell, your label would drop you.

In the 2000s, streaming music would flip the script: There isn't much money in recording new material these days, but bands can make a killing in concert. Today, tickets to a top-name act can set you back several hundred dollars or even into four figures.

Back then, it was a much different story. A ticket to a Zeppelin concert at the San Antonio Convention Center in 1970 might cost you $6. If you wanted to see Queen, Kansas and Mahogany Rush at the Morris Civic Auditorium in South Bend, Ind., it would set you back a whopping $6.50 in 1975. Even adjusted for inflation, tickets were dirt cheap compared with today's stratospheric prices.

Kiss had saved their career by capturing their live sound on vinyl (even though, admittedly, that sound was augmented in the studio) with *Alive!* But soon, they were innovating in another area as well: merchandising.

The band went well beyond the old faithful concert T-shirt, selling everything from lunchboxes to belt buckles to action figures of themselves. When a couple of teenage fans from Indiana started a fan club called the Kiss Army in 1975, the band took notice and began promoting it as their official fan group. You could join for $5 a year.

Kiss made their records like Cracker Jack boxes: There was always a toy surprise inside. *Rock and Roll Over* came with a sticker of the album cover, which immediately started appearing on school notebooks across the country. Their next release, *Love Gun*, included a cardboard pop-up toy gun, and *Dynasty* came with a poster.

In 1977, the band members mixed their blood with the ink that was used in their very own *Marvel Super Special* comic book, in which they appeared as superheroes. (A second issue appeared the following year.) Bally created a Kiss pinball machine in 1979, which later went on display at the Rock & Roll Hall of Fame.

This wasn't the kind of stuff that would appeal to a 20-year-old Motörhead fan with a few bucks in his pocket. It was geared toward a younger crowd, who could beg their much-more-

POP GOES THE METAL

affluent white-collar moms and dads to buy "stuff" for them.

Belt buckles.

Patches.

Tour books.

Posters.

Necklaces.

It was just the kind of calculated business move that Simmons and then-manager Bill Aucoin were known for. In the short term, it would make the band multimillionaires; in the long term, it would backfire and set the tone for a feud in the 1980s between hair and heavy metal.

(Even in the 1970s, battle lines were being drawn at junior high and high schools between Kiss fans on the one hand and Led Zeppelin fans on the other.)

Kiss could have gone the other way. They could have gotten even heavier and gone after the "real" metalheads. Frehley, in particular, appeared to lean in that direction — and would leave the band, at least in part, because they didn't rock hard enough in the early '80s.

In 1976, the band resisted recording "Beth" because they feared it would cost them credibility with more hard-core rockers. And they tried, on more than one occasion, to recapture these fans by recording heavier albums like *Creatures of the*

STEPHEN H. PROVOST

Night in 1982 and *Revenge* a decade later.

Still, they always wanted the best of both worlds and never seemed entirely at home in either. For about three years in the 1970s, they were able to keep a foot in both camps by carving out their own distinct niche, and during that time, they rode the crest of the wave. But the fact remained that they had always resonated more with young people.

Like the kids at Cadillac High School in Michigan.

After the Cadillac High football team began the 1974 season with two straight losses, assistant coach Jim Neff hit upon an idea to motivate the team, he decided to start playing Kiss songs like "Strutter," "Hotter Than Hell," and "Nothin' to Lose" in the locker room. The strategy worked: The Vikings started to win (they would finish the season as conference co-champs), and when Neff found out the band would be playing nearby just before homecoming, he decided to invite them to the school.

The band accepted, and the town responded by renaming Mitchell Street "Kiss Boulevard" for the day and giving them the key to the city. City officials and school staff donned Kiss makeup. The band had its own float in the homecoming parade. Kiss visited classrooms and performed in the school gym. Gene Simmons even breathed fire to start the traditional homecoming bonfire. He agreed, however, not to spit blood as he typically did in concert.

Principal John Laurent had asked him to refrain from that activity, telling the band, "I'm in enough trouble already." (Maybe a few parents had realized that "Strutter" sounded like an ode to a streetwalker, "Hotter Than Hell" told the story of an ill-fated attraction to a married woman, and "Nothin' to Lose" had been written about anal sex.)

The Cadillac visit was a great publicity stunt, but it was also a troubling omen of things to come: As the decade wore on, more and more Kiss fans were young teens and pre-adolescents. The band abandoned its early image as a hungry, dangerous metal act to play the part of increasingly cartoonish superheroes.

They set a new standard for self-promotion, and people beyond their fanbase started to take notice. In January of 1978, NBC News televised a special report called *Land of Hype and Glory*, in which staid newsman Edwin Newman asked band members what made them tick. His demeanor, and the segment in general, probably reflected what the older generation thought when they saw Kiss.

"What the hell is *this*?"

Newman's narration fell somewhere between dispassionate observation and mild disdain.

Instead of asking the band about the origin of their name, he declared, aloofly, that "their name, for no reason immediately apparent, is Kiss."

His assessment: "In a frenzied world of rock, where the audiences are young and volatile, Kiss has found a simple formula for success: Hit those audiences so hard with a barrage of gimmicks, stunts and theatrics that they won't be able to forget you."

Ironically, NBC and Kiss teamed up for even more "hype and glory," when the network aired a TV movie featuring the band that October. *Kiss Meets the Phantom of the Park*, a campy B-movie set in Southern California's Magic Mountain theme park, sought to build on their comic-book superhero image with a script that was supposed to be a cross between *Star Wars* and *A Hard Day's Night*.

By this time, it was becoming clear that overexposure was right around the corner, and overreach was inevitable.

When the four members of Kiss each put out a solo album

in 1978, the LPs were sent back to Casablanca in droves: The company had shipped a million copies of each record to ensure it would go platinum, and record stores couldn't find enough buyers. Frehley's album was the only one to produce a top-20 hit, and most fans seemed to agree that his and Stanley's (which sounded the most like an actual Kiss album) were the ones worth buying. Simmons' was a self-indulgent and inconsistent affair that featured the likes of Helen Reddy and his then-girlfriend, Cher. Criss' effort sounded more like easy listening than Kiss.

Further missteps followed: An ill-conceived concept album was supposed to be the soundtrack to a movie that was never made and the launching pad for a tour that never was. A Kiss amusement park was planned but never built.

More merchandising mayhem — such as a Kiss Koffin, a Kiss "Rock & Brews" restaurant chain, Kiss Kruise, Kiss miniature golf course, and L.A. Kiss indoor football team — would have to wait for the band's second wave of nostalgia-induced popularity, in the late '90s and 2000s.

Man of 1,000 Faces

Simmons had plenty to keep him occupied in the meantime. He appeared in movies, most notably as the villain in Tom Selleck's 1984 vehicle *Runaway*, and opposite Rutger Hauer three years later in *Wanted: Dead or Alive*. (Spoiler alert: Simmons was the "wanted" man in the movie, a terrorist, and his character wound up dead.)

In the 21st century, he would have his own reality show.

He also kept his eyes peeled for musical talent, and discovered a number of bands during his career — some more successful than others.

POP GOES THE METAL

Word had it that Jon Bon Jovi discovered '80s blues-pop-metal band Cinderella. But lead singer Tom Keifer confirmed in an interview that Simmons "was actually the guy who first took an interest in the band," although "his interest did not lead to a deal for one reason or another."

Simmons gave PolyGram a heads up about the band, but the label passed. It wasn't until Bon Jovi recommended them that the record company decided to sign Cinderella to a six-month "development" deal. Each of their first two albums went triple-platinum, and from 1988 to 1991, their singles hit the U.S. Rock Chart top 20 half a dozen times.

In 1987, Simmons formed his own record company and came across some demos from a band called Giuffria, which had already recorded two records with MCA and had notched a No. 15 single with "Call to the Heart" three years earlier. The band was led by keyboardist Gregg Giuffria, but Simmons didn't like the name. If he was going to sign the band, he wanted a different lead singer and a new name — "something that sounded classy, and not too heavy-metal."

The singer was replaced, the name House of Lords was chosen, and the band found some minor success after Simmons signed them. Their video of "Love Don't Lie," off their debut release, got some exposure on MTV, and their sophomore effort produced a No. 10 Album Rock hit with their cover of Blind Faith's "Can't Find My Way Home."

Giuffria was actually a known quantity to Simmons, who had previously discovered him playing in a Washington, D.C.-based band called Angel back in the mid-1970s.

Kiss' label, Casablanca, wound up signing the band. They took their name from a Jimi Hendrix song, but their long hair and white satin stage outfits made them seem like the antithesis of the demonic Simmons and his bandmates. Guitarist Punky

Meadows, with his long feathered locks and pouty lips, looked like a raven-haired male version of Farrah Fawcett. (Frank Zappa even wrote a song about him called "Punky's Whips," satirizing his feminine good looks.)

The marketing possibilities were endless.

Angel took the Kiss template and put a heavenly spin on it. Like Kiss, they played hard, melodic rock, put on larger-than-life stage shows and had a distinctive logo: one that read the same upside down as it did right-side up. But they wore white instead of black and were pretty boys in the tradition of the early-'70s glam bands, not demonic-clown caricatures like Kiss. One promotional poster posed the question: "Mirror, Mirror, on the wall, who's the prettiest band of them all?"

Casablanca was poised to milk both the similarities and the contrast for all they were worth.

A "Heaven and Hell" tour, in which Angel would have opened for Kiss, was apparently discussed but never came to fruition because — according Meadows — Simmons felt "a bit threatened" by his band. In fact, Meadows said, Casablanca signed Angel without even bothering to hear them play for precisely this reason. According to Meadows, label founder Neil Bogart wanted to have the band audition by opening for Kiss during an upcoming show in Anaheim. He even called Simmons to set it up, but Meadows got a call back from Bogart five minutes later.

The bad news: Angel would not be opening for Kiss, because Simmons, who had seen them play at the Capital Centre in Landover, Md., was having none of it. Simmons' band, which had earned a reputation of upstaging headliners like Blue Öyster Cult, apparently didn't want to have the tables turned.

The good news? Bogart had agreed to sign them anyway, apparently convinced by Simmons' reaction. If the Demon was worried about Angel opening the show, he figured, they *had* to be good. Meadows recalled Bogart telling him: "I'll sign the band sight unseen, because Gene Simmons says, 'Under no circumstances will Angel ever open up for Kiss.'"

Could Angel have really upstaged Kiss? Was that even possible?

Maybe not. But if anyone could have done it, it was Angel. Like Kiss, they were known for their live concerts, which featured a light show and illusions created by magician Doug Henning. Kiss had a huge flashing logo and an elevating drum kit. But Angel had an 11-foot talking angel head named Gabriel that served as a backdrop for their stage set and had been designed by Sid and Marty Krofft. This was before *Star Wars* revolutionized special effects, and — odd as it may seem today — the Kroffts were on what was then the cutting edge. They'd made a reputation in the early '70s by producing Saturday morning live-action children's shows such as *The Banana Splits*, *H.R. Pufnstuf* and, perhaps most memorably, the claymation-dinosaur series *Land of the Lost* (Sleestaks, anyone?)

Kiss concerts famously began with an announcer intoning, over ominous sounding music, "You wanted the best, you got the best. The hottest band in the world: Kiss!"

But that was nothing compared to Angel's introduction. The Gabriel logo would come to life, through the use of rear-projection technology, and begin reverently reciting a pseudo-biblical text:

"And it came to pass one day in heaven that Gabriel summoned his flock of angels unto him and spoke thus: 'I have watched my children on Earth at play, and I am saddened that they know not the pleasures of our music. Who of you will go forth and let the music of heaven echo throughout the lands of the Earth?' "

The angel head would go on to introduce the band members in turn, each one appearing in a mirrored plexiglass cube, amid a frenzy of smoke and lights. When all five of them had made their grand entrances, the angel head would conclude its script: "And thus it came to pass that there was music on Earth as it is in heaven."

Angel would then launch into its signature tune, "Tower," the heavy-prog lead track from their debut LP.

One difference between Angel and Kiss was their music, at least initially. Angel's approach started out as slightly more progressive than the hard-rock style of their labelmates, with Giuffria's keyboards helping to distinguish them from purely guitar-driven bands like Kiss. Angel's self-titled debut album, released in 1975, was so well received that readers of *Circus* magazine voted them the year's best new band; with more than 40,000 votes, they beat the likes of Boston and Heart.

But Angel's album sales didn't match their concert buzz or fan following, so Casablanca tried to make them more and more like Kiss. On their second album, they abandoned most of the prog-pomp aspirations of their debut in favor of a more straight-ahead rock sound, and Eddie Kramer — the guy who had produced Kiss' breakthrough *Alive!* album — was hired to head up their third release.

The cover of Angel's 1978 album, *White Hot*, was a color fantasy illustration that showed the band being burned at the stake, striking a similar tone to Queen's *News of the World* and, notably, Kiss' *Love Gun*, both released the previous year. But that album and its follow-up both failed to find a big audience, forcing Casablanca to borrow one last gimmick from Kiss' bag of tricks: A double-live album had launched Kiss' career, so why not try the same thing with Angel?

The problem was, it was 1980, not 1975. Kiss' own fan

base was shrinking, and public tastes were changing. As a result, *Live Without a Net* failed to replicate the success of *Alive!* and, instead of a breakthrough, it proved to be Angel's swan song.

Lead singer Frank DiMino went on to sing "Seduce Me Tonight" on the *Flashdance* soundtrack; Giuffria formed his own band; and bassist Felix Robinson played on White Lion's debut album in 1985.

Guitarist Meadows, meanwhile, nearly became a member of Kiss.

After Ace Frehley left after Kiss' *The Elder* LP, Meadows was apparently the band's top choice to replace him. According to Meadows, Simmons asked him to learn some Kiss material and sit in with him and Paul Stanley during a rehearsal. The audition must have gone well, because Meadows says he was invited to join the band. But when he told Simmons and Stanley that he and Giuffria were shopping for a record deal, they apparently thought he was turning them down, and "no one's ever turned down Kiss."

So that was the end of that.

Kiss ended up going through two other guitarists in rapid succession before finally settling on Bruce Kulick, while Meadows returned to D.C. and opened a tanning salon. He continued to play guitar on the side and explored country music before ultimately re-forming Angel with DiMino in 2019 for a release titled *Risen*.

But even though they never broke through in the States during their first incarnation (like Cheap Trick and the Runaways, they were big in Japan), Angel played a major role in bridging the gap between the glam power pop of the early '70s and the hair metal of the '80s. Their androgynous look, together with their Raspberries-influenced pop metal, made them the missing link between early Sweet and bands like

Poison.

But Angel wasn't the only band to bridge the gap between the 1970s and the '80s. Another, far more well-known band, played a crucial role in that, as well. And, as it just so happens, that band was *also* discovered by Gene Simmons.

Unchained

By the late '70s, rock's "dangerous" acts had started to seem a lot less dangerous. Alice Cooper had appeared on *The Muppet Show*. David Bowie had retired Ziggy Stardust and had joined Bing Crosby for a duet on "The Little Drummer Boy" at Christmas. Kiss, meanwhile, appeared in a bad TV movie and was in the midst of devolving — albeit temporarily — into a kiddie pop band.

Other artists were gone completely. Marc Bolan was dead, and Brian Connolly was out of Sweet, which had lost its way trying to compete with Queen.

Unsuccessfully.

Heavier bands were in similarly dire straits. The New York Dolls disbanded in 1976, having failed to gain any commercial traction. Deep Purple had imploded that same year after a series of personnel changes that saw Ian Gillan and Roger Glover leave, followed by Ritchie Blackmore. Ozzy was fired from Sabbath in 1979, and John Bonham's death marked the end of Zeppelin the following year.

Hard rock had been eclipsed by disco, anyway, and punk was the new "music your parents didn't want you to listen to." But there was a transitional force bubbling just below the surface in pop-metal out in Southern California, the land of surf, sun, and swimming pools.

And it wasn't the Beach Boys or Jan and Dean.

POP GOES THE METAL

"It makes me feel good that L.A. is finally developing some real rock bands again," Jett told the *Los Angeles Times* in 1977, when she was still a member of the Runaways. "All the good groups have seemed to come from New York or England for so long that people got the impression nothing happened out here. All the L.A. bands seemed to consist of these wimpy guys for so long."

She didn't mentioned any "wimpy guys" specifically, but Los Angeles at the time was known for the so-called Southern California sound, which featured a laid-back vibe that you could fall asleep to while working on your tan at Malibu. The sound was epitomized by the Eagles, but they weren't the only ones who'd latched onto the style. There was also Jackson Browne, Player, Jay Ferguson, and bands that weren't from the area at all but sounded like they were. Firefall and Pablo Cruise come to mind. British blues band-turned-pop-powerhouse Fleetwood Mac even relocated to the San Fernando Valley around that time.

Christopher Cross was sailing, Robbie Dupree was stealing away, and the Little River Band was reminiscing, while Rupert Holmes was drinking piña coladas and getting caught in the rain. They called it yacht rock, and it was about as far away from metal as you could get without locking yourself in an elevator for toxic dose of Muzak.

But things were about to get very different, and it all started with the Sunset Strip.

Rodney Bingenheimer's English Disco had closed in 1975, but that didn't mean the Strip was dead. Far from it. Over a stretch of just a couple of miles, you could find a smorgasbord of sex, drugs and rock and roll long before hair metal conquered the Strip in the 1980s. The Roxy, the Starwood (which closed in 1981 after repeated citations for underage drinking), and the

Rainbow Bar & Grill had both opened in the early '70s, while the Troubadour (a couple of blocks south on Santa Monica Boulevard), Gazzarri's and the Whisky a Go Go had been around even longer.

Record executive David Geffen, one of the Roxy's owners, said he wanted the Roxy to be "what, say, the Dorothy Chandler Pavilion is to concert halls."

The Rainbow opened in 1972 with a party for Elton John and featured an exclusive club upstairs called Over the Rainbow. When guitarist Ritchie Blackmore left Deep Purple to form a new band in 1975, he named it after the club.

Gazzarri's, which during the 1960s had featured the Doors as its house band, in 1974 began booking a then-unknown act led by a couple of brothers from Pasadena. In 1979, owner Bill Gazzarri — the self-described "godfather of rock 'n' roll" — sent a letter to *Los Angeles Times* music critic Robert Hilburn reminding him of its importance to the local music scene, based on the club's association that group:

"Way back in 1974, we auditioned a group called Van Halen," the letter read. "Upon booking said group, David Lee Roth of Van Halen, informed me that they had auditioned at 19 clubs and did not get one single job except at Gazzarri's. We continued to book Van Halen through the years 1974, 1975 and 1976, and were the ONLY Club in Los Angeles booking them."

As proof, the letter then provided a list of dates that Van Halen had played at Gazzarri's during each of the three years in question.

That's where Simmons enters the picture.

The story behind Simmons' involvement with Van Halen depends on who's doing the telling, and when. As with many bands, the it begins on the Sunset Strip, and, in this case, it began with Rodney Bingenheimer — the same guy who owned the club that had played a key role in the formation of the Runaways.

Bingenheimer's club closed in 1975, but he remained a prominent figure on the Strip and also hosted a radio show on KROQ. In the summer of '76, he caught Van Halen's act at Gazzarri's, where they were mostly a cover band. They played Deep Purple, Bad Company, the James Gang and the Stones. Sometimes, they'd close their show with "Make It Last," a song written by Sammy Hagar for Montrose.

"They were just doing top-40 stuff, but I was impressed and asked them if they had any original material," Bingenheimer told the *Los Angeles Times*. "They told me I should drop by and see their show at the Pasadena Civic (Auditorium). When I got there, they had something like 2,000 kids in the place. They had put the show together themselves. Amazing."

Van Halen hadn't just appeared out of nowhere. They'd been gigging since 1974, starting with clubs in the San Fernando Valley like the Rock Corporation in Van Nuys, where they played four sets a night six nights a week and were paid mainly to keep patrons going back for more drinks.

"We were supposed to make sure people got into the bar, not into the band," guitarist Eddie Van Halen told the *Times*. At the Rock Corporation, which billed itself as "The Valley's Home of Rock 'n' Roll," they were told to read announcements between songs like: "Remember, it's two-for-one night next Thursday."

Van Halen alternated between the Valley and the Strip, which is where Simmons first caught their act after hearing about them from Bingenheimer. The Demon was so impressed by what he saw that he flew them to Greenwich Village and had them record some demos at Electric Lady Studios (which had been built by Jimi Hendrix shortly before his death in 1970).

Simmons apparently wanted to change the band's name to Daddy Longlegs.

He told the *L.A. Times* in 1988: "I paid for the demo record, flew them to New York — I even bought David Lee Roth his first pair of leather pants. But my manager told me they'd never make it, that Roth looked too much like Jim Dandy (Mangrum, vocalist for Black Oak Arkansas). So I let 'em go."

In another interview, Simmons said he produced 15 songs

POP GOES THE METAL

for the band at Electric Lady, but gave a different reason for dropping the band, saying he "got too busy" and "tore up the contract" because he had to go back on tour. He told them if he had time once the tour was done, he'd help them get a record deal, but he didn't want to keep them waiting around in the meantime.

"So I did the right thing, and the guys, of course, got signed right away."

Actually, it took another year or so before that happened. By 1977, the band was playing at other clubs on the Strip besides Gazzarri's. The *L.A. Times*, in its entertainment calendar for Jan. 25, 1977, showed them scheduled to play at the Whisky, headlining a bill that also featured bands called Orange and the Berlin Brats. The announcement — right below a blurb for "W.C. Fields Night" at the Saratoga Restaurant — said you could see all three bands for a $4 cover charge and boasted, "Rock can't get much punkier."

Van Halen? Punk?

Not quite.

But the Berlin Brats were a New York Dolls-influenced act, and that was enough. Hard rock was comatose, punk was the next big thing, and promoters played up what was hot. Enough said.

Another calendar item in November of that same year got it right, announcing VH would be playing New Year's Eve at the Whisky. "This isn't new wave," Robert Hilburn wrote in the Times. "More a Led Zeppelin Meets Black Oak. ... If you're still into the heavy metal sound, this is your chance to see what it looks like up close."

Still, the implication was that metal was all but dead — or that only certain people were "still into" it. It wasn't the first time a reviewer had dismissed metal as a relic of a bygone era, nor would it be the last.

Van Halen was undeterred. After they sought, and landed, a regular gig at the Starwood (at Bingenheimer's suggestion), they shelled out some extra money for roadies to set up their equipment, so they could *look like* they were big time.

They didn't have much left in their wallets after that — but they soon would, because the gamble paid off. They'd been playing the Starwood for four or five months when it happened. It was a particularly rainy night and hardly anyone had showed up. But Milton Berle's nephew was there. Marshall Berle, who would later become their manager, took the band aside and told them to "play good" because there was someone in the audience there to see them.

That someone was Warner Bros. president Mo Ostin, who was there with producer Ted Templeman. After the show, the pair met the band backstage.

Ostin told them he wanted to sign them.

In separate interviews, Roth and Eddie Van Halen both described it as a scene "right out of the movies."

You Really Got Me

Hilburn, the *L.A. Times* reviewer, hadn't been wrong when he suggested that metal wasn't the hottest commodity. The reviewer himself was partial to a local punk band called X. He would, effusively, tout their debut album as "an extraordinary work whose maturity and power surprised even those who followed X's progress around town since 1977."

As for Van Halen, Hilburn admitted they had skills and the potential to build a big following, but bemoaned what he saw as their lack of imagination and songs that offered "mostly routine reflections on worn rock topics."

POP GOES THE METAL

Fans weren't buying hard rock, and even the most dynamic new bands, like Van Halen, elicited shrugs and skepticism from the critics.

Meanwhile, a number of other hard-rock bands were plying their trade in the L.A. area without gaining much traction beyond the clubs. Some of them would never get a shot; others would finally get their break when metal exploded in the '80s — but they'd be hitching their trailer to Van Halen's limo, not riding the band's Panama Express to stardom.

Yesterday & Today played the Starwood in the '70s before they shortened their name to Y&T.

Quiet Riot, which at the time featured a guitar hero of their own named Randy Rhoads, was among the bands working the Strip in the late '70s. And guitarist George Lynch, who would rise to fame with Dokken, was playing in a band with future Dokken drummer Mick Brown called The Boyz, which evolved into an outfit called Xciter.

George Lynch

There was plenty of competition.

Lynch's band was on the same bill with Van Halen when Simmons stopped by to hear them play. He was reportedly interested in making some demos for them — until VH took the stage and diverted his attention elsewhere.

Lynch would go on to audition for Ozzy Osbourne's band in 1979, losing out to none other than Rhoads. In a rather bizarre case of synchronicity, Lynch said, he wrote a guitar solo he never used, but showed it to Rhoads, who put it on an Ozzy album; much later, Lynch himself recorded it on an Ozzy *tribute* record.

Rhoads had to drop a teaching gig at Musonia, his mother's music school, when he joined Ozzy's band, and Lynch was his replacement on the staff. "I won the consolation prize," Lynch would quip. "Randy got to tour with Ozzy... and I got to teach at his mom's school."

At least a couple of tracks from Lynch's Xciter days would show up on Dokken albums: "Paris is Burning" (on *Breaking the Chains* in 1981) and "Sleepless Night" (on 1987's *Back for the Attack*).

While Rhoads and Lynch found success in '80s, a power trio called A La Carte wasn't so fortunate. The band was a fixture in the West Hollywood clubs, where they hung out with the Runaways and built a reputation for a loud, heavy sound that could pack 'em in. In 1976, they played to crowds of 2,000 on the Queen Mary and at a block party in Seal Beach, where their aural assault led the city to adopt a ban on amplified music.

Despite their popularity, A La Carte never got a record deal. Neither did Snow, a band that featured another future Quiet Riot guitarist, Carlos Cavazo (he actually replaced Rhoads in QR after Rhoads joined Ozzy's band). Snow did self-finance a five-song EP in 1980, but that was the extent of their recording history.

Several members of Wolfgang, which featured another hot guitarist named Lynch — Steve Lynch — would regroup in

POP GOES THE METAL

1983 to form a band called Autograph. Lynch joined fellow Wolfgang alums Steve Plunkett (vocals/guitar) and Randy Rand (bass) in the band, which took the inspiration for its name from Def Leppard's MTV breakthrough hit "Photograph." They'd soon have a hit of their own with "Turn Up the Radio," an anthem made it into Billboard's top 30 in March of 1985.

It's easy to forget that Van Halen, like its contemporaries, toiled for years in the clubs before they made it big. Before they signed with Warner Bros., the band had never played farther from home than Santa Barbara.

Strike that.

They'd *intended* to play Santa Barbara once, but the gig got rained out.

But even after they signed with Warner Bros., one member of the band was on shaky ground — although he didn't know it at the time. In his autobiography, producer Ted Templeman said he considered asking the band to replace David Lee Roth as its frontman.

With Sammy Hagar.

Templeman knew talent when he saw it. He'd gotten his start as a singer himself: His band Harpers Bizarre had reached No. 13 on the Hot 100 in 1967 with a cover of Simon and Garfunkel's "59th Street Bridge Song (Feelin' Groovy)." The band broke up in 1970, and Templeton went to work in an A&R job at Warner Bros. that same year. It was there that he discovered the Doobie Brothers and produced their first album.

Three years later, he produced the debut album for Ronnie Montrose's band, which featured Hagar on vocals and guitar. Hagar's "Bad Motor Scooter," which appeared on the first Montrose album, had earned a decent amount of FM radio airplay, along with "Rock Candy" and the riff-driven "Rock the Nation." The album eventually went platinum, but Hagar had quit the band after its second release over differences with Ronnie Montrose and had launched a successful solo career in 1976.

Why did Hagar's name surface now, with Van Halen already signed to a contract?

It turns out that Roth's vocals on Van Halen's demos had raised some red flags with Templeman. Some of them, he said bluntly, "just weren't acceptable."

But Templeman remembered Hagar and, in raising doubts about whether Roth could cut the mustard, he put an idea in engineer Don Landee's head: What about Sammy? When they started working with VH in the studio, Templeman recalled, Landee would hear something he didn't like about Roth's vocals and tell the producer, "You've gotta call Sam." Templeman would nod and say under his breath, "You're right." But for whatever reason, he never did.

Templeman ultimately decided that Roth's limitations as a vocalist were more than offset by his abilities as a lyricist, his intellect and, particularly, his sense of humor. So Roth stayed on board — at least until 1985, when the band replaced him with none other than Sammy Hagar.

Van Halen's debut offering was recorded in just three weeks during October 1977. The album didn't feature any hit singles, although a cover of the Kinks' "You Really Got Me" peaked at No. 36, and the heavy follow-up single, "Runnin' With the Devil," barely made the Hot 100 at No. 84. But both cuts, along with "Jamie's Cryin,'" "Ain't Talkin' 'Bout Love" (and, to a lesser extent, a cover of the 1953 John Brim blues number "Ice Cream Man") received heavy airplay on FM album-oriented rock stations.

Perhaps the most memorable cut on the record, though, was also the shortest: a 1-minute, 42-second instrumental piece titled

POP GOES THE METAL

"Eruption" that served as an intro to "You Really Got Me." It was, simply put, a guitar solo. But not just *a* guitar solo. It was one of those milestones in the history of rock that changed just about everything. Eddie Van Halen's frenetic finger work on the frets, known as tapping, established him as the heir to Jimi Hendrix's throne as the flashiest guitarist on the planet.

Tapping is just what it sounds like: tapping guitar strings with the fingers on one or both hands, rather than holding them down with one hand while strumming or picking them with the other. Eddie Van Halen wasn't the first guitarist to use the technique. Van Halen said he was inspired by Jimmy Page's solo on Led Zeppelin's "Heartbreaker," while George Lynch of Dokken and Steve Lynch of Autograph both said they saw Harvey Mandel of Canned Heat tapping on stage at the Starwood in the early '70s. Steve Hackett of Genesis said he was the first one to put it on a record, back in 1971, but it was Eddie Van Halen who inspired a generation of guitarists to start doing it.

Van Halen's debut album would eventually sell 10 million copies, but it was a slow build, initially peaking at No. 19 on the Billboard album charts, which was actually the *worst* showing of any VH studio album.

It just shows that sometimes, even the most accomplished bands need a little time to build a following.

Rolling Stone reviewer Charles M. Young put Van Halen in the same class with Deep Purple and Led Zeppelin, which would've have been a compliment except he predicted that, in three years, the band would be so "fat and self-indulgent and disgusting" that they'd "follow Deep Purple and Led Zeppelin right into the toilet."

"Van Halen's secret," he continued, "is not doing anything that's original while having the hormones to do it better than all those bands who have become fat and self-indulgent and disgusting."

Um, OK.

Terry Atkinson's review of *Van Halen* in the *Times* — which ran sandwiched between pieces on new albums by Barry Manilow and Art Garfunkel — was less cynical. He began his assessment by stating that the difference between great hard-rock bands, such as Zeppelin and the early Jeff Beck Group, and "runners-up" (he named Deep Purple and Ted Nugent) was that the great ones had both top- flight singers and guitar heroes. Those in the second tier had just one or the other.

Atkinson compared Edward Van Halen to Beck and Ritchie Blackmore, but he called David Lee Roth's vocals "the album's weakness."

He also questioned whether Warner Bros.' decision to issue Van Halen's cover of the Kinks' "You Really Got Me" as the first single was a smart move. He wondered: Wasn't Van Halen tired of playing covers in their bar gigs? And wouldn't it be "sadly ironic" if the band became known for that particular tune and got stuck playing requests for it the rest of their career?

He needn't have worried.

Still, the review highlighted the natural tension between the flamboyant Roth and the more introverted Eddie Van Halen, the guitar god who'd originally fronted the band but had given up the mic because he just wanted to play.

It was Edward's chops that gave Van Halen credibility. It was Roth's showmanship that made the band the template for what was to come in the 1980s.

But just as it took Van Halen a few years to break out of the club scene, it also took them a few years to become the reluctant godfathers of the 1980s hair-metal movement.

POP GOES THE METAL

And the Cradle Will Rock...

As the 1970s drew to a close, disco faded, Kiss retreated into pop, and Aerosmith's "Toxic Twins," Joe Perry and Steven Tyler, had gone their separate ways. Zeppelin had recorded its last album, and Sabbath had fired Ozzy. The self-destructive punk scene vied with safe, so-called "corporate rock" acts like Styx, Journey, Foreigner and Boston for musical supremacy.

Van Halen didn't fit into either of those two categories.

They concocted the perfect brew of power pop and heavy metal, of musical chops and showmanship, that became the formula for '80s pop metal. David Lee Roth pointed to the fact that they'd honed their style at party gigs in Pasadena, where the kids wanted tunes that were both heavy and danceable.

"Nobody could compete with us," he said, "because we were the only ones who could play rock music and you could dance to it."

Case in point: Van Halen's first hit top-20 single, off their second album, was their catchiest tune yet and was even *called* "Dance the Night Away." But the formula for success was already there on the band's debut, which touched all the bases with potential record-buyers. It had a scorching guitar solo in "Eruption" and a rockin' cover in "You Really Got Me." It also included a heavy, defiant rocker for the guys ("Runnin' with the Devil") and a catchy, more sensitive track for the girls: "Jamie's Cryin'," which postulated that love should mean "a little more than one-night stands."

(Considering Roth's reputation for womanizing, it's easy to wonder how sincere he was.)

In the late 1970s, Van Halen was doing some heavy lifting, carrying the banner for hard rock music alongside a shrinking number of bands: most prominently, Australia's AC/DC and

Britain's Judas Priest.

In fact, there were so few points of reference out there, one reviewer actually said Van Halen was being touted as Southern California's answer to Boston — even though the two bands sounded nothing like each other.

"I don't need a hit. I don't need a radio," Roth said. "Just give me an album and a stage. ... This is a personality band. We go on stage and we're ourselves. People can relate to that. That's why we named ourselves after a human being — Van Halen. That name won't lock us into anything."

Actually, two human beings: the Van Halen brothers. The band was a trailblazer in that regard, as well: In the decades ahead, bands like Bon Jovi, Dokken, Vandenberg, and Daughtry would name themselves after their most prominent members. Before Van Halen, there had been Montrose and Santana, which Roth said actually inspired the name. (The band had gone by Genesis — which was taken — and Mammoth before turning to the brothers for the name they'd use from 1974 onward.)

But one thing Roth said laid down the gauntlet for bands that would follow:

"This is a personality band."

For all of Edward Van Halen's guitar-slinging virtuosity, it would be Roth's personality that set the tone for the 1980s — at first on the Sunset Strip and then beyond.

Decade of Decadence

Passing the Baton

Van Halen didn't stop with its debut album, putting out five albums in as many years.

By 1982, the band stood alone atop the heap of guitar-rock bands in the U.S., having just put out its fifth multiplatinum LP in a row, *Diver Down*. Despite its success, though, many fans were dissatisfied. The album felt cobbled together and clocked in at a perfunctory 31 minutes, 4 seconds, with one-third of the cuts well under 2 minutes each. To make matters worse, nearly half the songs (five out of 12) were cover tunes, and three of the originals were instrumentals.

The Van Halen brothers' dad handled clarinet (clarinet?!) on the band's cover of "Big Bad Bill is Sweet William Now." And the final track was a cover of "Happy Trails," the theme song for cowboy icons Roy Rogers and Dale Evans. It wasn't quite as odd as Gene Simmons cover of Jiminy Cricket's "When You Wish Upon a Star" on his Kiss solo album, but it was up there.

What was going on?

Rolling Stone reviewer Park Puterbaugh called the album "a cogent case for consumer fraud."

"Van Halen, it appears, is running out of ideas: there's more excelsior here than in a shipment of glassware."

And what was the heck was with that stark album art: a red square interrupted with a white diagonal line?

Turns out, it's the flag for "diver down," which indicates there's a scuba diver underwater nearby. David Lee Roth tried to persuade potential listeners there was "something going on that's not apparent to the eyes." If you were diligent enough to look past Puterbaugh's "excelsior" (in this case, meaning wood shavings used as filler to pack fragile goods), you'd find some hidden gems.

But why should you have to go looking?

In an interview with Sylvie Simmons, Roth said: "You put up the red flag with the white slash. Well, a lot of people approach Van Halen as sort of the abyss. It means, it's not immediately apparent to your eyes what is going on underneath the surface."

To many listeners, *Diver Down* was, indeed the abyss in terms of quality. But it turns out, something was, indeed going on beneath the surface — even if it wasn't on this particular album. And what was "going on," or what would soon transpire, would both give Van Halen the biggest success of its career and winding up tearing the band apart.

In a word: synthesizers.

To many rockers, synthesizers were anathema. Queen had started proudly declaring that the band had played "No Synthesizers!" on their albums after a music critic had praised the supposed use of synths on their first release. Brian May had worked hard to create a unique sound using his guitar and felt it hadn't been appreciated. Synthesizers were widely viewed by rock fans as a phony shortcut — as the easy way out — and Queen wanted them to know that the band was putting in an honest day's work. (No offense to Greg Giuffria, Jon Lord, or Joey Tempest.) The disclaimer appeared on every album Queen released in the '70s, until the band finally relented and really *did* use synthesizers on 1980's *The Game*.

To be clear, Roth *wasn't* talking about synthesizers when he coyly referred to "something going on that's not apparent to the eyes." He wouldn't have made that sort of reference, because he didn't like synths. Neither did producer Ted Templeman. The idea came from what might have seemed like the most unlikely source: guitar hero Eddie Van Halen.

Van Halen had been introduced to music on the piano, learning musical theory from an aging Russian instructor: a former concert pianist who, "couldn't speak a word of English" and "would just sit there with a ruler ready to slap my face if I made a mistake."

Templeman had included some of Eddie's piano-playing on "And the Cradle Will Rock...," the single from VH's third album, *Women and Children First*. But the Wurlitzer electric piano he used is largely hidden on the track. Much of the sound was fed through a 100-watt Marshall amplifier and came out the other end sounding like a distorted guitar. And on the guitar solo, about halfway through (just before Roth asks, "Have you seen Junior's grades?"), you can hear the keyboards in the background if you listen for them, providing the foundation for Eddie's blistering attack.

He'd never played keyboards in the studio before, and the band sure as heck didn't want him playing them in concert. That task was assigned to bassist Michael Anthony, because, Eddie later recalled, "they didn't want a guitar hero playing keyboards onstage."

None of this stopped him from writing songs on his electric piano. In fact, on the same day he bought the Wurlitzer, he wrote a tune called "Jump" on the back of the band's tour bus. He pitched the song repeatedly over the next two years, but it was always vetoed by Templeman and Roth.

Other synth-based songs made the cut — but only after they were recorded on guitar in the studio. One exception, which appeared on band's fourth release, *Fair Warning*, was a low-register apocalypse-meets-the-gates-of-hell slow burn titled, ironically, "Sunday Afternoon in the Park."

Diver Down hit the stores in 1982. But then, for the first time since they'd started putting out records, the band took two years before releasing their next LP. The break allowed Eddie to finish up his home studio, 5150 (which would also be the title of the band's seventh release) and start creating new material. Without Roth or Templeman to discourage him in the studio, he worked on synth-based tracks like "I'll Wait" and the spacey "1984," an instrumental that would become the title track to the album released that same year.

Then there was "Jump," the song that had been floating around for a couple of years now. It was the second song Eddie recorded at his new studio, and this time, he, Alex and engineer Don Landee developed it more fully before they presented it to Roth and Templeman. Whether they liked it or just felt Eddie had invested too much in it by that point to turn back, Roth started writing lyrics for it.

The band would use the guitar riff in the background at the end of the song as the basis for their 1990 single "Top of the World." But "Jump" didn't just tee up another song in the VH catalog; it influenced everything that was to come in ways they couldn't have imagined.

First and foremost, it propelled Van Halen to the top of the chart. Not the mainstream rock chart, but the Billboard Hot 100, the upper echelons of which were typically off-limits to hard rock. Released four days before Christmas in 1983, it took two months to reach the summit, knocking off Culture Club's "Karma Chameleon" and staying there for five consecutive weeks.

But was "Jump" hard rock, or was it pop? That wasn't an easy question to answer. Eddie Van Halen's guitar solo rocked as hard as his previous efforts, but the poppy synth riff dominated the rest of the song. It wasn't the first time he'd lent his axe to a pop song: A year earlier, he'd supplied the solo to another No. 1 hit: Michael Jackson's "Beat It."

The synthesizer would play a key role in future Van Halen hits, as well, such as "Dreams" and "Love Walks In" off the band's next LP (where Sammy Hagar would walk in to replace the synthesizer-averse Roth). But the impact of "Jump" went far beyond Van Halen, thanks not only to the sound, but the video that dominated MTV. In that video, Roth's showmanship was on full display, with the flamboyant frontman mugging and pouting for the camera, and doing aerial splits to illustrate the song's title. Eddie, attired in a tiger-print top, spun around and showed off his axe work — at least when Roth didn't step in front of him to hog the spotlight.

"Jump" sewed the seeds for countless flashy, good-time pop-metal videos in the years ahead, putting Van Halen on top of the world.

Roth declared that the band was "like the world's greatest traveling circus — and I get to play ringmaster every night." When he came out with a solo EP in early 1985, it seemed like the definition of a side project: four cover tunes that took a week to record. It appeared to be a hiccup: a pit stop in Van Halen's full-steam-ahead road trip to conquer the world.

And then, it wasn't.

The EP, *Crazy from the Heat*, went platinum, and two of its four tracks were hit singles: A cover of the Beach Boys' "California Girls" went to No. 3 on the singles chart, and an update of Louis Prima's 1956 medley of the early 20th century standards "Just a Gigolo" and "I Ain't Got Nobody" made it to No. 12.

The songs' videos took Roth's flair for showmanship to new heights, building on the goofiness of Van Halen's "Hot for Teacher" video (which had featured kids dressed up to look like junior versions of the band members). "California Girls," narrated by a Rod Serling soundalike, cast Diamond Dave as a tour guide driving into a beachfront Twilight Zone. The Louie Prima cover was a song-and-dance routine built around a parody of pop culture that began with Roth doing a sendup of MTV as the host of "Dave TV." It was far more big band camp than heavy metal thunder, with lookalikes poking fun at the likes of Michael Jackson, Willie Nelson, and Billy Idol.

Roth himself became a target for lampooning: A Boston-based team of morning drive-time DJs released a single on Rhino Records in the fall titled "Just a Big Ego": There will come a day when I'll get old and gray / Oooh, what will they say about me? / When the end comes they'll know / I've got a big ego / The world revolves around me.

Roth wanted to make a movie based on *Crazy from the Heat* and asked Eddie Van Halen to score the soundtrack, but the guitarist apparently was more interested in focusing on the band's next project. By the summer, word got out that Eddie was planning to work with The Who's Pete Townshend and was working on songs with Patty Smyth of Scandal, who was asked to replace Roth.

She declined. She was pregnant at the time and didn't want to move to California, so the band moved on and asked Sammy Hagar — who accepted.

POP GOES THE METAL

David Lee Roth

According to Eddie Van Halen, it was simple: "Dave left to be a movie star."

Following the split, Roth put together his own band with his own guitar hero, Steve Vai from Frank Zappa's band, and released a solo album called *Eat 'Em and Smile*, a not-so-subtle reference to Roth's boast that his band was better than what naysayers had dubbed Van Hagar. (Van Halen would respond with an album title of its own: "OU812," implying that they were smiling first.)

Comparisons were, of course, inevitable, and Roth believed Van Halen was egging them on. "Well," he said, "I'll rise to the challenge. If we have to have a comparison, then fine, I eat you for breakfast, pal. I eat you and smile."

Van Halen released its first album with Hagar, *5150*, in March of 1986 and hit No. 1 on the album charts, propelled by the No. 3 single "Why Can't This Be Love." Roth answered four months later with the aforementioned *Eat 'Em and Smile*, which got to No. 4 and produced the top-20 hit "Yankee Rose."

"Van Hagar" had won the first round, if narrowly, and would stay one step ahead of Roth's solo career for the next decade. Both, however, continued to have success, and the debate about which version of the band was better appears no closer to being resolved now than it ever was.

But the larger point is, there was room for both of them. Because of the musical pop-metal template Eddie Van Halen created and the larger-than-life glam-boyant theatrics of Roth, the sky was now the limit for imitators, who started coming out of the woodwork on the Sunset Strip.

They were, in all, a motley crew.

Wild Side

"There are a lot of imitators out there," David Lee Roth said in early 1985, when the imitation was just getting started. "The easy way out is to simply go as far as the footsteps lead and stop there. So you see a lot of clones: funny little clones, and they last maybe a year or two, then they go by the wayside. Most of these folks are more dependent on their shoes and haircuts than the music. If the music is great, people will tolerate any kind of shoes and haircuts."

POP GOES THE METAL

One has to wonder whether future underdressed grunge pioneers like Eddie Vedder and Kurt Cobain were taking notes.

Regardless, others certainly were paying attention, and were trying to carve out their own niche in the shadow of Diamond Dave — on their way to a place at the top.

At the head of the pack was a band called Mötley Crüe, which consisted of mastermind bassist Nikki Sixx, bleach-blond vocalist Vince Neil, and Tommy Lee, whose real last name was Bass (not Jones), but who actually played drums, not bass.

The three got an apartment together above the Whisky after Sixx quit a band called London, which he'd formed with two others in 1978. Over the years, a revolving door of rockers — Blackie Lawless (W.A.S.P.); Fred Coury (Cinderella); and Izzy Stradlin, Steven Adler, and Slash (Guns N' Roses) among them — passed through London's ranks. But Sixx, disillusioned with the band's instability, left around 1979.

Sixx then teamed up with Lee and guitarist Greg Leon in a band called Suite 19, with Sixx himself on vocals. Leon left, and the band saw an ad in *The Recycler*, a weekly newspaper full of classified ads that helped a number of SoCal rock stars connect over the years. "Loud, rude, and aggressive guitarist available," the ad read. It had been placed by one Mick Mars, formerly of a band called White Horse. That band, one of its members once said, looked like a "motley looking crew."

Mars had written down the words (as Mottley Cru), and it became the basis for his new band's name. The spelling was changed slightly, and umlauts were added to complete the look. They didn't mean anything; the band just happened to think they looked cool on a bottle of Löwenbräu beer.

The fourth member of the ensemble was Vince Neil, who'd gone to high school with Lee. Neil stood out because of his blond hair and attitude; when he donned the black leather attire

Whisky a Go Go

favored by the band, he looked like a satanic surfer dude. Neil patterned himself after none other than David Lee Roth.

"Dave was kind of like me — born and raised in Los Angeles and had that kind of beachy vibe," he said in an interview for the *Metal Evolution* video series. "I saw myself, you know, in him."

Sixx also named Van Halen as an influence, along with the New York Dolls and Aerosmith. But more than anyone, they resembled Kiss — not the watered-down, pop band that was, by this time, most popular with the preteen set, but the version from 1974, which dressed in leather and face paint, put on the craziest show you'd ever seen, and cranked out, raw, heavy rock with melodic undertones.

All those things described the Crüe in 1981.

The words Sixx used to describe the band's approach might

just as well have been uttered by Simmons a few years earlier: "We would go see other bands and go, 'We can top that.' You have to experiment musically and visually to push the envelope."

Simmons famously lit his hair on fire when learning to spit out gasoline in a fire-breathing stage stunt; Neil would use a fiery sword to light Sixx on fire. Kiss painted their faces; Sixx and Lee would paint black lines on theirs. Kiss' Ace Frehley was a spaceman; Crüe's Mick Mars looked like a vampire. The finale of a Kiss show featured the drum set rising up on hydraulics behind the band; Mötley designed a rotating drum set that looked like a roller-coaster or a gyroscope and turned Lee upside down while he continued to play.

But the band's on-stage antics were tame compared to their offstage debauchery. Excess might as well have been their middle name. Their autobiography, *The Dirt*, would be subtitled *Confessions of the World's Most Notorious Rock Band*, and their 1991 greatest hits compilation was called *Decade of Decadence*. That applied to the entire Sunset Strip scene, but Mötley Crüe was at the top of the list.

They had an image, and they lived up to it. Sixx once said he didn't care if people saw them drinking, as long as no one saw them drinking milk.

There was a steep price to pay for the band's dedication to excess, but they usually weren't the ones to pay it.

In 1981, Neil assaulted a drag queen for selling him baby powder at a nightclub, pretending it was cocaine. In 1993, Mars took a woman named Rebecca Mettling to a remote high-desert spot north of Los Angeles for some target shooting, but one of the bullets ricocheted off a rock and hit her in the stomach. Those, however, were relatively minor incidents.

The worst occurred on Dec. 8, 1984, when Neil got behind

the wheel of his red 1972 Ford Pantera, with Nicholas "Razzle" Dingley in the passenger's seat. Dingley, an English drummer, had hooked on with an up-and-coming band from Finland called Hanoi Rocks, which was in the midst of its first U.S. tour.

The tour had hit a rough patch on stage in Syracuse, when lead singer Michael Monroe slipped and broke his ankle after jumping off a stack of amps into a puddle of alcohol. So the band had taken a break, with the other members heading on to L.A. Dingley, 24, found himself partying at Neil's Redondo Beach home. They'd both gotten drunk and, having run out of booze, decided to do a liquor store run to replenish their supply. Neil was doing 65 in a 25 zone along the beach just south of the pier, when he suddenly found himself coming up on a firetruck that was stopped in the road. He swerved to avoid the truck, lost control, and veered into oncoming traffic.

There was a crash.

Neil, amazingly, was uninjured, even though he wasn't wearing a seatbelt. Unfortunately, the same couldn't be said for Dingley, who perished in the accident.

He wasn't the only victim. The two occupants of the VW that Neil hit head-on — one of two other cars involved in the crash — were both injured and rushed to the hospital. The driver, 20-year-old Daniel Smithers, had a broken leg, and his girlfriend Lisa Hogan, 18, was taken to ICU, where she was listed in critical condition. She had suffered a fractured arm and two broken legs; when she finally emerged from a coma at the end of the month, she was left with brain damage that made her prone to seizures.

There was more than one cruel irony surrounding the crash: It happened on the very first day of National Drunk Driving Awareness Week, and Lisa Hogan was en route to a meeting of recovering alcoholics at the time of the crash.

POP GOES THE METAL

"She spent three years getting her life together, trudging through that hard road of staying sober and clean, and in five minutes, some fool wrecks it," one of her friends told the *Los Angeles Times*.

Neil, whose blood-alcohol level measured 0.17 percent, was arrested and charged with vehicular manslaughter and drunken driving. He faced as much as eight years in prison, but he was ultimately sentenced to just to 30 days in jail. The reason? The district attorney pointed to lawsuits filed against him by the victims and the fact that Neil, despite his success, didn't have any money in the bank. A private investigator working on the case said he was living a "hand-to-mouth" existence, so the victims wouldn't be able to collect any monetary damages from him unless he earned more cash — which he couldn't do from a prison cell.

Ultimately, Neil agreed to enter a guilty plea in exchange for avoiding prison time and instead performing community service (lecturing about the dangers of drug and alcohol use), while paying $2.6 million to the victims. It seemed like a win-win situation: Neil avoided prison, the victims received restitution, and fans got to hear more music from Mötley Crüe, which released their third album (*Theatre of Pain*, which they dedicated to Dingley) around the same time Neil entered his plea.

But did Neil learn his lesson? Apparently not: In 2011, he was sentenced to two weeks in jail and two weeks of house arrest for driving his Lamborghini on the Las Vegas Strip while drunk. Neil called the sentence "a little harsh" and complained that the courts wanted to make an example out of him "because of my past."

Theatre of Pain turned out to be Mötley Crüe's biggest success yet, reaching No. 6 on the Billboard album chart and, just as significantly, producing a blockbuster power ballad in "Home Sweet Home." You wouldn't know it by looking at the singles chart, where the song topped out at No. 89 in the U.S., but the video was an absolute phenomenon, becoming the most highly requested song on MTV's *Dial MTV* (a precursor to *MTV's Most Wanted* and *Total Request Live*) for three months running. The video's hold on the top spot was so unrelenting that *Dial MTV* adopted the so-called "Crüe Rule," limiting any video's reign to 30 days. The video itself was pretty straightforward: After a goofy intro, it segued into scenes of the band in concert at the Houston Summit. But it opened the floodgates for the power ballad, making it something pop metal bands pretty much *had* to record on every album from that point forward.

It wasn't as though bands enjoyed doing power ballads (although they certainly enjoyed the female attention that came with them). Dokken's biggest power ballad, "Alone Again," actually predated "Home Sweet Home" by a year, but guitarist George Lynch viewed songs like that as a necessary evil:

"Personally, the things I liked least about Dokken were some of the things that we were recognized for the most and had the most success with," he said, adding that, "when you get to the point when you start making music because it's the music you're supposed to make rather than what you want to make, you're definitely compromising. But that's what we did."

Sure enough, each of the next two Mötley Crüe releases included a power ballad: the somewhat disturbing "You're All I Need" (about an obsessive relationship that ends in violence) and "Without You," which was not the Nilsson hit.

Crüe's fourth album, *Girls, Girls, Girls*, was released in 1987 and hit No. 2 on the charts, paving the way for 1989's *Dr. Feelgood*, which went all the way to the top. The title track charted at No. 6, and the second single cracked the top 30. Titled "Kickstart My Heart," it was based on the band's second brush with death, which hit even closer to home.

Barely three years after Neil's tragic, alcohol-fueled crash, substance abuse once again nearly brought down the Crüe. This time, it was heroin. Sixx had been using the drug since 1983, and, as with the crash that killed Razzle Dingley, a sportscar was involved.

Except this time, it was a Porsche, and the drug use *followed* the crash.

Sixx had been using substances since the age of 6, when his stepfather offered him a joint and a bottle of Jack Daniels. But he didn't start using heroin until he wrapped his Porsche around a telephone pole and wound up in the hospital, hopped up on painkillers. Afterward, he started taking heroin to cope with the continued pain.

His complexion turned yellow. He had the sweats constantly. He nearly killed himself during a tour with Cheap Trick, blacking out only to wake up on his drug dealer's shoulders, where he was being carried "like an old trash bag." The dealer evidently had given up on reviving him and planned to dispose of his body in a dumpster.

But the worst was still to come. On Dec. 23, 1987, he joined members of Megadeth, Guns N' Roses and Ratt for a party where the he had a dealer inject him with heroin. In the band's biography, *The Dirt*, he described a sensation of leaving his body and being pulled upward toward a bright white light.

But he also recalled the paramedic saying, "No one's going to die in my fucking ambulance!"

You've heard of the phrase, "live by the sword, die by the sword." For Sixx, it was "die by the needle, live by the needle." He was reportedly clinically dead for 2 minutes before he woke up to find two syringes sticking out of his chest, the contents of which — adrenalin — had brought him back to life.

British Steel

Another New Wave from Overseas

At the dawn of the '80s, Judas Priest stood at the vanguard of what was called the New Wave of British Heavy Metal: the next generation of bands that took the mantle from Led Zeppelin, Black Sabbath and Deep Purple. But despite the furious twin-guitar assault of Glenn Tipton and K.K. Downing, they had yet to break through in the States. Their best showing to date had been 1978's *Hell Bent for Leather*, which had only gotten to No. 128 on the Billboard album chart.

AC/DC got their start in Australia but moved to London in 1976 and gained significant airplay on album rock stations in the U.S., hitting No. 17 on the album chart in 1979 with *Highway to Hell*, despite the lack of a hit single. But just as they appeared poised to take off, lead singer Bon Scott — who was making a name as one of rock's most distinctive voices — was found dead in his own car after a night of heavy drinking, apparently having choked on his own vomit.

Also in 1979, a band from Sheffield called Def Leppard had released *The Def Leppard EP*, a three-song effort recorded in just two days at Fairview Studios in Hull, England. The 7-inch record featured "Getcha Rocks Off" and "Ride into the Sun" on the A side, backed with a nearly 8-minute opus titled "The

Overture" that was recorded in just one take.

The initial release was just 1,000 records, 100 of which came with a signed lyric sheet. The front cover featured a clever takeoff on RCA's iconic logo of a dog cocking its head to one side as it stares into a record player's megaphone-style speaker. (The dog was bemused at hearing "his master's voice" issuing forth from the contraption.) Instead of a dog, Def Leppard's sleeve showed a leopard roaring as it turned its head away from the band's music — presumably because it was so loud. The back cover included photos of the band and a track listing, along with production and art credits. Lead singer Joe Elliott's picture was captioned as "Joe 'Zeff' Elliott."

It was an ambitious project for a band so young. Elliott, at 19, was the senior member; guitarist Pete Willis was 18, and bassist Rick Savage just 17. They had to borrow Frank Noon of The Next Band to play on the two-day recording session because they'd parted ways with their original drummer, Tony Kenning, a couple of months earlier.

(Kenning's ultimate replacement, Rick Allen, was even younger at 15. He signed on after Noon declined an invitation to join permanently.)

To pay for the recording, Elliott had to borrow money from his father, who "took every penny out of his bank account" to cover the cost, the singer later said.

After Elliott's father "literally emptied his life savings" to get the EP recorded, the band had to borrow money from a woman at the local steel foundry — at 25 percent interest — to finance actually pressing the record and printing the sleeve.

The band used Noon's contacts to send copies out to radio stations and journalists, including Geoff Barton of *Sounds* magazine, who took them up on an invitation to see them play live in Sheffield. They also contacted record store owner Pete Martin, who agreed to distribute the EP and eventually teamed up with publicist Frank Stuart-Brown to manage them.

Stuart-Brown's reaction upon hearing "Overture" was that it reminded him of the progressive band Yes around the time they'd recorded *Fragile*, back in 1971. That assessment gets at the heart of the problem with defining Def Leppard: Most of their early material was definitely hard rock, as epitomized by the most popular track on the EP, the driving "Getcha Rocks Off." But there was a lot more to them than that, even then.

The band's first LP, *On Through the Night* continued in the vein of their EP — it even included new versions of two songs from that self-release: the slightly retitled "Rocks Off" and "The Overture." But their sound would evolve as time went on: Their second release, *High 'n' Dry*, featured one of the decade's first widely played power ballads, "Bringin' on the Heartbreak," and the Middle Eastern-sounding "Mirror, Mirror."

Their breakthrough third album, *Pyromania*, which hit the No. 2 spot on the Billboard album chart, firmly established them as leading purveyors of melodic metal, with the No. 1 U.S. Rock hit "Photograph" a favorite on MTV. The follow-up album, *Hysteria*, cemented that reputation, spawning *seven* charting singles.

Hysteria was four years in the making and marked a time of transition for the band.

Original guitarist Pete Willis had been fired toward the end of the *Pyromania* sessions over his problems with alcohol, and Phil Collen had been brought in to finish up. Collen was coming off a three-year stint in a band called Girl, which also featured future L.A. Guns front man Phil Lewis (with whom Collen collaborated on much of their material).

Mutt Lange, who had produced Def Leppard's previous two albums, bowed out early in the process and was replaced by Jim Steinman, who'd written all the tracks on Meat Loaf's multiplatinum *Bat out of Hell* LP in 1977. But Steinman didn't click, and enough time passed that Lange eventually returned.

In the meantime, the band endured a tragic setback when drummer Rick Allen's left arm was severed in a high-speed crash on New Year's Eve, 1984. The car went off the road on a curve and overturned, and Allen was taken to the hospital, where he was unconscious and listed in critical condition after undergoing microsurgery to have the arm reattached.

Allen survived, but the arm developed an infection and had to be amputated.

Four days later, Allen's brother said he fully intended to get back behind the drum kit and had already talked to an American drum manufacturer about creating a custom-built electronic drum that would allow him to play with just one arm.

"He is determined to get back, and I believe he will," Robert Allen told the press. "He has the willpower to do it. I think there is a strong possibility Rick will be playing with Def Leppard later this year."

Robert Allen's confidence proved to be well-founded: His brother did, indeed, return to the band and appeared on the next album — not to mention all the albums, and tours, after that. In fact, it was Allen who supplied the title for the song that became the title track when the band decided not to call the album "Animal Instinct."

Hysteria alienated some fans of Def Leppard's harder-rocking earlier releases by including more polished pop-rock and fewer straight-ahead rockers. But that was a tradeoff the band was ready to make. The disc was *designed* to be a crossover hit, with something for everybody: "a hard rock version of 'Thriller,'" as Collen described it, referring to Michael Jackson's massively successful 1982 album.

It lived up to every bit of those expectations, selling more than 12 million copies in the U.S. alone and spending 96 weeks in the top 40, a record for the 1980s that it shares with Bruce Springsteen's *Born in the U.S.A.*

The power ballad "Love Bites" made it all the way to the top of the Billboard Hot 100, while the album's signature cut,

"Pour Some Sugar On Me," just missed at No. 2, and the cheekily titled "Armageddon It" (recalling Iron Butterfly's "Inna Gadda Da Vida") checked in at No. 3. For good measure, the title track also squeezed into the top 10 at No. 10.

But although Def Leppard's mastery of melodic metal separated the band from the New Wave of British Heavy Metal, it wound up grouping them together — at least in the minds of some critics — with the bands that had come out of the Sunset Strip scene.

"We were always getting lumped in with this so-called new wave of British heavy metal when we first started out," Elliott would recall in an interview with *Loudwire*. "Cut forward like 10 years, and some moron — I use the word not lightly, moron — comes up with the phrase 'hair metal' and we're going, 'Dude, we couldn't have been so far removed from that if we tried.' Literally, while everybody else is poncing around Sunset Boulevard doing whatever they did, we were in Holland living next to a windmill recording the 'Hysteria' album."

Elliott told *Rolling Stone* he'd been to the Strip at least once, when the band was on tour with Billy Squier, to celebrate guitarist Steve Clark's 23rd birthday back in 1982. They stopped by the Rainbow and invited some folks back to their hotel room, but word got out and, as everyone made a beeline for the Sunset Marquis, where they were staying.

"We wound up having like 65 people trying to walk into Steve's room. It just got stupid. We had to start turning people away — and it was guys like Dio. But we had to say, 'Dude, we can't let you in.' Imagine saying that to Dio! But it was crazy, I mean, we were a band from Sheffield. We had never seen a scene like that."

Def Leppard may not have been hair metal, but there were some common threads. Like many of the West Hollywood bands, they wrote catchy, hook-laden songs. In fact, they did it better than most, if not all of them. Beyond that, both the band and their U.S. peers were heavily influenced by the glam-rock movement of the early '70s.

Collen's previous band, Girl, had covered Kiss' "Do You Love Me" and had adopted an androgynous look, with Collen himself looking like a dead ringer for Rod Stewart in a (yes) *leopard*-skin top.

If you have any doubt about Def Leppard's influences, just listen to "Rocket," the second cut from *Hysteria*, which reference Queen, Bowie and Elton John, among others.

When Def Leppard recorded an entire album of cover songs in 2006, it didn't have a single selection from Led Zeppelin, Deep Purple or Black Sabbath. Instead, the band chose songs by glam pioneers like Bowie, Roxy Music, T. Rex, Mott the Hoople, and Sweet, along with power-pop tunes originally done by bands like the Nerves and Badfinger.

Collen, appropriately, sang lead on a cover of the Faces' "Stay With Me," which Elliott later called "his best Rod Stewart impression."

Except maybe for the one he did with Girl.

You Can't Kill Rock and Roll

Sometimes, new decades start without a clear cultural or artistic break from what came before. There's a sense of continuity, until some major event, such as the end of World War II or the release of "Rock Around the Clock" draws a line in the sand between then and now.

On other occasions, though, a new decade really does mark a new beginning. In the U.S., the election of Ronald Reagan meant the ascendance of a new kind of conservatism that would define the 1980s. Disco was dead, CNN launched the age of cable news, John Lennon was killed in front of his apartment, and Pac-Man launched the era of the video game.

Meanwhile, overseas, several acts from the British Empire launched a second, more metallic, invasion of the radio dial.

Iron Maiden, which had formed five years earlier, released its self-titled debut album on EMI, sending it to No. 4 on the U.K. album charts. After a less successful follow-up, Bruce Dickinson replaced Paul Di'Ano on vocals, resulting in *The Number of the Beast*, the first of five No. 1 albums and the second of 11 top-five showings for the band.

Nineteen-eighty was also the year Judas Priest broke into the U.K. top 10 for the first time with *British Steel*, featuring one of the most iconic album covers in the annals of metal: A hand stretched forth, holding a razorblade at the straightedges — somehow, without getting cut. The album's highlights included "Breaking the Law" and one of the first true metal anthems of the '80s, "Living After Midnight," both of which ascended to No. 12 on the U.K. singles chart.

It was the first Priest album to go platinum in the States.

In September of 1980, the singer Black Sabbath had fired released his first album as a solo artist: *Blizzard of Ozz*. Ozzy Osbourne's debut was the first of eight consecutive platinum LPs over a span of 20 years. It spawned a pair of singles: "Crazy Train," which rose to No. 9 on the U.S. Mainstream Rock chart, and "Mr. Crowley," inspired by occultist Aleister Crowley.

Ozzy had assembled a band that included SoCal guitar prodigy Randy Rhoads, who had developed a reputation more formidable than anyone this side of Eddie Van Halen (his rival on the L.A. club scene.) Although he taught guitar himself at his mother's music school, which she'd established in 1948, Rhoads was always eager to learn more.

POP GOES THE METAL

When asked once who his teacher was, he responded: "Anybody. I just take lessons from anybody, like when I have a day off or something. I'll find someone in town and just pick their brain."

Rhoads had been playing with a band called Quiet Riot for five years. The band got its name after vocalist Kevin DuBrow got into a discussion with Rick Parfitt, guitarist for the British band Status Quo. Parfitt mentioned that, if he ever were to start another band, he'd name it "Quite Right." But because of Parfitt's cockney accent, DuBrow heard it as "Quiet Riot."

The band had gone on to score a record deal with CBS and had recorded two albums, but the label only released them in Japan. Frustrations were mounting, and tensions were running high, compounded by the fact that bassist Kelly Garni had an anger problem and didn't get along with DuBrow.

One night, Garni robbed a bar of its liquor and then got drunk at home with Rhoads. Garni, who had a gun with him, wanted to fire DuBrow from the band, but Rhoads wasn't convinced. At some point in the evening, Garni fired the gun at the ceiling, and the rumor got started that he wanted to kill the guitarist: a rumor he denied. They *did* get into a fistfight, but DuBrow was the guy he wanted dead.

So after Rhoads left, Garni got in the car and started driving toward the studio where DuBrow was recording vocals for *Quiet Riot II*. But 25 miles later, he realized he was too drunk to drive, so he turned around. Unfortunately for him, as he approached his house, he was pulled over by a police officer who noticed the gun in his holster as he got out of the car. He wound up under arrest for DUI and possession of a concealed weapon. As a result, it was he — not DuBrow — who ended up getting kicked out of the band.

Rudy Sarzo replaced Garni on bass, but Rhoads was getting

fed up with the band, especially since he didn't want to play rock 'n' roll all his life: He aspired to eventually get a degree in classical music.

That's when he got a call that Ozzy Osbourne was putting together a band and was looking for a guitarist. Rhoads wasn't a Sabbath fan, so he wasn't particularly enthusiastic about the idea, but he decided to give it a shot. He was just warming up at the audition when the inebriated Osbourne declared he had the job — and promptly passed out.

Rhoads wasn't just a great guitar player. He also helped Osbourne write songs like "Crazy Train," "Flying High Again," "Over the Mountain" and "Mr. Crowley" that established Ozzy as a solo artist.

Later, when Osbourne needed a new bass player, Rhoads suggested Sarzo, who left Quiet Riot, which basically ceased to exist at that point. DuBrow teamed up with guitarist Greg Leon, and ultimately went on to form a new band (called DuBrow). Leon was replaced by Carlos Cavazo, and the name of the band eventually reverted — with Rhoades' and Sarzo's blessing — to Quiet Riot.

Sarzo, meanwhile, joined Ozzy's band in time for the *Diary of a Madman* tour supporting Osbourne's second album.

It was during that tour that tragedy struck. En route to a music festival in Orlando, Fla., the air conditioner blew, and the bus driver stopped for the night to fix it. Rhoads, Sarzo, and the Osbournes (Ozzy and his wife, Sharon) were all on board, as were keyboardist Don Airy and drummer Tommy Aldridge. Tour manager Jake Duncan and Rachel Youngblood, the band's 58-year-old seamstress, cook and makeup artist, were also along for the ride.

Everyone went to sleep for the night, but early the next morning, bus driver Andrew Aycock woke up with an idea in his head. They were parked near a friend's house — a friend who had a plane and a small airstrip. Why not take it out for spin? Aycock had a pilot's license. Sure, it was expired, but what did that matter? There wasn't anyone around, and he'd just take a couple of quick flights.

(The plane was a 1955 single-engine Beechcraft: the same kind of aircraft that crashed on Feb. 3, 1959, the infamous "day the music died," killing Buddy Holly, Ritchie Valens and J.P. "The Big Bopper" Richardson.)

Aycock asked Airey and Duncan if they wanted to go for a ride, and they agreed, so he took them up and brought them back down safely, then asked Rhoads if he wanted to go up next. He did, and roused the still-sleeping Sarzo to ask him if he wanted to join them. But Sarzo wanted to get some extra shuteye, so he stayed in his bunk on the bus. Youngblood decided to join them instead.

Once they were aloft, Aycock decided to have some fun, flying low and buzzing the tour bus. After making two close passes, he began his approach for a third.

But he miscalculated.

He got too close to the bus, and clipped it with one of the wings, sending the plane tumbling out of control.

The aircraft ripped off the top of a pine tree and slammed full-force into the garage of a nearby home. The pilot and his two passengers, Rhoads and Youngblood, were all killed instantly.

No one on the bus was injured, but the sound of the plane clipping the vehicle woke everyone who'd been sleeping. Sarzo expected to find himself on the freeway and was surprised to see they were still at their stop. Ozzy thought they'd gotten going again, too, and had hit a car.

They soon realized what had happened, and once the

implications sank in, they never got over it.

More than 30 years later, Sarzo said it was still difficult to talk about that morning. He wound up leaving Osbourne's band because it was too hard for him to go out on stage every night knowing Rhoads wasn't there. Sarzo ended up rejoining his old band, Quiet Riot, in time for their breakthrough album, *Metal Health*.

Osbourne said: "I swear to God, the tragedy of my life is the day he died."

The last thing Rhoads said to him was an admonishment for Osbourne, whose alcohol problems were well known, to take better care of himself.

He told Osbourne: "You'll kill yourself, you know? One of these days."

Back in Black

Without question, the biggest success story of 1980 was AC/DC's *Back in Black*, their first album with new singer Brian Johnson. The band had decided to soldier on after Bon Scott's death and hired Johnson, who'd previously fronted a glam band called Geordie that had opened for both Sweet and Slade in the early 1970s.

Geordie had taken its name from the word for residents of their hometown, Newcastle upon Tyne, as well as their distinctive regional dialect. They'd had a couple of top-20 hits in 1973 but hadn't been able to attain the level of stardom some of their contemporaries achieved, despite 15 appearances on *Top of the Pops*. Like other glam bands, they faced a decline in popularity during the second half of the decade and eventually broke up. Johnson had been trying to resurrect the band with new members before he joined AC/DC.

POP GOES THE METAL

Brian Johnson

Oddly enough, Johnson and Scott had actually met before *Scott* joined AC/DC. Scott had been part of a soft-rock and bubblegum act called the Valentines in the '60s before moving on to front a progressive rock act called Fraternity in 1970. That band opened for several more establish acts — including, as fate would have it — Geordie.

At one of those shows, Johnson recalled, he went onstage in excruciating pain.

He explained: "I had a terrible case of appendicitis, and I

went down on my side, kicking and going, 'Ooh!' But I kept on singing. Apparently, (Scott) told the boys when he joined AC/DC, 'I saw this guy Brian Johnson sing, and he was great. He was on the floor, kicking and screaming — what an act!' Of course, it wasn't an act. I was really ill."

Johnson's moderate success with Geordie didn't prepare anyone for what he was about to experience with AC/DC. How often does a successful band with a distinctive lead singer find even greater success with his replacement? The best that can usually be hoped for is to maintain at least something close to the same level of popularity — usually amid complaints that the new guy can't compare to the original. (Prime example: Sammy Hagar taking over for David Lee Roth in Van Halen.)

Johnson didn't make anyone forget about his predecessor, and he didn't try. In fact, he wrote the title track as a tribute to Scott. The song was one of two from the album to hit the U.S. top 40, the other being "You Shook Me All Night Long." But the album didn't need a hit single to succeed. It exploded on the charts, hitting No. 1 in several countries and No. 4 in the United States. It would go on to become one of the top-selling albums of all time, both in the U.S. and worldwide.

With 25 million certified sales as of 2019, it had sold more than the combined total two other huge hard rock albums from the '80s — Bon Jovi's *Slippery When Wet* and Def Leppard's *Hysteria*.

Combined.

The bands at the forefront of the New Wave of British Heavy Metal were not, by and large, in what was known as the "hair metal" category, although they were often placed there casually by fans or critics who didn't know any better. Some of them, most notably Def Leppard and Ozzy Osbourne, did move more toward melodic or pop metal as the decade progressed.

POP GOES THE METAL

Judas Priest briefly dabbled in pop metal, most notably on their 1986 album, *Turbo*, before returning to the more aggressive heavy metal for which they were known.

One notable exception was a blues-rock outfit fronted by the man who had replaced Ian Gillan as the lead singer of Deep Purple. David Coverdale had recorded three albums with Purple before the band broke up, and he went on to record a couple of solo albums, the first of which was titled *White Snake*. The name served as the inspiration for a new band he formed in 1978, Whitesnake.

L.A. Times reviewer Terry Atkinson described the band's debut, *Snakebite*, as medium-to-hard rock that was "in the Bad Company/Deep Purple mold" and achieved "only the level of those bands' more mediocre efforts." He went on to compare the style to that of Foreigner, which itself had been likened to Bad Company.

Whitesnake scored its biggest hit to date in 1980 with "Fool for Your Lovin'" which failed to chart in the U.S. but hit No. 13 in the U.K. with a sound that did, indeed, sound a lot like Bad Company. It was catchy, but instrumentally, it bore little resemblance to the pop metal that would start coming out of West Hollywood later in the decade.

Coverdale would stick with that sound for the band's first four albums before suddenly changing things up with 1984's *Slide It In*.

If you want to hear the difference between the kind of hard rock music that evolved from blues rock and the metal sound that grew out of power pop, you need only listen to Whitesnake before 1984 and the same band after that date. The band even recorded new versions of "Crying in the Rain," "Here I Go Again" and "Fool for Your Loving," so it's easy to hear the difference.

The latter two songs both missed the U.S. charts completely in their original versions. But "Here I Go Again" topped the Billboard Hot 100 the second time around, while the updated version of "Fool for Your Loving" made it to No. 2 on the Mainstream Rock chart.

What a difference a makeover makes.

Indeed, the band's sound wasn't the only thing that changed during Whitesnake's transformation. Coverdale lightened up his dark hair and began applying makeup until he and his band started looking — and sounding — a whole lot more like Poison and less like Bad Company.

It was part of a template that had preceded 1980s metal, having been established by frontmen like The Who's Roger Daltrey and, especially, Zeppelin's Robert Plant: the singing Adonis. Now, however, it was everywhere: Bret Michaels of Poison, Jani Lane of Warrant, Jon Bon Jovi, Kip Winger, David Lee Roth. And David Coverdale.

"In some of the pictures, it's difficult to tell the difference between Whitesnake and Poison unless you hear the records," he said in an interview with Sam Dunn for Dunn's documentary series on the evolution of metal. "We worked with the same stylist who was doing Van Halen, Mötley — it actually became just more of a joke to us, you know, 'cause it was just kind of out of control. You know, 'How much eyeliner should we use? I don't know. Let's look like girls.'"

But Coverdale added that he wouldn't change a thing.

"MTV was the icing on the cake," he said. "It saved me three to five years' hard road work in the United States to achieve that kind of success."

In 1989, Coverdale became one of several pop metal stars to marry a model (others included Gene Simmons of Kiss, Jani Lane of Warrant, and Axl Rose of Guns N' Roses) when he tied the knot with Tawny Kitaen. She'd come out to L.A. — where Coverdale had relocated — with then-boyfriend Robbin Crosby of Ratt, whom she'd known since high school, and wound up appearing in several Whitesnake videos.

The pair would divorce two years later. Coverdale decided to disband Whitesnake in the meantime and returned to his blues-rock roots in collaboration with former Zeppelin guitarist Jimmy Page. In a notable twist, Page had previously worked with Paul Rodgers, former vocalist for Bad Company — the band to which Coverdale's Whitesnake had been compared. It seemed like a natural fit. Except now, Coverdale was being measured against former Zeppelin vocalist Robert Plant. Critics and fans often viewed him as merely a clone of or stand-in for Plant, who himself derisively referred to him as "David Cover-version."

The Coverdale-Page partnership yielded a platinum album that hit the top 10 on both sides of the Atlantic, but the pair went their separate ways after that, as Page reunited with Plant for an acoustic album under the auspices of MTV, while Coverdale eventually re-formed Whitesnake.

Turn Up the Radio

Turn on the Video

Metal had never gotten much respect on the radio dial. One reason hard-rock bands had to tour so much was radio DJs wouldn't touch them, at least for the most part. Alice Cooper was never really metal in the '70s, but he did have a reputation as a hard-edge, dangerous hard rock act.

Radio had played "I'm Eighteen" and "School's Out" (the latter during the first week of June every year), but after that, all that reached the airwaves were ballads like "You and Me," or "I Never Cry." One of his biggest hits was another ballad called "Only Women Bleed." Teenage guys who listened to it thought it was about a woman's period — which made no sense except for the fact that teenage guys have pretty much one thing on their mind. Women who heard it realized it was a sad tale of domestic violence.

"I didn't realize it would end up as a woman's anthem," Cooper told *Mojo*. "I just needed a ballad for 'Welcome to my Nightmare.'" (Apparently, the "token ballad" strategy was a thing long before the '80s.)

Kiss needed a ballad of their own, "Beth," to break them on the radio in 1976, but it wasn't as though that paved the way for a future assault on the airwaves. In the years that followed, you might hear "Hard Luck Woman," "Christine Sixteen" or "Rocket Ride" once in a blue moon, but that was about it. Oh, and when 1979 rolled around, you might hear the discofied "I Was Made for Lovin' You" every now and then — but if you were a rock fan, that didn't count. If anything, it was a strike against the station that played it.

By that point, much of FM radio had gotten stale and had morphed into a slightly harder-edged version of the bland and predictable AM broadcasting they'd once rebelled against.

In the late '60s and early '70s, FM radio had broken away from the rigidly programmed AM top-40 format, which served up the same pop songs over and over and over again ad nauseam. Listeners wanted more variety and more innovation. AM music, by contrast, had grown "safe," at least relatively speaking, and by the late 1960s, top-40 radio was inundated by bubblegum pop and watered-down psychedelia: "Sugar, Sugar" and "Aquarius" were the top two singles of 1969. The closest you could get to real rock was the Stones, who had been sort of grandfathered in by that point, and Creedence Clearwater Revival.

The restrictive format meant established acts got most of the airtime. There were only a couple of ways to break onto the airwaves: Get an influential DJ to play your song (and hope it generated requests), or go out and buy up a bunch of copies at the local discount store or record shop. If you did enough of the latter, you could boost sales figures, which factored into whether a song cracked the local top 40. Then, maybe other stations would pick it up from there.

Clearly, an alternative to the AM model was needed, and FM provided it in the form of something called Album Oriented Rock, or AOR (not to be confused with adult-oriented rock or soft rock). The idea was to play a bigger variety of music, including album cuts, not just 3-minute singles.

Stations in the Metromedia chain, which included such heavyweights as WMMR in Philly, KSAN in San Francisco, and KMET in L.A. — aka, "The Mighty Met" — all labeled themselves as progressive rock stations, which didn't refer to progressive *acts* like Yes or King Crimson. As described by KMET general manager David Moorhead, a progressive station was simply "a station which is against any and all established radio traditions."

They also hired DJs for the morning "drive time" block, roughly 6 to 10 a.m., who often created humorous skits that ran between songs during their programs. These were usually geared toward teens, who were driving/being driven to school and hanging out in the parking lot, listening to the radio as they waited for classes to start. Starting in 1972, Sunday evenings at KMET were the domain of Barret "Barry" Hansen, aka Doctor Demento, who spun sometimes crass and often hilarious tunes like "Diesel Smoke and Dangerous Curves," the Halloween staple "Monster Mash," and "Big Ten-Inch Record" (a penis joke set to music that was later covered by Aerosmith).

Album-rock radio would play everything from Bob Dylan to Jethro Tull to Led Zeppelin, with lesser-known acts like Cat Mother & the All Night Newsboys, Mahogany Rush or Cold Blood thrown into the mix, as well. But that didn't mean it wasn't formatted, too. It wasn't as though the DJs at KMET got to play whatever they wanted.

"Every cut that gets on the air is an approved cut, in general," KMET's Moorhead, told *Billboard* in 1972. "The music director and creative director check every album before it goes into the library. The specific cuts not to be played are so indicated."

There was a system that rated album cuts on a scale of 1-10, and those that didn't get a number were "obviously not worth playing," Moorhead said. The Stones, he added, received a lot of 10s, while "Fanny Tablelegs from East Jesus, Neb., would be lucky to even get one cut listed."

In other words, the more popular bands still got played more, just as they had on top-40 stations. They just happened to be a little more cutting-edge, and the tracks that got played were more than just their singles. (This is how Led Zeppelin's "Stairway to Heaven" became the most-played song in FM radio history, even though it was never issued as a single.)

By '72, Moorhead was already declaring progressive radio to be dead. "On the West Coast, unfortunately, the term came to mean undisciplined radio — a bunch of freaks sitting around smoking dope," he said. "That type of radio had to evolve."

Or devolve.

Into a slightly more mature version of top-40 radio, which Moorhead himself described as "adult rock." By the late '70s, it had come to be called something else, derisively, by those who missed the more freewheeling early days of dope-smoking DJs playing whatever the hell they wanted. That something else was "corporate rock."

Boston, Journey, Styx, Foreigner, Kansas, Asia, Heart, Toto, Loverboy... If you were listening to an album rock station in the 1970s or early '80s, it was impossible to avoid any of these bands. What you didn't hear, except for the occasional ballad, was metal. The closest thing resembling it that might turn up on an album rock station was the aforementioned bands' heavier tunes: "Miss America" by Styx, or Journey's "Chain Reaction." REO Speedwagon was another example: They were *almost* pop metal at times, but they broke through with a ballad ("Keep on Loving You") and were fronted by a guy with a high voice who'd started out as a folk singer.

POP GOES THE METAL

Some rock radio stations did play songs from the likes of AC/DC, Led Zeppelin, Rainbow and a few other acts. Black Sabbath, Judas Priest, and Kiss? Not so much.

Rock radio's overall disdain for heavier bands meant they had to tour to gain a following, then hope that touring translated into album sales.

That, however, was before MTV.

I Want My MTV

"The generation that grew up on television and rock 'n' roll is about to get both. Together."

That's how the *Los Angeles Times* introduced the concept of MTV, five months before its debut on Aug. 1, 1981. The channel would be geared toward viewers 12 to 34 years old and would be programmed, for the most part, like an album-rock radio station.

It's not as though rock bands had never been on TV before. The Beatles famously broke big on *The Ed Sullivan Show*, and there was always the possibility of lip-synching on Dick Clark's *American Bandstand*, which was mostly for pop acts but did occasionally welcome rockers like Aerosmith, Kiss, and Dokken. If you wanted to stay up late, you could catch your favorite bands on NBC's *Midnight Special* or the syndicated *Don Kirshner's Rock Concert*, both of which debuted in 1973 and went off the air the same year MTV made its entrance.

American Express had recently bought Warner Cable, and the original idea was to use its new acquisition to sell credit cards. MTV would be the third leg in a trinity of channels being offered by Warner/Amex, joining Nickelodeon and The Movie Channel. Its mission wasn't to offer a variety of programming, it was to create an TV channel that would cater to the audience that listened to album-rock radio with a near-continuous stream of 3- and 4-minute promotional videos.

"We're not trying to be all things to all people," said John A. Leak, executive vice president of MTV's parent company, Warner/Amex. "We're going after the rock audience that grew up on television and music."

Cable was still in its infancy then, transitioning from its original mission — providing a static-free picture in areas where broadcast reception was fuzzy — to offering a smorgasbord of viewing options.

The new channel quickly issued a call for prospective video jockeys, or VJs, to auditions in New York, Chicago, and L.A. Among them was Marc Bird, a senior at Columbus East Senior High School in Indiana, whose massive record collection included 38,000 albums and singles, and who ran a radio station out of his parents' home. He entered the process "with high hopes," but he didn't make the cut: The five VJ slots went to Nina Blackwood, Mark Goodman, Alan Hunter, J.J. Jackson, and Martha Quinn.

MTV was a low-cost, low-risk endeavor that would offer music videos, supplied free of charge by record companies promoting their talent, similar to a radio station. It started out with somewhere between 250 and 400 videos in its catalog, which it would play in varying rotations, while sandwiching in 8 minutes of commercials every hour. It would also carry live concerts, such as an REO Speedwagon show that was slotted in to kick off the channel's second week.

REO, naturally, got a big push from the network on opening day, with eight different videos played a total of 15 times. It made sense: The band's *Hi-Infidelity* was the year's biggest rock album and would go on to sell more than 10 million copies.

That first day also featured a couple of metal songs: Iron

POP GOES THE METAL

Maiden's "Wrathchild," which got played four times, and two songs from Blackmore's Rainbow — "Can't Happen Here" and "All Night Long" — which showed up five times between them. Both bands hailed from England, which isn't too surprising because most of the material MTV had in hand at the outset were promotional videos produced across the Atlantic, where record companies were cranking out 15 to 20 a month.

MTV beckoned viewers to give it a try with the tagline, "You'll never look at music the same way again." But it wasn't as though the channel showed up all over the country in one big splash. On the contrary, it made its debut mostly in rural and suburban locales, where cable had already been laid to bring regular broadcast stations to areas beyond easy reach of rabbit ears.

Only later would it hook up to homes in urban areas, where it cost more to lay cable.

In sync with its rural audience — and in line with AOR radio — MTV didn't play any black acts, at first. This was supposed to be a rock channel, not soul or funk or R&B, and executives would hold the line on this until public pressure and the success of Michael Jackson's *Thriller* album forced them to change their tune.

That was still a year or two away in 1981, and there was plenty of room for the channel to grow its catalog. There was a clear void that could be filled by metal bands.

Kiss had already produced a concept video for "Shandi" off its *Unmasked* album a year earlier, and put out a video for "A World Without Heroes" off its ill-fated *Elder* concept album just after MTV debuted, but the band was at its commercial nadir and neither song could properly be considered anything close to metal.

The genre wouldn't really blow up on MTV until '83, when Def Leppard released the video to "Photograph" off its third LP, *Pyromania*. A lot of people point to the band's next album, *Hysteria*, as their milestone release, and while it was certainly

POP GOES THE METAL

their commercial *high* point, "Photograph" was their *turning* point. Performance video of the band was interspersed with scenes from a loose concept; the plot revolved around the murder — tied to the song's "passion killer" lyric — of a Marilyn Monroe lookalike, played by model Kay Kent. Midway through, singer Joe Elliott does the splits as he leaps off the drum riser, a move emulated by David Lee Roth in Van Halen's "Jump" video a year later.

Together with the video for "Rock of Ages," also from *Pyromania*, "Photograph" not only made Def Leppard a major player in mainstream music, it helped give metal videos parity with Men at Work, Stray Cats, Culture Club and other MTV staples.

Within a year after Def Leppard blew the lid off MTV, pop metal bands from across the landscape had started showing up on the channel. By 1984, bands like Quiet Riot, Twisted Sister, and Ratt were all in heavy rotation, accomplishing something their forerunners could never have dreamed of achieving on FM radio. And this was more than a thousand times better, because radio reception, even for 50,000-watt "blowtorch" stations, only extended between 50 and 100 miles from its broadcasting tower. MTV, by contrast, was national.

But not everyone liked metal's newfound accessibility, including some folks at the channel itself.

With the success of bands like Quiet Riot and Def Leppard, record companies had rushed to sign metal acts — and to produce videos for them. MTV soon found itself scrambling to keep up, and by the beginning of 1985, it was playing one heavy metal video every three or four songs.

"We played an enormous amount of metal music last summer, but we've gotten to the point where we feel the music has become overexposed," MTV president Bob Pittman said in

March of 1985. "It seems as if every record company has signed a bunch of metal bands, all of whom had videos they wanted us to play."

So Pittman, a former Detroit disc jockey, announced he would be cutting back on metal's presence by a whopping 75 percent, playing just one video every hour or even every 90 minutes.

"These guys don't deserve to dominate the channel," he said. "They're not as popular as the Police or Mick Jagger." The channel, he said, would continue to feature some mainstream pop metal acts like Van Halen, while reducing screen time for bands "that you've never heard of."

Pittman's purge wouldn't last.

The Police, which he'd referenced as a popular act, never put out another original studio album. And Jagger's Rolling Stones released just one more album before Pittman's departure, a disappointing effort titled *Dirty Work* that *People* magazine called "old and tired."

Pittman's fate was sealed when he tried to buy MTV Networks from Warner/Amex, but the channels were sold to Viacom instead.

Before he left, the channel introduced a new call-in request show in early '86 called *Dial MTV*, which was promptly dominated by Mötley Crüe's video for "Home Sweet Home." As previously noted, it would maintain a stranglehold as the No. 1 most requested video for more than three months.

Clearly, there was still a huge appetite for metal among MTV viewers.

Pittman departed as chief executive in August. The following year, metal acts were back in full force.

POP GOES THE METAL

Nothin' But a Good Time

Music videos started off simple: Most were either concert videos or staged performances. But it wasn't long before the clips started getting more creative, and video became something of an art form.

The Cars, a power pop New Wave band, won the inaugural MTV Video of the Year Award in 1984 for their lighthearted, special-effects-laden video, "You Might Think." There's a clear plot, in which singer Ric Ocasek plays a guy who wears down the reluctant object of his affection by morphing into various forms, ranging from a coat hanger to a horsefly.

Two years later, an unknown Norwegian synth-pop band called A-ha caught everyone by surprise with its video of "Take On Me." The song itself was catchy enough to have been a hit anyway, but it's impossible to separate it from the video that aired on MTV, which featured a full-fledged plotline that was resolved in the space of just 4 short minutes: A woman at a diner picks up a sketch comic book about a motorcycle racer, who reaches up out of the book and invites the woman to join him. She becomes part of the sketchbook world, where the hero woos her before they're chased by a pair of two-dimensional villains; he then tears a hole in the page and allows her to escape back into the diner. In the end, he's able to follow her, and the video ends with them united in the real world.

The video won six awards at the 1986 MTV Video Music Awards, losing out to "Money for Nothing" by Dire Straits for the top honor. (The Dire Straits video was a worthy effort, but the lyrics also opened with the signature line "I want my MTV," which couldn't have hurt its chances.)

Metal bands, too, began creating videos with storylines, but with less critical success. Perhaps the most popular "story" clip produced by a metal act was Twisted Sister's "We're Not Gonna Take It," which opens with a nearly minute-long intro before the music even starts. The clip depicts a confrontation between an abusive father and a defiant son, during which the father famously screams at the boy, "What do you want to do with your life?" and the boy, holding a red guitar, responds, "I Wanna Rock."

He then plays a power chord on the guitar, which sends the father flying out a second-story window, and the song begins as the boy transforms into the band's lead singer, Dee Snider.

The video, though, wasn't even nominated for Video of the Year; in fact, only two metal videos would receive nominations during the 1980s. Both were by David Lee Roth, and both were off his 1985 EP *Crazy From the Heat*.

Both lost.

Ironically, the first metal band to win the award was Roth's former band, Van Halen, which won for "Right Now" in 1992 with Sammy Hagar on vocals.

When metal videos tried to get ambitious, they often just looked silly. Krokus' "Screaming in the Night" served up a variation of the same theme used in "Take On Me." As the video opens, singer Marc Storace has been taken prisoner in a cheesy post-apocalyptic fantasy world (think Mad Max meets Conan the Barbarian) before escaping through a trapdoor and popping up, of all places, in a diner.

One might be tempted to say Krokus had taken a page out of A-ha's comic book, but the video for "Screaming" actually came out first. A key variation: In Krokus' version of the tale, the main character's love interest dies.

Women were often treated as props in the world of heavy metal. Videos were targeted to suburban white males in their teens and early 20s, and showed them what they wanted to see:

images of women — often scantily clad and nearly always attractive, unless they were there for comic relief — and sportscars, trucks or motorcycles.

Van Halen's "Panama" was among them. It wasn't about the country, but a race car called the Panama Express that David Lee Roth recalled seeing at a Las Vegas track. When a critic assumed that every Van Halen song was about women, partying and fast cars, Roth balked. It might have been a reasonable assumption, but it was an assumption. And it was wrong. Roth realized he'd actually never written a song about a car — so he decided to come up with one. The fact that the double-entendre lyrics also could have applied to a woman, well, that was just a nice bonus.

Roth is seen driving both a classic red convertible *and* a motorcycle in the video. But the car is not the Panama Express, and the engine that's heard in the song is from a third car: Eddie Van Halen's Lamborghini. There's no real plot to the video, most of which consists of a staged performance with different members of the band goofing off as they "fly" across the stage on a wire.

Plotlines, such as they were, were thin in most metal videos, with brief and banal theatrical scenes often interspersed with concert re-enactments. They weren't actually stories, but rather "conceptual videos," which made them sound a lot more highbrow than they actually were. Often, as with the Krokus video, they played out on low-budget fantasy, dystopian, or gritty street sets designed to make the band members look tough or heroic.

Kiss put out a series of videos like this after they removed their makeup in the mid-'80s. The video to "All Hell's Breakin' Loose" opens with the band fending off a series of attacks from street people in a seedy alley (trashcan fires are everywhere) as they make their way to an equally seedy basement club. Once there, they play a gig while fights break out between women in the crowd — two of whom go at it with fencing swords. (You can almost hear teenage guys watching the video shout, "Girl fight!") When the band finishes playing, they leave, and the video ends with them walking off like conquering heroes.

As skimpy as that plot was, the band's video for "Tears Are Falling," produced a couple of years later, was even worse: It had no story line at all. It opened with a shot of a woman crying, and similar shots appeared occasionally throughout the video. But the woman was little more than a glorified extra: Most of the 3 minutes and 46 seconds was taken up by shots of the band playing and mugging for the camera in front of a fake volcano.

Dokken's video for "It's Not Love" begins with a blonde in bright red lipstick, jeans and a cowboy hat climbing into the cab of a big-rig and hitting the road. She's on the screen for about 5 seconds, tops. Her role is simply to drive the band members through L.A. while they play a concert on a flatbed to enthusiastic fans lining the streets. The blonde never appears again, although rock radio stations KMET and KNAC get some free exposure.

Jackyl came relatively late to the scene, arriving in 1992 with a blues-flavored Southern metal entry, "The Lumberjack." But that didn't mean metal videos had gotten any more mature — or any less confusing — in the meantime. "The Lumberjack" intermingles three seemingly unrelated scenes: A performance in which lead singer Jesse James Dupree wields a chainsaw like a guitar on stage; one in which the band performs in front of an old man's tin-roof home, apparently somewhere in Appalachia; and a third scene in which the band invades a one-room schoolhouse full of bored teens.

When it came to schoolhouse scenes, Van Halen's "Hot for

Teacher" from 1984 was far more inventive. It enlisted four young Van Halen lookalikes to play their roles in a classroom alongside a highly insecure, nerdish boy named Waldo. The real classroom is presented in black and white, juxtaposed against a full-color fantasy in which the teacher is reimagined as a bikini-clad beauty queen.

Most of the video takes place at some point in the past, and it concludes with a "where are they now" sequence that shows drummer Alex Van Halen as a gynecologist, Michael Anthony as a sumo wrestler, Eddie Van Halen "relaxing" in a mental ward, and David Lee Roth as a game-show host. "No one's really sure what became of Waldo after graduation," the text on the screen declares, but the video shows a pimped-out adult version of the once-shy boy, wearing a fur coat and reclining against a classic purple car surrounded by three skimpily clad women.

Whether this is meant to be seen as reality or the fantasy Waldo was suppressing all along is left to the imagination. But the scene brought together two of the most common components of MTV metal videos — beautiful, objectified women and cool cars — and aimed them directly at real adolescent males in real classrooms across the country: teenage boys who with raging hormones who had crushes on their teachers and were bored to death in school.

It hit the bullseye.

No wonder pop metal bands like Van Halen had become so popular by 1984.

Metal Health

By that time, they were on the radio, too — at least in some places. Album-rock stations hadn't played much metal during the '70s, but MTV exposure had created more demand on the airwaves, too. Some stations were playing metal, but others were more reluctant to do so.

Shortly after its first surge in popularity, in 1984, *Billboard* described radio acceptance of metal as "inconsistent," even though sales were up at record stores. Camelot Records, a chain of 161 stores based in Ohio, had embarked on a radio ad blitz of 28 stations offering $1 off hit albums from 19 different metal acts. Meanwhile, Denver-based Budget Tapes & Records was touting metal acts with a monthlong "Metal Mania" push, even though radio stations in the Colorado city were "basically chicken about metal."

Those were the words of ad director Jeff Klem.

"Everybody's playing Ratt and Twisted Sister and maybe Helix," he said, "but not much else."

Still, that was more than most album-rock stations had been playing in years past, and there were signs that the genre's popularity was beginning to broaden. KLOL in Houston had dropped metal six months before *Billboard*'s 1984 article, but was bringing it back. Four thousand people had shown up when the station brought Ratt and Twisted Sister in for an appearance at a local record store.

Those bands' fortunes declined as the decade progressed, but others were more than filling the void as MTV started playing more metal again, spearheaded by the likes of Bon Jovi, Def Leppard, and Whitesnake.

Late in 1986, radio jumped on the bandwagon when a new syndicated format called Z-Rock debuted in Chicago. The following year, a radio station in Denton, Texas, celebrated Independence Day by shedding its municipally inspired call letters, KDNT, and pulling the plug on the "500 Miles of Country Music" it had been broadcasting from its powerful

POP GOES THE METAL

radio tower in Gainesville.

Henceforth, it would be known as KZRK.

On-air talent like "Shootin'" Jim Newton and the Midnight Cowboy were replaced with personalities named Killer Craig, Wild Bill, and Madd Maxx.

The format was also in place at stations in Grand Rapids, Columbus, and Cleveland, all of which played the same songs at the same time via an emerging technology that cut costs through the use of satellite programming. You didn't need to pay local talent anymore, because operations were all centralized on the Satellite Music Network (SMN). Z-Rock was actually just the latest format to be offered by SMN, which had already set up shop with distinct networks broadcasting country, Big Band, oldies, adult contemporary, and contemporary hits. Affiliated stations each paid a fee of $1,150 to $1,750 a month, depending on their market size, to carry the programming, and agreed to pass along 2 minutes of national advertising each hour.

The stations mixed thrash metal with pop metal and classic metal from the '70s. Its playlist included Tesla, Anthrax, Slayer and King Diamond; its top 10 in March of 1987 looked like this:

	Artist	Album
1	Slayer	*Reign in Blood*
2	Stryper	*To Hell With the Devil*
3	Iron Maiden	*Somewhere in Time*
4	Deep Purple	*House of Blue Light*
5	Tesla	*Mechanical Resonance*
6	Jack Starr	*No Turning Back*
7	Megadeth	*Peace Sells*
8	Lizzy Borden	*Menace to Society*
9	Dokken	*Dream Warriors*
10	Malice	*License to Kill*

"There's enormous record sales in this kind of music, and it doesn't get radio airplay," vice president Dennis Grandcolas said of heavy metal in announcing the Denton format change. "We want to get into the Dallas market and see this as a way to do it."

And the airplay, once it started, boosted record sales even more. The results in Cleveland, where the format went on the air in January at WBEA, were immediate and striking.

"The minute it went on, the kids found the station, and we felt it," said Brad Hunt, vice president of AOR promotion for Elecktra/Asylum Records. "Not just with Dokken and Metallica and Mötley Crüe, but also with development bands like Metal Church."

The latter band had sold just 922 units of *The Dark* in Cleveland as of Jan. 26, but that figure had jumped to 12,866 just five weeks later. That was comparable to the sales the label had seen for the band in Los Angeles, a city that was several times larger, Hunt said.

The network broadcast live concerts, aired a show called *Blistering Leads* that spotlighted guitar solos, had an all-request show, a classic rock show, and a news show produced in conjunction with *RIP Magazine*. Z-Rock was to radio what MTV was to television: a place that offered national exposure to metal acts.

It was, however, rawer and more in-your-face. Some of the bands that got airtime on Z-Rock were nowhere to be found on MTV, which preferred "safe" power ballads by established acts to thrash metal by underground favorites. It would have been hard to imagine MTV adopting a slogan like Z-Rock's "If it's too loud, you're too old!" let alone taglines such as "Flip us on and flip them off," or "Lock it in, and rip your knob off."

Even when metal became more popular on MTV, the cable

channel kept a tight rein on what it would allow. Not every metal video made it on MTV, even those put out by popular, established acts.

In 1987, Mötley Crüe's video to the power ballad "You're All I Need" followed on the heels of "Home Sweet Home," which had dominated MTV's request lines a couple of years earlier. But the channel banned this one because the song dealt with a relationship obsession that turned deadly.

Wait. Hadn't that been the theme of Def Leppard's "Photograph" video? And what about The Police's "Every Breath You Take," which — far from being a tender ballad — was sung from the perspective of a stalker? Hmmm.

By that time, Twisted Sister was already history. The band's sax-infused, zombie-themed offering "Be Chrool to Your Scuel," with guest vocals by none other than Alice Cooper, was deemed too gruesome by MTV. (One can only guess what the censors might have said if they'd been able to flash forward to the next century and catch an episode of *The Walking Dead*.)

It was the beginning of the end for the band.

Twisted Sister took off their makeup for 1987's *Love Is for Suckers*, release, which was, to all intents and purposes, a Dee Snider solo album. The album sank like a stone and vanished almost without a trace.

Despite these setbacks, pop metal was once again as popular as anything else on MTV in 1987, spurred by the likes of Bon Jovi's monster *Slippery When Wet* album and Whitesnake's self-titled release. It would retain that popularity through the rest of the decade on MTV, on newly popular CD players, and in the places where it was born, the most prominent of which was West Hollywood's Sunset Strip.

STEPHEN H. PROVOST

Out of the Cellar

Metal in the Mainstream

Woodstock was the culmination of 1960s counterculture youth movement. Hippies. Free love. Pot. Long hair. Tie-dye. Psychedelic music. It was the high point, but it was also the beginning of the end. And it lived on in our cultural mythos as the symbol of what could be, of what might have been; of hopes dared, attained, and vanquished, all in one.

Concert promoters have tried to replicate it ever since, with varying degrees of success.

In 1982, Apple cofounder Steve Wozniak had a big idea: a music festival to mark the end of the "Me Decade" (the 1970s) and usher in an "US" generation. He decided, appropriately, on the name "US Festival," not realizing that its biggest success would involve some of the most hedonistic, self-absorbed musicians on the planet: the superstars of pop metal.

Ah, the irony.

Actually, Wozniak's first US Festival didn't feature any metal acts. The event was dominated by pop and New Wave acts like the Talking Heads, Fleetwood Mac, the Police, and the B-52s. The hardest rockers on the bill were Santana, Eddie Money, the Kinks and Pat Benatar.

It wasn't the first time Southern California had played host to a huge music festival. The massive Cal Jam and Cal Jam II had packed the Ontario Motor Speedway (and the surrounding freeways) in 1974 and again in 1978. But those had been one-day affairs; Woz's first US Festival would span three full days on a stage he built especially for the event at Glen Helen Regional Park in San Bernardino.

The event, staged in the blistering triple-digit heat of late summer, drew 425,000 fans... and lost $10 million.

So Wozniak, naturally, decided to do it again just nine months later, on Memorial Day weekend 1983.

Wozniak had money to burn, so he did, handing Van Halen a $1 million contract that guaranteed they'd be the highest-paid act on the bill. When the ink was dry, however, he realized he wanted David Bowie, too. The festival was fully booked, but Wozniak was adamant: He had to have Bowie.

Unfortunately, Bowie was in the middle of a European tour and would have to charter a 747 to interrupt it for Wozniak's whim. For his inconvenience, he demanded to be compensated to the tune of $1.5 million.

But since Van Halen's contract demanded that the boys from Pasadena receive top pay, Wozniak had to give them an extra $500,000, meaning it cost him $2 million total to get Bowie (who earned his pay with a 22-song set including everything from "Life on Mars?" to "Modern Love").

The Clash, who'd signed to play for "just" $500,000, were indignant, so they held a news conference, defiantly declaring that they weren't going to play. Positioning themselves as champions of the fans, they complained that they'd been told tickets would cost just $17 each, but were instead being sold for $25. Ultimately, they did, in fact, play — and festival organizers got back at them by flashing a huge picture of the $500,000

MEMORIAL DAY WEEKEND & JUNE 4

US '83

Glen Helen
Regional Park,
San Bernardino

The Clash

Van Halen

The Music Event of
the Eighties Continues...

SATURDAY, MAY 28TH
THE CLASH
MEN AT WORK
STRAY CATS
A FLOCK OF SEAGULLS
THE ENGLISH BEAT
OINGO BOINGO
WALL OF VOODOO
INXS
DIVINYLS

SATURDAY, JUNE 4TH
WILLIE NELSON
ALABAMA
WAYLON JENNINGS
HANK WILLIAMS, JR.
EMMYLOU HARRIS
RICKY SKAGGS
RIDERS IN THE SKY
THRASHER BROTHERS

SUNDAY, MAY 29TH
VAN HALEN
SCORPIONS
TRIUMPH
JUDAS PRIEST
OZZY OSBOURNE
JOE WALSH
MOTLEY CRUE

MONDAY, MAY 30TH
DAVID BOWIE
STEVIE NICKS
JOHN COUGAR
PRETENDERS
MISSING PERSONS
U2
QUARTERFLASH
BERLIN
LITTLE STEVEN & THE
DISCIPLES OF SOUL

Willie Nelson

David Bowie

• World's Largest Stage
(435 Feet Across)
• World's Most Powerful
Sound System (400,000
Watts of Sound Power)
• 8 Computerized Sound
Delay Towers, For The
Greatest Sound Ever —
EVERYWHERE In The
Amphitheatre
• Spectacular Laser Light
Show
• More Giant Video
Screens, Including
Diamond Vision For
Daytime Viewing
• More Camping Facilities
• More Parking
• Complete Convenience
Store, Concessions and
All Facilities
• All New '83 Career-
Technology Exposition

US '83

TICKETS ON SALE AT TICKETMASTER™ TICKET CENTERS
including Music Plus, Federated Group, and Sportmart
TICKETMASTER/CHARGIT: 213-480-3232 VISA/MC

THE 'US' FESTIVAL 1983 . . . MORE THAN A CONCERT!

Advance Tickets: $20 Per Day Plus Service Charge — Prices Will Be Higher at the Gate.

check they'd received behind them during their set.

The second US Festival differed slightly in format from the first. Wozniak expanded it to four days, each of which featured a different style of music. Saturday would belong to New Wave acts like Stray Cats and Divinyls; Monday would be dedicated to mainstream rockers like Bowie, the Pretenders and Stevie Nicks; and the following Saturday would be devoted to country music.

Sunday, however, turned out to be the main attraction: Heavy Metal Day. An astonishing crowd of 350,000 fans turned out, more than half the attendance (670,000) for the entire event.

"There were so many people that the curve of the earth hid you from seeing it all," Quiet Riot vocalist Kevin DuBrow recalled.

Mötley Crüe took the stage second, following Quiet Riot, which had just released its landmark album, *Metal Health*. From there, the lineup featured, in order, Ozzy Osbourne, Judas Priest, Triumph, Scorpions, and Van Halen.

It was the last US Festival, but it was just the beginning for pop metal in the '80s.

Said Mötley Crüe singer Vince Neil: "It was the day New Wave died and rock 'n' roll took over."

Paradise City

The explosion of Quiet Riot's "Cum On Feel the Noize," and Van Halen's *1984*, ignited a new gold rush to California. Except this time, the prospectors came searching for gold (and platinum) records. They all converged on the burgeoning mecca of '80s metal: West Hollywood, where they competed for exposure at clubs along the Sunset Strip.

Ratt came from relatively close by: San Diego, to be exact. The band had started off as Mickey Ratt (like Mickey Mouse, get it?) had been chosen simply "because we needed a name, because we needed to play," guitarist Robbin Crosby said. "It was almost like a temporary joke. We almost changed it a couple of times, but our following kept getting so strong, we didn't want to say, 'so-and-so, formerly Ratt.'"

The name would pave the way for plenty of wordplay. The band called its style of music "Ratt & Roll" (also the title of its greatest hits collection), and dubbed its debut album *Out of the Cellar* — which they supported with a "World Infestation Tour." They teamed up with Poison a couple of times for Ratt-Poison tours.

Like Mötley Crüe and Def Leppard, the band released its first record, an eponymous seven-song EP, on its own label, with the backing of Marshall Berle. The nephew of pioneering TV funny man Milton Berle had previously managed Van Halen, and he'd produced some rock shows on the Strip.

The EP sold 60,000 copies, and DJs at Los Angeles rock stations KMET and KLOS gave the single "You Think You're Tough" some exposure before Atlantic Records signed the band and released *Out of the Cellar*. The album featured Crosby's then-girlfriend Tawny Kitaen on the cover and broke the band into the mainstream with the No. 12 hit "Round and Round."

The video to that song featured none other than Milton Berle, who played two parts: a cigar-smoking snob in black tie at a fancy dinner party, and (in drag) his date. The party is disrupted by the band's loud music and a waiter who serves up live rats on a platter. It wasn't Berle's nephew who asked him to appear, but the band members themselves. "Uncle Milty" also appears at the end of the video for "Back for More," another song on the album, which was filmed at the Roxy on the strip. The club had an after-hours VIP area upstairs where Hollywood madam Heidi Fleiss served as host.

Side note: Ratt would appear in another video in 2020, only this time, it was in a commercial for Geico, the insurance company. As in the video for "Round and Round" (which they perform in the ad), they show up and play loud music where they're not wanted: this time, in the new home of a couple who sing the house's praises but admit, "We do have a rat problem." Actually, a Ratt problem.

Lead singer Stephen Pearcy appeared in that commercial, looking a bit older (it *had* been almost 40 years, after all). But back in the day, Pearcy's jet-black hair always seemed to be falling over his eyes and he became something of a sex symbol, basing his pirate look on New Wave icon Adam Ant. The band was one of the first to set the standard for the look and feel of '80s pop metal.

Crosby explained in a 1984 interview: "We're all sexy. We play it up. We're fashion conscious. Our music is very melodic and singable. All that makes us different than a lot of other new heavy metal bands.

"We're maybe more melody and more hook-oriented than a lot of bands. I think that appeals to more females than a lot of other heavy metal bands. We're shooting for songs and song writing. I think that's what sets bands apart from one another. ... If you can't write songs, you're up a river. No guitar solo can save a bad song."

But a good song can make a band's career, and that was the case with Ratt. "Round and Round" kickstarted a string of four consecutive platinum albums and also launched the career or Beau Hill, who would produce not only all four of those albums but would also handle albums for Alice Cooper, Kix, Winger, Warrant, and Europe, among others.

While Ratt arrived on the Sunset Strip from relatively nearby, the members of a band named Paris traveled a lot farther to pursue their dreams. They hailed from Mechanicsburg, Pa., hardly a hotbed of music, let alone metal, so after hearing about the US Festival in 1983, they decided to buy an old ambulance and take it on a cross-country trip to L.A. Soon, they'd ditched the name Paris in favor of a new one: Poison.

"Poison" also happened to be the name of a song by the Baltimore-based band Kix, who came west themselves for some shows at places like the Troubadour, the Roxy, and the Reseda Country Club (not a golf course, but a nightclub built in an old Sav-On drugstore). Both bands were playing the L.A. area in the fall of '85, and a calendar entry in the L.A. Times even showed the two scheduled to play the Strip on the same night.

Kix had been around longer. They'd started out as the Shooze in 1977 before changing their name to the Generators and, for a few moments, the Baltimore Cocks. They finally became Kix in 1981, when they released their self-titled debut on Atlantic Records, making them one of the first '80s-era pop-metal bands to ink a deal with a major label.

The name was slightly confusing, especially if you heard a DJ play it on the radio and thought he was saying, "Kiss." The band shared its name with a brand of cereal, which invited comparisons with another cereal-sounding pop-metal band of slightly later vintage, Trixter.

In comparison to Poison, Kix played pop-metal but had a harder-edged sound; they wore jeans and leather instead of flashy colors and eyeliner. But several people remarked how similar their stage show was to Poison's — or, rather, vice versa, since Kix had gotten there first.

In a 2002 interview with Metal Sludge, Kix vocalist Steve Whiteman was asked directly whether Poison "blatantly ripped off" Kix's entire show. His response?

"Yes, they did."

He cited, specifically, the use of the color green in Poison's logo and the similitude between the band's name and the Kix song, released in 1981.

But even Whiteman acknowledged that Poison "busted

their balls to get where they got."

Poison certainly wasn't above sticking it to another band to get ahead. Drummer Rikki Rockett, a former hairdresser whose skills came in handy during the age of high, teased hair, recalled an early gig when Poison was the opening act. He suggested that Michaels tell the audience the boys would be having a party up the street immediately after their set: The first 100 people in the room, he said, would get free beer.

The outcome? No one stuck around for the headliner, and everyone remembered Poison.

The band had to scratch and claw its way up the ladder, because it started at the very bottom. When they first hit the Strip, Rockett recalled, they hung around outside the Rainbow Bar & Grill because they didn't have enough money to go inside. Instead, they'd hand out fliers, then head back home to a meal of Top Ramen.

(The members of Poison weren't alone. Blackie Lawless of W.A.S.P. said he spent a year and a half living on $5 a week in a 3-by-12-foot closet with zero heat and zero electricity. He recalled seeing another aspiring rocker steal slats from his landlord's picket fence and using them for firewood.)

Handing out fliers was huge. At night, band members would go out and plaster fliers to phone poles, the sides of buildings and anywhere they could find an empty space. Then again, it didn't have to be empty. One band would staple up their fliers over another's, and if they were paying attention, the first band would come back later to return the favor.

In fact, frontman Bret Michaels says the neon green that became Poison's signature color happened by accident (not because the band was copying Kix or anybody else). The band was so poor, he said, they couldn't afford any of the normal paper colors at the local print shop. But the store had a surplus of green, sparkly paper, so the band took it. As it turned out, it was perfect: It made their fliers stand out from all the others.

"You've got to promote in order to get people out there," Poison singer Bret Michaels said. "You've got to go out and distribute fliers plugging the shows. After a show like Loverboy at the Forum, I'll be passing out fliers and saying, 'Come out and see us.' They'll crumple 'em up and throw 'em in my face. But I'll give out a thousand fliers and a hundred people will show up because of it — which is a hundred people that have never seen us before."

Every band that hit the Strip was competing to make the big time, and every band thought they would. The reality, however, was much different.

Home Sweet Home

"Due to the erratic lives of L.A. musicians and the capricious personalities of booking agents, all of the following bookings are subject to change for no apparent reason."

That was the disclaimer that topped a listing of club dates in Los Angeles, as printed in *LA Weekly* during the first week of November 1985.

All the drugs floating around in what amounted to a sea of West Hollywood chaos made it a necessary caveat. Rehearsals led to parties led to shows led to promotions led to fights led to drugs at more parties, which sometimes led to overdoses. Vince Neil called it a cesspool.

Poison's Bret Michaels recalled his first impression of the place in an interview with *Rolling Stone*: "When we finally pulled onto the Strip it was, 'Holy shit!' We're driving past the Rainbow, Gazzarri's, the Roxy, the Whisky, and there's gotta be, like, 100,000 people walking around. And they all look like they're in a band. For a bunch of small-town guys, that's a lot to take in."

With so much going on in such a confined space, it was like the bands and their friends were in their own little world. A lot of them lived on the Strip and frequented the same businesses — and not just nightclubs. So many rockers ate at the nearby Denney's and shopped at the neighborhood Ralphs supermarket that they became known, colloquially, as Rock 'n' Roll Denney's and Rock 'n' Roll Ralphs. Tattoo parlors popped up around the neighborhood, and bands were frequent customers. They could also be seen at Tower Records and its competitor, Licorice Pizza.

The Tower Records parking lot was a gathering spot for musicians, some of whom — including Axl Rose and Slash of Guns N' Roses — worked inside to earn pocket money while they waited for their big break.

Bands in town to play gigs would stay at places like the Sunset Marquis, Chateau Marmont, and the Continental Hyatt House. Rowdy rock 'n' rollers' antics at the hotels predated the '80s. The venerable Chateau Marmont, where comedian John Belushi died of an overdose in 1982, had been converted into a hotel during the Depression after being built in the 1920s as the first earthquake-proof apartment building in L.A. Singing cowboy Gene Autry had opened the Hyatt — which was nicknamed the "Riot House" somewhere along the way.

It earned the name. Led Zeppelin, which stayed there whenever they were in town, rented the entire top floor of the building, which, conveniently, included the rooftop swimming pool, so they could have privacy for their wild parties. Drummer John Bonham rode motorcycles through the Hyatt's corridors. They threw TV's (and other things) out the windows. When you were making so much money, everything was disposable.

POP GOES THE METAL

Tower Records

Including women. Bands used their money to pay for the right to trash hotel rooms; they used their fame to get any girl they wanted.

Groupies (and misogyny) were everywhere, and had been for years. Starstruck teenage girls on the lookout for rock stars had been regulars at Rodney Bingenheimer's English Disco during the '70s, and they weren't off limits to rock stars who thought the rules didn't apply to them.

Bingenheimer himself had been immortalized on vinyl by an all-girl group called the GTOs in their only release: a 1969 record produced by Frank Zappa. The group's name was short for "Girls Together Outrageously," and they were actually a collection of Sunset Strip groupies — the most famous of whom was Pamela Des Barres.

On the spoken-word track titled "Rodney," the GTOs offer commentary as Bingenheimer regales them with an abbreviated version of his life story, most of which involves bragging and name-dropping. He boasts about having lunch with Grace Slick, and getting his picture taken with George Harrison. And he notes that, after the photo appeared in *Tiger Beat* — a magazine marketed to adolescent girls — girls were lining up at his door to sleep with him for a week solid.

The track ends with this from the GTOs: "Oh, Rodney, if you introduce me to Mick Jagger, I'll let you meet my little sister. She's only 12 years old."

"Baby groupies" Sable Starr and Lori Maddox started hanging out at places Rodney's in their early teens. Maddox met Zeppelin guitarist Jimmy Page when she was 14 and said the two were involved in a sexual relationship; photos taken in the early '70s show the two together. Starr, whose real name was Sabel Hay Shields, also said she slept with a number of rock stars, including Iggy Pop — which Pop appears to confirm in his 1996 song, "Look Away." The song contains the lines "I slept with Sable when she was 13. Her parents were too rich to do anything."

Zeppelin, meanwhile, recorded a song by Page and Robert Plant that declares: "One day soon you're gonna reach 16, painted lady in the city of lies." That line, in the opening verse of 1975's "Sick Again," has been interpreted as a reference to Maddox. If it is, however, the songwriters used some poetic license: The second line of the song refers to the painted lady's "pretty blue eyes," but Maddox's eyes were brown.

Other bands wrote odes to teenage girls, too. Among them: Kiss' "Christine Sixteen" and "Goin' Blind," and Winger's "Seventeen."

Who slept with whom may not always be clear, but there's no doubt that a lot of people were sleeping together — or, rather, doing something other than sleeping. Ratt's Stephen Pearcy wrote in his autobiography that he saw so many people doing it on the grass behind Gazzarri's that he started to throw empty beer cans at them.

POP GOES THE METAL

The Body Shop and Seventh Veil strip clubs, meanwhile, were immortalized in Mötley Crüe's "Girls, Girls, Girls."

Face Dances

Fans cruised the Strip looking for rock stars and sex and drugs. Rock stars cruised the strip looking for sex and drugs, too, when they weren't passing out fliers, rehearsing or partying. They all knew each other, and partied together.

"There is definitely a lot of unsafe sex and (drug) needles in the Hollywood rock scene," said Riki Rachtman, owner of the Cathouse club. "And the community is so small that a lot of guys have slept with a lot of girls that have slept with a lot of guys. If you find a girl who hasn't slept with the singer of at least three bands, keep her. I haven't found her."

When they weren't partying, chances are they were mixing it up with their fists. According to Nikki Sixx, he and Vince Neil got in a fight after the very first Mötley Crüe show. And Rikki Rockett estimated the members of Poison got in something like 30 fights on the Strip, often because of their glam look.

Rockers from thrash/speed metal outfits like Anthrax, Metallica, Slayer, and Megadeth didn't want anything to do with the spandex crowd, and neither did their fans.

A lot of guys liked thrash, but the girls liked hair, and the thrash fans (and bands) went to hair-metal shows for the girls, not the bands or the music. It came down to a simple choice: Do you want to look tough or do you want to meet girls? For most guys, the choice was an easy one. But the situation could be more fluid than either side wanted to admit.

Pantera, from Texas, started out as a glam band but changed their image four albums in and became a thrash metal outfit.

STEPHEN H. PROVOST

After that, they didn't want anyone to remember their previous records, none of which had charted. Their "real" history, they insisted, started when they signed with Atco and released *Cowboys from Hell* in 1990.

Change was the only constant. Bands formed, disbanded, regrouped and switched names. Musicians hopped from one band to another. In the words of bassist Rik Fox, "It was definitely every band and man for themselves, and there was no such thing as loyalty; musicians changed bands as easily and as fast as you changed your shirt."

In an interview with *The Cosmick View*, the New York native talked about how eye-opening it was to move from the tough, streetwise vibe of NYC to the cutthroat atmosphere that awaited him in SoCal, where bands had a "crabs-in-a-barrel mentality," with "everyone climbing over each other, pulling each other down over and over in a repeating pattern."

They'd smile and say nice things to your face, but then, "as soon as you turn around, they're talking shit about you because you represent some sort of inferred territorial threat, because the scene was packed with so many bands per capita."

The L.A. scene, he came to realize, was "very plastic, two-faced, backstabbing (and) competitive."

Fox himself epitomized the volatility of that scene: He was, in fact, the common thread running through a number of bands.

Back in New York, his camera had become his ticket to the rock scene while he was still in high school: In the early '70s, he would sneak into a club called the Coventry in Queens, to shoot photos of the New York Dolls and other bands, like the Brats, who were popular there.

Around the same time, he started dating the sister of a drummer who lived around the corner. The drummer eventually landed a job with a band that would also play its first gig at the

POP GOES THE METAL

Coventry — which was called the Popcorn Club at that point. The drummer was Peter Criss, and the band was Kiss.

Fox would later recall that Criss gave him is first rock 'n' roll haircut, and would become like the big brother he never had. He shot a number of Kiss' early shows before joining a band himself after graduating in 1975: The band was called the Martian Rock Band, and Fox donned green makeup to make him look like a reptile from outer space when the group played shows. Taking a cue from Kiss' Gene Simmons, he even spat up green blood onstage.

One day, he got a call from a fellow New York native who had relocated to Los Angeles. The guy's name was Blackie Lawless, who'd played a few live gigs with the New York Dolls in 1976 after founding guitarist Johnny Thunders quit the band. Later that year, Lawless had moved to L.A., where he fronted a band called Sister that, at one time, also included future Mötley Crüe bassist Nikki Sixx.

Sixx left to form a band called London, and Lawless joined him in 1979, but Sixx subsequently departed to form Mötley Crüe, while Lawless left to found a new incarnation of Sister. That's when he phoned Fox and, despite his own impoverished state, scraped together enough cash to fly the bassist out to West Hollywood.

Fox joined Sister, but Lawless quickly decided he wanted a new name. With Twisted Sister and Reseda-based White Sister both making music, he didn't want his band to get lost in the crowd. He went outside and stepped on a hornet, and it dawned on him that Wasp would be a great name for the band. Lawless liked the idea and adopted Fox's idea, in all caps, but didn't keep Fox himself around, kicking him out of the band shortly after that.

Fox would try out with Ratt and the Greg Leon Invasion,

whose namesake guitarist had played with Quiet Riot after Randy Rhoads' departure, as well as on Dokken's first EP, and in Suite 19 with future Mötley Crüe drummer Tommy Lee.

Fox joined his friend, drummer Eric Carr (who had succeeded his other friend, Peter Criss, as Kiss' drummer) at a show put on by Steeler, which included vocalist Ron Keel and hotshot guitarist Yngwie Malmsteen. Shortly afterward, he got a call from Keel, who'd seen an ad Fox had placed in a music magazine. Fox got the job, but the band didn't last long, and Keel went on to form his own eponymous band.

Sixx and Lee, meanwhile, went on to success with Mötley Crüe, whose members hung out with the members of Ratt. Sixx and Ratt guitarist Robbin Crosby were both heroin addicts, and it was Crosby's dealer who supplied Sixx with the drug that stopped his heart for two minutes before a paramedic's shot of adrenalin brought him back from the dead. Crosby and Sixx were both partying with Guns N' Roses drummer Steven Adler and guitarist Slash at the time.

Slash wouldn't have been with GN'R at that point if he'd won a tryout with Poison — yes, Poison — in 1985. He scored a tryout with the band after their original guitarist, Matt Smith, quit and went back home to Pennsylvania. The band liked his playing, but his look wasn't flashy enough, so they chose C.C. DeVille instead.

Guns N' Roses itself was a convoluted combination that of three bands: Hollywood Rose, L.A. Guns, and Road Crew. The band ultimately took its name from the first two bands, but its deepest roots lay in Road Crew. Guitarist Saul Hudson (aka Slash) and drummer Steven Adler were L.A. kids who had known each other since they were 11; they placed an ad for a bassist and recruited Duff McKagan. The three would form the core of GN'R, but they couldn't find a singer, so they called it

FRESH FROM DETOX

Photo: Jack Lue

GUNS "N" ROSES
'Rehab Show'   Sat. July 20

Troubadour
8:30PM
$2.00 off with this ad

For Band Info:
SASE to 9000 Sunset Blvd. Ste.405 W. Hollywood, CA 90069

quits. Slash and Adler subsequently hooked up with singer Axl Rose and guitarist Izzy Stradlin, childhood friends who had come west from Lafayette, Ind. They played together in Hollywood Rose before Slash left in 1984, with Rose and Stradlin merging the remnants of their band with L.A. Guns to form Guns N' Roses.

That band consisted of three members of L.A. Guns, along with Rose and Stradlin. The name made a lot more sense at the time than it does now, because all three members of L.A. Guns (including Tracii Guns) departed just a couple of months after the merger to re-form their original band, eventually recruiting Phil Lewis, who'd worked with Def Leppard guitarist Phil Collen in Girl, as their lead singer.

Meanwhile, Slash, McKagan, and Adler joined Stradlin and Rose in what was basically a reconstituted Hollywood Rose, but was operating now under the GN'R nameplate.

Confused?

Hold on. There's more.

Ratt drummer Bobby Blotzer and bassist Juan Croucier got their starts as members of a band called Airborn, which had been formed by singer Don Dokken in 1976. Dokken opted to change the band's name because it was already being used, in slightly modified form (as Airborne), by a group that featured a guitarist named Beau Hill.

This time, Dokken just used his own name.

Hill's band landed a deal with Columbia Records that led to one album before they split up and Hill eventually moved into a new role as a record producer. His first major project was the debut album by an L.A. band that sold more than 3 million copies. That band was Ratt.

Croucier, who was a member of Ratt at the time, was also still a member of Dokken. He played bass and co-wrote a couple of songs on Dokken's first album before leaving to devote his full attention to a Ratt lineup that, by then, already included Blotzer.

Livin' On a Prayer

If it sounds like a game of musical chairs or an Abbott and Costello skit, that's how it often went on the Strip, sometimes out of necessity.

POP GOES THE METAL

"I was in about five bands at the same time," drummer Frankie Banali said. "One fed me. The other one I could stay at somebody's house. The third gave me enough for drumsticks. The latter two were better than the other ones... One of those bands happened to be Quiet Riot."

Still, West Hollywood was — even in the midst of all the chaos — quickly becoming the gateway to the big time.

In the spring of 1987, MTV went all-in on metal with the debut of *Headbangers Ball*, a late-night show that showcased videos from top bands as well as lesser-known acts hoping for a breakthrough.

In baseball terms, West Hollywood's nightclubs were a farm system for MTV and the major record labels. The Strip was the minor leagues, the proving grounds; MTV was the majors. The only difference between rock and baseball was that the bands who made it to The Show came back around a lot to party with the ones still waiting for a call-up.

And there were a lot of bands in that second category.

For every Poison or Guns N' Roses, there were dozens of bands you'd never heard of, or who maybe got a minor record deal and never went anywhere. Angora, Odin, Tuff, Seduce, and others never got very far beyond the Strip. Do the names Mary Poppinz, Harlot, Ragged Lace, or Merger ring a bell? All were playing at the Roxy on the night after Halloween in 1985.

"I think a lot of those bands didn't have that much substance, and so they only would last for so long and then the interest level would then sort of wane," Slash said in the *Metal Evolution* video.

It got to the point that it was hard to tell even the successful acts apart. Bands ran out of ideas about what to call themselves, and names started to blend together. There was Great White and Whitesnake and White Lion. They all sounded different on disc or in concert, but if you weren't familiar with any of them, it was hard to know where to start.

Then there were the "W" bands: Winger and Whitesnake (again) and Warrant and Warlock and W.A.S.P. and White Lion (again, again), and White Tiger (big cats, anyone?).

W.A.S.P. may have stood for something, or maybe it was just meant to keep the question of *what* it stood for — and the band — at the top of people's minds. The band inscribed the first printing of its debut release with the words "We Are Sexual Perverts," but when asked whether that's what the acronym meant, singer Blackie Lawless replied, "We ain't sure, pal."

Lawless was the Marilyn Manson of his time, a shock-rocker who outdid Alice Cooper. He performed with green skulls as a backdrop and threw raw meat at the audience as part of his show. Streaks of white through his long black hair made him look every bit the part of a wicked witch. And if Michael Jackson seemed obsessed with grabbing his crotch, he had nothing on Lawless, who wore several different codpieces in concert. One featured a circular saw; another spewed out sparks and fire. The one with the saw was also adorned with tiger stripes and emblazoned with the words "I Fuck Like a Beast."

Those words weren't chosen at random: "Animal (Fuck Like a Beast)" was the title of a W.A.S.P. song.

The codpiece with the circular saw posed a unique problem: It extended vertically from Lawless' crotch, so he couldn't sit down when he had it on. The only solution was to find a bench with slots in it.

Pretty Boy Floyd gave Lawless a run for his money, at least when it came to crotch-wear. The band took its name from a notorious bank robber who became the FBI's "Public Enemy No. 1" in 1934 and was shot to death by law enforcement that same year.

POP GOES THE METAL

The band never made much of a mark nationally (their debut album got to No. 164 on the Billboard 200), but they were determined to make an impression. One photo showed the nearly naked band, in heavy makeup, mugging for the camera. The guy standing second from the right, wearing silver-pink lipstick and a red outfit, is holding his crotch protectively; the band member at the far left is wearing nothing but silver-studded leather straps wrapped around his legs and lower torso. Nothing, that is, except a huge silver skull with devil's horns affixed to his groin.

The photo appeared on Twitter in 2013, along with this caption: "Pretty Boy Floyd: 'We will never, ever regret this photograph.'"

The band's first LP was titled "Leather Boyz with Electric Toyz."

What was it with the z's, anyway? It wasn't just Pretty Boy Floyd. Bands seemed to have a penchant for using x's and z's in their names and album titles: Nikki Sixx, Alcatrazz, and Kix were some of the better-known examples. Then there was the lesser-known LixxArray, an Orange County foursome not to be confused with the later Swedish glam-metal band Crazy Lixx or another band, just called Lixx, that featured a guitarist named Nazz E. White.

Kiss may have started the whole thing with their lightning-bolt S's, which looked like backwards Z's.

At least Anthrax was an actual word.

There were a lot of umlauts, too. Mötley Crüe, Motörhead, Queensrÿche, Blue Öyster Cult... They were so prevalent they were lampooned by Spın̈al Tap.

They didn't change the pronunciation one bit.

Understandably, a lot of these bands tended to get lumped together, but despite all the knock-offs and rip-offs, they were

often very different. Each group had its own gimmick, or at least its own take on the typical schtick. Poison was all lipstick and eyeshadow. W.A.S.P. was a shock to the system. Mötley Crüe was warpaint (sometimes) and motorcycles. Twisted Sister were macho drag queens.

Slither

Some bands played bright, hook-infested pop metal, while others favored a rawer sound with rougher production that seemed closer to the blues.

POP GOES THE METAL

These "dirtier" bands often employed a slithering, sliding guitar sound rather than jangly electric power pop and lightning-fast solos. "Sleaze metal" acts retained their long hair but didn't glam it up as much as contemporaries like Warrant and Poison. Many were descendants of Aerosmith's *Rocks*-era look and sound. In fact, Oni Logan's vocal intro to the title track of Lynch Mob's 1990 release *Wicked Sensation* sounds about as close to Steven Tyler as you can get.

Along with Lynch Mob — formed by George Lynch after he split from Dokken — bands in the sleaze metal category included Cinderella, Faster Pussycat, Skid Row, Guns N' Roses, L.A. Guns, and Dangerous Toys. To hear a hybrid of sleaze and pop metal, take a listen to Whitesnake's "Slow an' Easy," which deftly balances a beguiling, bluesy intro with an anthemic, hook-laden chorus.

This particular brand of metal seemed to be gathering steam toward the end of the '80s as an alternative to the lighter pop metal that was dominating MTV. Even Poison started turning more toward this style with songs like "Something to Believe In" and "Bastard Son of a Thousand Blues."

Guns N' Roses was already there.

"We never did the spandex or anything," GN'R guitarist Slash said on *Metal Evolution*. "There was a little bit of makeup in the early days. There was a little bit of hairspray that happened in the very beginning. And there was definitely a glam influence, but it was more from, say, Marc Bolan than it was from the Bay City Rollers."

Guns N' Roses and Faster Pussycat were two of the hottest bands in West Hollywood near the end of the decade. Faster Pussycat lead singer Taime Downe even had his own club on the Strip called the Cathouse with future *Headbangers Ball* host Riki Rachtman. They started the club because they wanted their own place to party, where they could meet appropriately dressed girls (the fewer clothes, the better) and drink for free.

Rachtman was sort of a Rodney Bingenheimer for the next generation. He sang in a couple of bands, but he was mostly known as a DJ, and his brainstorm was to start a club that played hard rock instead of dance tunes. The Cathouse grew out of that idea. Rachtman issued membership cars that gave you $2 off the $10 cover charge.

The Cathouse put the sleaze in sleaze rock, and Rachtman once boasted it had been called "the sleaziest club in the world." But what else would you expect from a club whose name was another word for "brothel"? Faster Pussycat even had a song on their first album called "Cathouse" that was originally titled "Whorehouse." An ad for the grand opening of its new location promised bikers, booze, and broads, with free reserved parking for Harleys and "more bars to serve your over indulging needs."

The place drew everyone from L.A. Guns to Alice Cooper, from Suicidal Tendencies to Pearl Jam. When Cooper played the Cathouse on Halloween, it gave Rachtman a particular sense of satisfaction. When he was a kid, his dad hadn't let him go to a Cooper concert because he'd gotten bad grades. Not only did the legendary shock-rocker play at the club, he name-checked the Cathouse in the opening line of a 1989 tune called "Trash."

Rachtman said he knew the club had made it when Lita Ford got so drunk she puked in the bathroom.

Guns N' Roses were regulars at the Cathouse. They shot a video for "It's So Easy" there, but it stayed in the can until 2018 because, like the club itself, it was too extreme for the MTV crowd. As Axl Rose told the Cathouse audience that night: "What we're makin' this for is ourselves. ... If we made a *nice* video for MTV and put it out, (we'd) sell more records and shit. But instead we're gonna spend 150 grand just to make something we want to see."

Erin Everly, the daughter of Everly Brother Don and Rose's girlfriend at the time, shows up during the video in bondage gear.

One of the people in the audience that night was none other than David Bowie. This was still a couple of years before his marriage to Iman, and he was on the prowl, so to speak, like most other Cathouse patrons. He'd arrived at the club early, apparently already intoxicated, and tried to make a move on Everly.

Rose got wind of it and was livid.

The story goes that Rose started hurling insults at Bowie — who was in a band called Tin Machine at the time. At some point, they came to blows, and Rose started chasing Bowie down the street, yelling, "I'm gonna kill you, Tin Man!" The pair made up later.

An incident at the Cathouse involving another member of GN'R, guitarist Izzy Stradlin, carried over to the MTV awards. Again, it involved a woman: this time, the wife of Mötley Crüe singer Vince Neil. It seems that while Neil was away in Idaho on a whitewater rafting trip, his then-wife went out to the club, where she was allegedly assaulted by Stradlin.

When Neil heard about it, he confronted Stradlin backstage at the MTV awards. Actually, he did more than confront him: "I decked him good, right in the face," Neil said, claiming that he'd broken Stradlin's nose. "He fell to the ground like a tipped cow."

According to Rose, though, Stradlin was asked if he wanted to press charges and responded, "Naw, it was like bein' hit by a girl."

Faster Pussycat and Guns N' Roses released their debut albums within two weeks of each other in July 1987.

One took off like a rocket.

The other vanished almost without a trace.

Faster Pussycat's biggest hit would be the power ballad "House of Pain," which hit No. 28 on the singles chart and featured a video directed by Michael Bay of *Armageddon* and *Transformers* fame. But that wouldn't come until their second album. Their self-titled debut didn't include any hit singles and stalled out at No. 97 on the album chart.

GN'R's entry, meanwhile, shot to No. 1 and went on to sell 18 million copies.

The album called *Appetite for Destruction* took its title from a piece of artwork by Robert Williams of the same name, which Axl Rose wanted to use as the album cover. It was about as far from glam as you could get: The gruesome cartoon image shows what appears to be an open-mouthed alien monster leaping over a fence to attack a robot, which is assaulting a woman.

Williams told Rose the record company wouldn't like it, and after Tipper Gore asked the company to cover it with a paper bag, the band agreed to move the image to the inner sleeve and replace it with a painting of the band members' skulls laid out over a cross.

The title, however, stuck.

Who was Tipper Gore, and why did she have that kind of power?

Read on.

Teenage Wasteland

The Suburban Incubator

Prog-metal act Rush captured the situation perfectly. Neil Peart, known for his thoughtful lyrics, had penned a hit called "Subdivisions" for the band's *Signals* album in 1982, the year before metal started to break big at the US Festival.

The song set the scene for the imminent rise of metal. Its title referred to the *cultural* subdivisions that had arisen between parents and children, and between teenage peer groups, in *literal* subdivisions: the tract homes that were popping up like weeds across the suburban landscape. The message: The cookie-cutter society of Middle America was a threat to young people seeking to form their own identity as they came of age.

"Conform or be cast out," Rush's Geddy Lee sang. "Any escape might help to smooth the unattractive truth. But the suburbs have no charms to soothe the restless dreams of youth."

For many suburban youths, metal was that escape.

Billboard began a story on metal in the spring of 1986 by declaring: "As long as there are high schools and high schoolers, heavy metal always seems to find an audience."

At the time, that seemed like a safe prediction. Metal was huge among teenagers, who were some of the most loyal fans out there. They bought metal albums by the thousands, or even the millions, and made pilgrimages to local arenas for concerts, where they lit up, pledged allegiance to their favorite bands, and banged their heads to the thundering sound issuing forth from stacks of Marshall amps.

The Arizona Republic reported that 60 undercover officers issued 428 drug and alcohol citations during a Van Halen show at the Veterans Memorial Coliseum in Phoenix.

"We want to assure (parents) that we're going to take the necessary enforcement action," public safety officer Roy Van Orden said. "We want them to know that their children are safe when they come to the Coliseum."

The newspaper reported that streams of beer and other kinds of liquor were pouring into the streets around the arena as the officers dumped out the contents of "hundreds of cans and bottles."

It was pretty typical.

A 17-minute film called *Heavy Metal Parking Lot* offered viewers a glimpse at what it was like to hang out before a metal concert — in this case, a show with Judas Priest headlining and Dokken as the supporting act at Baltimore's Capital Centre in the spring of '86.

The film captured a crowd of rockers, most of them in their teens and 20s, drinking beer and Jack Daniels as they partied in the parking lot before the concert. They played air guitar, showed off their T-shirts and talked about how great Priest was.

The filmmakers, Jeff Krulik and John Heyn, pretended to be from MTV so people would talk to them. (One guy standing in line wasn't buying it. When they told him they were from the video music channel, he had a one-word response: "Bullshit!")

Colorful characters included a shirtless guy who introduced himself as "Graham, man, like gram of dope," and said he was on acid. His big idea? "They should make a joint so big it fits across America. Everybody'd smoke it."

One of his friends said he'd "get in line for that one."

Heyn and Krulik asked one girl: "What do you want to do when you go to a heavy metal concert?"

"Party!"

"Are you fucked up?" they asked.

"Half and half," she said.

Another concertgoer, who stood out in a zebra-striped suit and a Joe Elliott-style haircut, was asked about his philosophy on life. He promptly went into a rant about the virtues of metal compared to every other style of music: "Heavy metal rules," he declared. "All that punk shit sucks. It doesn't belong in this world. It belongs on fuckin' Mars, man. What the hell is punk shit? And Madonna can go to hell as far as I'm concerned. She's a dick."

A guy wearing an Ozzy shirt stuck his head in front of the camera to tell the filmmakers: "We are not juvenile delinquents, although we act like that. We try to be civilized but we can't."

But a parking lot party or a two-hour concert was just a snapshot of what it meant to be a metalhead in the 1980s. A rock show was like a church service: It brought together thousands of the faithful, who lifted their voices as one to cheer on their heroes. Yet their apparent unity of purpose belied the fact that these were very different people from very different backgrounds, tied together only by this single common bond: the music.

They were as different as the band members themselves, who came from diverse backgrounds. Sure, some of them, like Black Sabbath, came from the same working-class backgrounds. But the Van Halen brothers' early alliance with David Lee Roth brought two immigrant boys together with a rich kid from

Pasadena who had his own PA system that was his ticket to a spot in the band.

In junior high and high schools across America, kids were slapping band stickers on their notebooks, sewing patches on their jackets, and scrawling logos on the paper bags they cut and folded to create makeshift covers for their textbooks. But not all logos were created equal. The cooler the logo, the more you saw it: Van Halen, AC/DC, Aerosmith, Dokken, and Led Zeppelin, and Kiss were among the most distinctive.

Kiss is mostly known for its makeup and stage show, but without the lightning-bolt S's in the logo, they wouldn't have been KI⚡⚡.

Band logos were a way to represent. Whether you slapped them on your notebook or wore them on your T-shirt, they said something about you and generated one of two responses: "(Insert band here) rules!" or "(Insert band here) sucks!" Not all bands were created equal, and not all fans were anything like the same.

A few wanted to be rock stars. But far more used metal as the soundtrack to a perpetual party. And others still just liked the music. Or the attitude. Metal offered a sense of identity at an age when forging one's identity is a top priority; it provided a form of empowerment to kids feeling disempowered in a world run by adults.

Adults saw the worst of the worst, and imagined their own children were just as bad — which of course made them feel as though their own parents didn't respect them and had absolutely zero confidence in their ability to make smart choices.

When they saw news stories about satanic cults and ritual violence, parents worried that metal might brainwash *their* kids into killing someone. Paranoid Christian fundamentalists pushed a cause-and-effect narrative that led from metal to self-destruction, and the media, eager to boost their TV ratings and circulation figures, ate it up.

When Ricky Kasso killed his 17-year-old friend on Long Island while they were high on LSD in 1984, metal-haters came out of the woodwork. Fearful parents, judgmental pastors, and the headline-hungry press quickly latched on to Kasso's affinity for metal, and played it to the hilt. He was wearing an AC/DC shirt when the cops came to arrest him, and he was a fan of Ozzy, Priest, and Sabbath.

The fact that the killing took place in an affluent suburban community, the kind of place that was supposed to serve as a sanctuary from such horrors, made it all the worse in the minds of a panicked public. More disturbing still were Kasso's demand that his victim "say you love Satan" before he killed him, and subsequent boasts to his friends about the murder.

Two days after his arrest, Kasso hanged himself in his cell.

But Kasso wasn't your typical metal fan, despite what the Moral Majority and the media were saying about the supposedly inherent dangers of the music.

The kids, of course, knew better. They just had a hard time getting their parents to listen.

"If a criminal kills someone wearing a Brooks Brothers suit, do we say Brooks Brothers is responsible?" asked Gerald Rothberg, publisher of *Circus* magazine. "Of course not. It's a preposterous conclusion. ... To push it to an extreme, and say that violent behavior can be tied to music, well, they're barking up the wrong tree."

Young metal fans agreed. In 1990, a syndicated columnist named Willard Abraham printed a letter from a teenage girl named Tamra in Central California who listened to bands like Skid Row, Anthrax, Ozzy, and Cinderella: "I'm 13 years old, my favorite color is black, and I listen to heavy metal," her letter began. "I don't do drugs, and I've been on the honor roll both quarters. ..." She'd been prompted to write by a segment she'd seen on *A Current Affair*, a syndicated tabloid news show, that linked rock music and satanism. "I'm speaking out because I'm tired of hearing about all that," she said.

A lot of metal fans were.

It seemed even the mainstream press had taken a tabloid tone, and they were sick of it.

When Abraham invited teens to share their own views and experiences for future columns, his mailbag started to fill up with letters supporting Tamra.

Bobby from Portsmouth, Ohio, replied: "I get A's B's and an occasional C in school. I'm not crazy, not into drugs and I am a full-fledged Catholic (and proud of it)."

Lisa from Towson, Md., wrote: "I am 16 and have never received a grade lower than a C+ in my gifted and talented program. I don't do drugs or drink, I'm in Students Against Drunk Driving, I don't wear lots of black and I'm very active in my church. My favorite band is Motley Crue."

An anonymous letter-writer from Ottawa, Ill., sent this: "So-called experts say metal is not normal. If you don't call being a cheerleader, a basketball player and two B's away from straight A's in school normal, then you have a problem."

By the time these letters were written in 1990, the author of this book had moved out of the house and had a steady job, having graduated summa cum laude with a bachelor's degree four years earlier. He'd gone from nearly flunking out as a high school freshman to graduating with honors, all while listening to Kiss, Aerosmith, and Van Halen. He never became a pothead or a cokehead or a junkie. He would go on to become a career journalist and a published author, and metal would be the soundtrack to his life.

POP GOES THE METAL

Everybody Wants Some

The false belief that metal was an automatic gateway to drugs and satanism only reinforced the sense among teenagers that, in the words uttered by Will Smith on his own MTV video debut, "parents just don't understand."

Teens who listened to metal weren't plotting to take over the world in the devil's name, shooting up heroin or shooting off guns. Most of them had very little in common with the most hedonistic rock stars; they just liked listening to the music. It struck a chord — a power chord — with those who felt powerless.

They wanted the power their parents had, they just wanted it on their own terms. Metal fans soaked in everything Mom and Dad had been teaching them, subconsciously, about what was important in life. In the Reagan '80s, that meant the so-called "American Dream": a home, a fancy car, a backyard barbecue. The message to adolescent males was clear. If you can obtain material wealth, you'll reap the benefits: a beautiful wife who'll dote on your every need and a life that's one big party. In the music world, nothing fit that definition of success better than the flagrant self-indulgence of pop metal.

When David Lee Roth sang, "Everybody wants some!" he was preaching to the choir. "I want some too!" It wasn't just rock stars who wanted to live a life of luxury and ease; their listeners did, too. "Everybody wants some! How about you?"

Metal fans wanted some, just like their parents did. Their goals, though, were shaped, not by Wall Street, but by their own world: a world in transition away from the playground, but one which had yet to hit the reality of the 8-to-5 grind. These kids still remembered the candy store, and the bands they saw on MTV were an adolescent version of a Cracker Jack box.

A novelty store in Fresno, Calif., that was popular with teens offered posters of rock stars and other pop-culture icons, gag gifts, crass humor, and adult cards.

The owners named it Penny Candy.

"We forget we're not 21," said Gerald Rothberg, publisher of *Circus* magazine. "These bands are singing to these kids. They're trying to deal with dating, self-awareness, pimples — they're going nuts. We forget what it was like. But these bands, they're hitting these kids' wavelengths."

Teens shopped for blacklight posters and raunchy games at Spencer's in the mall. They grew up in the kind of subdivisions shown in *E.T.: The Extraterrestrial* and *Poltergeist*, and they served as real-life models for the characters in John Hughes' coming-of-age movies.

The Sunset Strip might as well have been halfway around the world for most kids growing up in tract homes on the other side of the Santa Monica Mountains, to say nothing of their peers in Cleveland or Shreveport or Peoria. To them, "Sex, drugs, and rock 'n' roll" was a rallying cry for suburban angst and rebellion. At worst, it meant cutting class, smoking pot, or getting your older brother to buy a beer for you at the 7-Eleven. It was *The Breakfast Club* and *Fast Times at Ridgemont High*. It didn't mean shooting up, destroying your liver, or suffocating on your own vomit.

The kids and the rock stars they loved had one thing in common: a spirit of rebellion, of wanting to be able to do what they wanted when they wanted. The music reflected that, and it bound them together. But there was no "typical" metal fan; kids who listened to the music weren't brainwashed zombies intent on destroying civilization as we know it. They just wanted a voice and a way of expressing themselves.

That's what a lot of adults didn't understand.

POP GOES THE METAL

And the fact that they didn't made those kids love the music even more.

Cover of (not) The Rolling Stone

While their parents were reading *The Wall Street Journal* and *The New York Times*, teenagers in Metalville were building their own press library around magazines that delivered news (and pictures!) of their favorite bands.

That didn't mean *Rolling Stone*, which was almost as bad as what their parents read. In some ways, it was worse. It was stuffy and pretentious and seemed to have less than zero respect for metal. Why should they care what that rag had to say? They had other magazines that didn't treat them or their favorite acts like second-class citizens.

Dr. Hook, in their tongue-in-cheek 1972 classic, had asked why "big rock singers with golden fingers" who made "$10,000 a show" couldn't make the "Cover of the Rolling Stone." They might as well have been any metal band in the 1980s. (Indeed, Poison would end up covering the song, by which time inflation had taken its toll: The lyrics were revised to suggest the band was making $10 *million* a show.)

A lot of *Rolling Stone*'s covers depicted people like Robin Williams, the cast of *Star Wars* or the Ghostbusters. Not only were these people not metal acts, they weren't even musicians. Who needed Jan Wenner when you had *Circus*, *Creem*, and *Hit Parader*? During the 1980s, magazines like those provided metal fans with everything they ever wanted to know, and some things they didn't, about their favorite bands.

None of those three '80s metal magazines started out that way. *Hit Parader* dated back to 1942, well before the birth of rock 'n' roll. *Circus* began its life as *Hullabaloo* in 1966, then changed its name three years later. *Creem* launched in March of 1969 and proclaimed itself to be "America's Only Rock 'n' Roll Magazine."

In fact, however, the magazine started out covering an array of styles. In September of 1971, it printed poetry by proto-punk icon Patti Smith, and the May 1972 cover featured T. Rex, Al Green, Bob Seger and Aretha Franklin: plenty of soul, but nothing about Sabbath, which released its fourth album that month, or Deep Purple, which had issued its sixth just a couple of months earlier.

In 1971, reviewer Dave Marsh wrote up a concert by ? and the Mysterians, by then long past their "96 Tears" prime. In it, he referred to the band's music as "punk rock," reportedly the first time anyone had used that term. (Before that, "punk" had occasionally been used to describe musicians themselves, but not their music.)

By the end of the decade, though, the magazine had taken a decisive turn toward hard rock. Four years after the T. Rex/Al Green cover, the band showcased David Bowie, Led Zeppelin, the Stones, Sweet, and Queen on the cover.

Creem knew which side its bread was buttered on. Its 1976 readers' poll named *Rocks* by Aerosmith as the year's top LP and *Destroyer* by Kiss as album cover of the year. Aerosmith, Kiss, and Zeppelin ranked 1-2-3 in the poll of best bands; Kiss was named the top live band, followed by Aerosmith and The Who.

The trend toward heavier acts would continue into the '80s. *Creem* would later start an offshoot that focused exclusively on heavy metal and, in 1987, moved its offices to L.A., the epicenter of the pop metal scene.

Similar changes were taking place elsewhere, too. By 1984, *Hit Parader* had transitioned completely to a hard rock/metal format, and *Circus* was going the same route. Reader appetites were driving the changes. Metal was, quite simply, what kids wanted to hear about. And not just once. They wanted every detail in every issue.

"Rolling Stone would do a cover on Van Halen when the song 'Jump' became so huge," said Ben Liemer, who served as managing editor of *Circus* from 1985 to 1989. "We would do Van Halen month after month after month. Do you know why that occurred? The fan questionnaire in every issue of the magazine."

If the survey indicated readers wanted stories about Mötley Crüe, they'd run stories about Mötley Crüe for 15 straight issues, he said. Covers were dominated by Mötley, Def Leppard, Metallica, and Van Halen. When the magazine put Bon Jovi on the cover, it sold 480,000 copies in a month. It was all about turning a profit, Liemer explained: "*Circus* went all-metal for economic reasons."

At their height, metal magazines took what *Rolling Stone* was doing, turned it on its head, and added elements of *People*, *Tiger Beat*, and *Mad Magazine*. They offered reviews, glossy full-page photos and centerfolds of the bands that could be cut out and pinned to your bedroom wall like mini-posters, and humor.

Creem was known for its sarcastic photo captions. A shot of Led Zeppelin posing on board a jet in the February 1978 issue came with the cutline: "The tour will commence as soon as someone convinces the boys to get off the plane." The same issue contained a publicity shot of a newly popular band that was captioned, "Tom Petty and the Heartbreakers check each other for body lice." Kiss' Gene Simmons got a nearly two-page photo spread and a caption that read: "Mrs. Simmons' son Gene breaks in his new disco outfit, and (inset) shows off the hair knob that launched a thousand split ends..." Funny stuff. Of course, the joke only worked if you didn't know "Simmons" was his stage name, and his mom was Flora *Klein*.

They had fun with headlines and cover teasers, too:

- **Huey Lewis** is No Duck!
- **Police** Beat Their Rap
- **Yes** Will They Say No?
- **Asia** Major or Minor?
- **Squeeze** Too Tight?
- **Ozzy Osbourne** From Iron Man to Bat Man!
- **The Motels** Rock 'N' Roll Room Service
- **Bob Seger** Bites The Silver Bullet
- **Boomtown Rats** Of Mice and Men

If you were looking for a fake ID or some spandex to complete your look, you could check the classifieds. You could submit your poems to be set to music, buy unused backstage passes, or learn to "play guitar in 7 days."

The magazines also included giveaways, celebrity rate-a-record features, and reader letters, which could turn into a fierce give-and-take between fans of competing genres. Punk and metal fans got into it on the pages of *Creem* in 1979, with letter-writers on both sides showing their defensiveness. And with good reason. Punk wasn't getting much exposure in the magazine, while metal was struggling, as several bands were showing their relative age — or the effects of their substance abuse.

Punks targeted David Lee Roth as effeminate and said the music was crass and antiquated.

POP GOES THE METAL

Metalheads, meanwhile, accused punk bands of being no-talent flashes in the proverbial pan.

But fans of different metal bands also went at it, debunking the idea that all headbangers were the same. A Kiss fan wrote to *Hit Parader* in July of 1986, declaring that his favorite band was far superior to Van Halen. "If Van Halen is so good why the hell did they cut only six albums and break up?" he asked. "Paul Stanley can play (guitar) better than Eddie Van Halen, and he's only a rhythm guitarist. ... Kiss rules. Van Halen drools."

The writer was probably one of the few human beings on the planet who thought Stanley was a better guitarist than Van Halen, but he was hardly alone in taking pen in hand to defend his favorite artist — and attack those perceived as less worthy.

A letter signed "Miss Gonzo" in Pittsburgh blasted *Hit Parader*'s taste in guitarists: "I don't know where the hell you come off saying Eddie Van Halen, Jimmy Page, Jimi Hendrix or Angus Young rules," she wrote. "Wake up! There is only one man who can crush any guitarist on earth today."

Her choice: Ted Nugent.

Some letters came from abroad, where the opinions were just as... opinionated. Monica from Bogota, Columbia wrote *Hit Parader*:

"This is my opinion about Slayer, Venom, Motorhead, and Possessed — I've never heard anything that bad before. They stink. I'm a headbanger and I like The Scorpions, Queensryche, Ratt, Iron Maiden (except that song *Number of the Beast*), Stryper, Aerosmith, Led Zep and I love Bon Jovi."

Destiny from Vancouver was just as adamant in her beliefs. "People who are fans of 'bands' like Twisted Sister or Motley Crue are twisted themselves," she wrote, lamenting that there was "no such thing as a good band anymore, with the exception of Whitesnake, Triumph, Deep Purple, Kim Mitchell, etc. Thanks for listening to the truth. (Facts are facts.)"

Readers weren't the only ones to sound off. Some of the bands themselves had a love-hate relationship with metal mags. They needed the press, but the criticism — both from fans and the publications themselves — could be brutal. In a 1985 interview, Ratt drummer Bobby Blotzer said, "Calling me fat and stuff... I think it's totally ridiculous and uncalled for. We don't make fun of *Creem*."

Two things are worth noting.

First: Blotzer didn't like what the magazine had said about him. Second: He did the interview anyway, even taking the call when he was just waking up, because the band needed *Creem* to sell records.

Axl Rose quite wasn't so tolerant. In 1991, he included his grievances against *Circus* and *Hit Parader* in the lyrics to "Get in the Ring," a track on Guns N' Roses' *Use Your Illusion II*. Rose name-checked both magazines, along with *Hit Parader* editor Andy Secher, blasting "all you punks in the press that want to start shit by printing lies instead of things we said."

By that time, *Creem* was already out of business, having ceased publication in 1989. *Circus* and *Hit Parader* struggled as revenues declined in the grunge era. *Circus* finally shut down in 2006,

Circus publisher Gerald Rothberg said he'd sold his home and everything else he owned in hopes of keeping the magazine afloat. He'd lost it all. "I'm broke," he said. "I feel like Humpty Dumpty who had a great fall."

Hit Parader folded two years later, following the December issue.

Editor Andy Secher reflected on the magazine's mission in an interview with Steven Ward: "*Hit Parader* isn't *The New York Times*," he said, "it's a frikkin' fanzine, and proud to be exactly that. Our target demographic is some 17-year-old kid in Iowa, not a socialite in Manhattan."

And in the '80s, they hit the target time and again.

We're Not Gonna Take It

So did Twisted Sister, at least in the early part of the decade. Like some other bands of the era, they wore makeup that gave them a more feminine look.

Kind of.

Kiss drummer Peter Criss would write in his autobiography that, when the band tried to emulate the New York Dolls by dressing in drag, it was "a disaster." They couldn't pull it off: Ace Frehley was a dead ringer for Shirley MacLaine, but they all looked like "bad transvestites."

Which is pretty much what Twisted Sister looked like. In 1972, founding guitarist Jay Jay French had auditioned for Kiss founders Paul Stanley and Gene Simmons, who were looking for a guitarist to play in their band Wicked Lester. He didn't get the gig, but later in the year, he answered an ad from the same two guys, who had pulled the plug on that band and were starting a new one. He must have seen the ad too late, because Stanley and Simmons had already hired Ace Frehley as their guitarist. Still, they let French stay to watch the rehearsal.

"They didn't have the makeup yet," he said, "but they had the platform shoes and these big Marshall stacks. I was just stunned."

French regrouped to form his own glam-rock cover band, called Silver Star, which one website would describe as a New Jersey version of the New York Dolls.

The band later became Twisted Sister and, in 1976, hired Danny "Dee" Snider as its lead singer. Snider would be Twisted Sister's songwriter and the face of the band, even appearing alone on the cover of their breakthrough 1984 album, *Stay Hungry*.

Not that it was a particularly pretty face. One fan described the band as "a bunch of tormented Avon ladies"; another description might have been drag queens on steroids. Snider, at 6-foot-4, made himself look even bigger by wearing football shoulder pads and platform shoes.

"I don't think Twisted Sister is 'glam,' because that implies glamour, and we're not glamorous," he said. "We should be called 'hid,' because we're hideous."

Snider was, in fact, a tough guy who didn't back down from anyone or anything. The title track of Twisted Sister's 1985 album, *Come Out and Play*, referenced a line from a 1979 action movie called *The Warriors* that focused on a Bronx street gang. Snider called Vince Neil a murderer for driving drunk in the crash that killed Razzle Dingley; in the same sentence, he called Donald Trump his best friend and "legally insane."

POP GOES THE METAL

Once, when Twisted Sister supported Motörhead, the rest of the band didn't want to wear their makeup.

Not Snider.

"The guys wanted to not wear the makeup and costumes for the first time in six years," he told *RockUnited* in 2007, "and I'm going, 'Listen, I've been wearing this shit in every fucking bar in every situation... I've been fighting every night of my life, literally to wear this, and I'm not taking it off now. No way.'"

Instead of reflecting some feminine ethos, the clothes and makeup made an entirely different kind of statement: We're gonna do whatever the hell we want, even if you disapprove. *Especially* if you disapprove. Go ahead and make fun of us. We dare you.

"Oddly," Snider would write in his autobiography, "the more feminine I got visually, the more aggressive and hostile I got as a person."

Snider's songs reflected the band's provocative, in-your-face attitude. They were about empowerment and rebellion — and that much was clear long before the band made their mark with "We're Not Gonna Take It" and "I Wanna Rock" on MTV in '84.

The previous year, they'd released an album that was just as bold and defiant: *You Can't Stop Rock 'n' Roll*. The title track was a minor FM radio hit and cracked the top 50 in the U.K., but their biggest hit there (No. 18) was the equally anthemic "I Am (I'm Me)," which opened with the fist-shaking verse: Who are you to look down at what I believe? / I'm on to your thinking and how you deceive / Well, you can't abuse me, I won't stand no more / Yes, I know the reasons, yes, I know the score.

The chorus followed with a chant of pride and personal integrity: "I am, and I'll be! I will, you'll see. I am, and I'll be. I am. I'm me!" Lyrics like these weren't the exception; they were par for the course with Snider. It was an us-against-the-world mentality, but with the assurance that "us" would prevail by standing up for what "us" believed in.

It's no wonder Snider's lyrics resonated so strongly with teens who felt alienated from their parents' world in 1984. Nor is it any surprise that Snider jumped at the chance to defend rock 'n' roll before a panel of senators who represented those same out-of-touch parents the year after that.

Running with the Devil

The Backlash Begins

Hundreds of spandex-clad, hunk-fronted bands continued to appear, seemingly out of nowhere, in the second half of the 1980s, hungry for a piece of the pop-metal pie. Even a Christian pop metal band called Stryper hit the mainstream, attired in distinctive yellow-and-black outfits that made them look like a swarm of human bees.

Like so many other, secular bands of the era, they came out of Southern California, and like them, they played the West Hollywood clubs. They'd started out calling themselves Roxx Regime, and had discussions with guitarists C.C. DeVille and Doug Aldrich about joining the band. Aldrich would go on to play in Lion, Hurricane, Dio and Whitesnake, among others. DeVille, of course, would wind up joining Poison. His problem with Roxx Regime, lead singer Michael Sweet said, wasn't their faith but that yellow-and-black wardrobe. Little did he know that he'd wind up in a band known for its neon green.

Stryper styled themselves as "a Van Halen for Jesus" and sometimes threw pocket-sized copies of the New Testament into the audience. But they didn't preach much, expecting fans to read those scriptures themselves and listen to the lyrics of their songs.

"We don't preach," drummer Robert Sweet, Michael's brother, said in 1984. "I'm turned off by people who try to force Jesus on you. All we're saying is that Jesus changed our life, and we believe that Jesus can do the same for you.

"We don't believe the music (rock) is (inherently) bad, it's what you put into it. Instead of stressing negatives, we try to make the lyrics positive and uplifting. We're here to rock 'n' roll."

The band's name was based on a Bible verse: "By his stripes we are healed," from the prophet Isaiah, and the band drew criticism from both directions. To some, Christian metal was antithetical to the whole point of rock music: rebellion. To others rock was "the music of the devil" no matter who was singing it or what the lyrics said.

"You can't rock 'n' roll your way into heaven," televangelist Jimmy Lee Swaggart was quoted as saying. "Rock 'n' roll is one of the most destructive forces in the country and world today," he also said, decrying the "smoke bombs, prancing and display of flesh" at live performances.

Ironically, it had been Swaggart whose televised sermons had led vocalist Michael Sweet and drummer Robert Sweet to Christianity in the first place. "I saw him in 1975, and he was totally different," Robert Sweet would later recall. "By 1984, he was... holding up pictures of us and trashing us in front of the television cameras."

Maybe Swaggart was a little sensitive because his cousin, Jerry Lee Lewis had been one of the first flamboyant concert rockers. And as to the criticism of "flesh," maybe that hit a bit close to home, too. In 1988, Swaggart tearfully confessed on television that "I have sinned" after pictures surfaced showing him outside a no-tell motel in Louisiana with a prostitute who said she'd posed nude for him. He later failed a polygraph test.

POP GOES THE METAL

Three years later, a patrol car pulled him over in Indio, Calif., for driving on the wrong side of the road and found him in the company of another self-described prostitute, who said, "He asked me for sex. I mean, that's why he stopped me. That's what I do. I'm a prostitute."

Swaggart was less repentant this time around, telling his congregation after the news surfaced: "The Lord told me it's flat none of your business."

Despite their obvious disagreements, Stryper had something in common Swaggart and other celebrity preachers beyond their gospel message: The band was filling arenas for their concerts, while Swaggart and his brethren were filling megachurches for their sermons.

They were both filling their coffers, too. Those tithes and offerings were pouring in, and the merch was moving at Stryper shows. An album insert in *To Hell With the Devil* included a $14 offer that would get you a "No Devil" T-shirt with the Stryper logo on one side and the word "Devil" struck out on the other. A Stryper cross earring would set you back $5, and you could buy a 777 button for $1 if you wanted an antidote to the satanic "number of the beast," 666.

Christian rockers like Larry Norman — who had blended Christian fervor with street sense and a Dylanesque approach to songwriting — had been caught in the crossfire between disdainful secular rock fans and self-righteous preachers before, so it was really nothing new. Norman had once asked, in the title to one of his songs, "Why Should the Devil Have All the Good Music?"

Christian teens answered: "He shouldn't."

Christian parents countered: "You call *that* good?"

To them, the beat itself was evil, no matter what the lyrics said, and copying a sinful world's approach to music was compromise at best, corruption at worst.

Nevertheless, Stryper found a niche among fans who felt they were tapping into the original message of Jesus (who was, after all, crucified for being a rebel) and who wanted to listen to something with more of a beat than Pat Boone, the Second Chapter of Acts or the Maranatha Singers.

Stryper's popularity peaked with their third album, *To Hell With the Devil*, which went double-platinum and produced their only top-40 hit.

Titled "Honestly," it was (of course) a power ballad.

It charted at No. 23.

Other popular songs from the LP were "Calling on You," a song that would have fit neatly into the repertoire of Europe or Poison, and "Free," which told listeners they were "free to do what you want to: choose your own destiny."

To Hell With the Devil was released in 1986, which was not just the high-water mark for Stryper, but in many ways, for pop metal in general. It was the year Van Halen topped the album chart with *5150*, its first album with Sammy Hagar. Poison released its debut, *Look What the Cat Dragged In*, which would go triple-platinum, and Cinderella made its entrance with *Night Songs*, which would do the same. Bon Jovi served up *Slippery When Wet*, which would go on to be the bestselling album of the entire following year.

Also in 1986, a band called Europe emerged out of... well... Europe (Sweden, to be exact), came out with an album that would sell 3 million copies in the U.S. and 15 million globally. Its immediately recognizable keyboard-flourish intro helped propel the title track, "The Final Countdown," to the No. 1 spot in eight countries around the world and No. 8 on the Billboard Hot 100. Two follow-up singles, "Rock the Night" (No. 30) and the power ballad "Carrie" (No. 3) were also U.S. hits.

POP GOES THE METAL

While new bands were emerging left and right to ride the coattails of Ratt, Quiet Riot and Mötley Crüe, acts that had built a following by playing traditional hard rock during the 1970s were also taking notice.

Whitesnake was just one example. Bands that could tweak their look and sound to hitch a ride on the new bandwagon, did so.

German rockers Scorpions didn't shift their image, but their penchant for hook-driven tracks and anthemic choruses helped them fit right in. They'd been around for 10 years when they first hit the U.S. charts with "No One Like You" in 1982, which they followed with their signature anthem, "Rock You Like a Hurricane" off their *Love at First Sting* album a year later. That track went to No. 25 and was followed by the band's first charting power ballad, "Still Loving You" (No. 64).

Scorpions highest-charting single: another power ballad, "Wind of Change," which got to No. 4 in 1991.

Kiss had tried disco, power pop, and a concept album with diminishing returns in the late '70s and early '80s before they decided to remove their iconic makeup on MTV in 1983. They returned to playing anthemic rock and, with the release of their 1985 album, *Asylum*, put on the eyeliner, blush and colorful clothes they'd ditched more than a decade earlier in trying *not* to compete with the New York Dolls. Their biggest hit of the decade — and the second biggest of their career — was the power ballad "Forever," which Paul Stanley wrote with rocker-turned-crooner Michael Bolton. It reached No. 8 in 1990.

Van Halen continued on the trajectory they'd begun with "Jump," scoring four straight No. 1 albums and eight No. 1 singles on the U.S. Mainstream Rock chart with Sammy Hagar out front.

Aerosmith, whose career had been sidetracked by internal

bickering and drug use, became relevant again with the help of a rap act. In 1986, Steven Tyler and Joe Perry guested on Run-DMC's cover of the band's No. 10 hit from a decade earlier, "Walk This Way." The new collaboration went even higher: It climbed all the way to No. 8, making it the rappers' biggest single and setting the stage for Aerosmith's return to the prominence a year later with the album *Permanent Vacation.*

The "Walk This Way" video opened the door to Aerosmith's comeback and, over the long haul, to rap's eventual dominance of MTV, with *Yo! MTV Raps* coming to the U.S. channel in August 1988. But it wasn't rap that sustained Aerosmith's second wave of popularity, which included six straight top-10 studio albums from 1989 to 2012. Instead, it was pop-metal hits like "Love in an Elevator," "Janie's Got a Gun," and "Livin' on the Edge," along with power ballads such as "Angel," "Crazy," "Cryin'," and "Amazing."

Capping it all was "I Don't Want to Miss a Thing," the band's chart-topping hit from the blockbuster Bruce Willis film *Armageddon* (which featured Tyler's own daughter Liv in a supporting role). The song was written by Diane Warren, who'd also penned the No. 1 Bad English power ballad "When I See You Smile," as well as seven other chart-toppers, all for different artists.

Ozzy Osbourne's new output was nothing like what he'd recorded with Black Sabbath. It was still hard rock, but much more melodic and "accessible," to use a term often applied to pop metal when it's contrasted with traditional heavy metal or speed metal. The charts, of course, reflected this. Although just one of his singles cracked the top 10 on the Billboard Hot 100 — his duet with Lita Ford, "Close My Eyes Forever" — 15 of them made the U.S. Mainstream Rock top 10.

POP GOES THE METAL

Shout at the Devil

But with that success came blowback, as it always seems to. And it wasn't just from heavy metal's harder-rocking vanguard, which viewed the pop metal bands as "wimps" and "sellouts." It was from the same self-righteous critics who imagined that Kiss stood for Kids in Satan's Service and conjured up echoes of demonic backward masking on Led Zeppelin's "Stairway to Heaven."

With the rising influence of Jerry Falwell's Moral Majority and other right-wing Christian groups following the election of Ronald Reagan, such criticism began to gain new traction. And new targets.

Pseudo-satanic imagery, meant to shock and sell albums more than anything else, drew the angst and ire of conservative parents in white suburbia: insecure — and sometimes absentee — moms and dads already scared that rock was fueling rebellion in the souls of their impressionable teens.

Of course it was.

First off, that's what it's always done. Second, teens don't need rock in order to rebel. They're gonna do it anyway: It's in their pubescent hormones, not the music.

Be that as it may, acts like Osbourne and Judas Priest and Mötley Crüe were convenient targets for these hand-wringing middle-aged misanthropes. How could a band named Judas Priest be anything *but* satanic? At least, that's how the thinking went.

As for Osbourne's *Blizzard of Ozz* album cover, it shows him half-lying on the floor, holding a cross aloft and staring into the camera with a half-crazed look on his face. There's a black cat, a skull and what looks to be antelope horns in the background. What more could you want than that — especially from a guy who used to be in a band called Black Sabbath?

Mötley Crüe was another easy mark, and not just for their drug abuse, drinking, and ode to strip clubs ("Girls, Girls, Girls"). It would have been understandable if parents didn't see a band that included a heroin addict and guy who'd killed someone while driving drunk as good role models for their kids. But most of those kids just liked the music. And most of the parents seemed less concerned with the band's bad behavior than they were with its kitschy, pop-satanic symbolism.

Not only was the Crüe's second album titled *Shout at the Devil*, but its all-black cover, accented with red lettering, also featured an inverted pentagram — a symbol of evil in some occult traditions.

AC/DC, whose hits had included "Highway to Hell," "Back in Black" and "Sin City" (a tribute to Las Vegas), supposedly stood for "Anti-Christ/Devil's Child," at least in the minds of the self-righteous and paranoid. Then, in 1985, the band came under further scrutiny when it was linked to a string of murders committed by Richard Ramirez, who was dubbed the "Night Stalker."

That link was based on the flimsiest of so-called evidence. The band had recorded a song called "Night Prowler," which had nothing to do with killers (serial or otherwise), but was still taken as "proof" that AC/DC had somehow inspired the killings.

"That song is not called 'Night Stalker,'" AC/DC's Malcolm Young pointed out. "It's called 'Night Prowler' — and it's about things you used to do when you are a kid, like sneaking into a girlfriend's bedroom when her parents were asleep."

Those pointing fingers didn't care about such distinctions. They'd already made up their minds. Even more damning to those looking for a scapegoat was the fact that an AC/DC cap had been left at the scene of one of the crimes, and that a childhood friend of Ramirez's said he'd been a fan of the band.

The *Ukiah Daily Journal* in California even ran a headline: "Richard Ramirez' 'Highway to Hell.'" It reported that the words "Jack the Knife" had been scrawled in lipstick at the scene of another Night Stalker crime, and used those words to link it to lyrics in a Judas Priest song.

There was no doubt that Ramirez was disturbed: At his arraignment, he shouted "Hail, Satan!" as he left the courtroom. But that didn't make AC/DC responsible for his crimes. Nevertheless, nearly every newspaper report found a reason to regurgitate the information about that baseball cap, and the connection stuck in the public's mind.

It wasn't as though a satanic army was running rampant across the nation, using heavy metal as a clarion call to butcher or brainwash every man, woman, and child in suburban white Christian America. Richard Couzens, a Superior Court judge in Placer County, Calif., said he, for one, hadn't seen any evidence of such activities, nor had he noticed any link between heavy metal and devil worship.

"To my knowledge, it has not played a prominent role in any case," he said in the fall of 1985. "I am certainly not aware of any large-scale expressionism of satanism in the county. It's just not there."

Often, though, people see what they want to see. Or what they expect to see. This tendency led to an imagined epidemic of satanism across the country, with an emphasis on supposed ritual abuse, torture and even sacrifice of young children at daycares and elsewhere.

In an NBC special report titled *Devil Worship: Exposing Satan's Underground*, Geraldo Rivera talked about a "secret network" of more than a million Satanists who were allegedly spreading covert messages with the help of heavy metal. The proof of this was about as substantial as what Rivera found in Al Capone's vault — which is to say, nothing.

Accusations that 48 children at the McMartin Preschool in Southern California had been sexually abused in bizarre satanic rituals led to 321 criminal charges. The case lasted seven years, cost $15 million and resulted in zero convictions. A teacher at the preschool had spent five years behind bars by the time the 20th century witch trial was over.

No evidence of any broad satanic cult was ever found, and most of the accusations were roundly discredited as the product of coerced testimony and manufactured "memories" of events that had never really happened. Still, at the height of the craze, a television poll found that 87 percent of respondents believed the defendants were guilty.

Talk Dirty to Me

In a climate like this, it's hardly surprising that rock bands should have gotten swept up in a campaign to expose and condemn their music as satanic, evil, or simply a bad influence on America's teens.

In 1985, Tipper Gore, then wife of the future vice president, Sen. Al Gore, and Susan Baker, the wife of Treasury Secretary James Baker, helped co-found the Parents Music Resource Center (PMRC) and started a crusade against what the group saw as sexually and/or violently explicit lyrics in popular music.

Gore got the ball rolling after she took her 11-year-old daughter, Karenna, to the record store because Karenna wanted to buy Prince's album, *Purple Rain*. Karenna liked a song on the record called "Let's Go Crazy," but the lyrics to another track caught Gore's attention, and set off alarm bells. "Darling Nikki" described a meeting with a girl who was "masturbating with a magazine" in a hotel lobby.

Gore contacted Baker and two other Washington wives, and together they formed the PMRC. The group gained support from the CEO of Coors Brewing Co., a supporter of Ronald Reagan who had donated $250,000 to form the conservative Heritage Foundation. Coors gave them an office in northern Virginia, on the fringes of D.C., to use as their headquarters, and Beach Boys singer Mike Love, another conservative, donated $5,000.

Gore, Baker and other members of the PMRC presented themselves as concerned mothers.

Said Gore: "I'm saying I don't want it for my child. I don't want to censor music for anybody else. I'm just saying I want some guidance before I buy the record for my children."

Her concern was no doubt real, but the fact remained that she and most members of the PMRC weren't just moms. They were Washington residents who with tight political connections. And while they used their image as loving parents to gain support at the grass-roots level, they wielded their clout as movers and shakers to make the record industry sit up and take notice.

PMRC leaders wanted to alert radio stations to songs they found objectionable by asking record companies to send them lyric sheets for all new releases. But programmers, especially at heavy metal stations, were cool to the idea, pointing out that they were already prohibited from playing songs that included vulgar language (famously recited by comedian George Carlin in his 1972 skit, "Seven Words You Can Never Say on Television").

When Baker complained about the song "Sugar Walls" by Sheena Easton, she was told it didn't contain any obscenities. Her response: "You should hear the way she sings those lyrics, using this very, very erotic voice."

If beauty was in the eye of the beholder, outrage was in the ear of the listener.

Undeterred by resistance from programmers, especially at hard-rock radio stations, the PMRC focused its attention on another of its priorities: proposing that record labels adopt a ratings system similar to the one used by the Motion Picture Association of America, with letters to denote different kinds of objectionable lyrics:

- X for sexually explicit content or profanity
- V for violence
- D/A for drugs and alcohol
- O for occultism

Not only would records carry warning stickers, the group proposed, but they would be kept behind the sales counter at record stores, the same way pornographic magazines were often kept behind the counter at liquor stores.

The group singled out 15 songs for condemnation, dubbing them the "Filthy Fifteen." Predictably, metal tracks made up more than half the list, which (just as predictably) included songs by the likes of Mötley Crüe, Judas Priest, Black Sabbath and Twisted Sister.

Band	Song	Rating
AC/DC	Let Me Put My Love Into You	X
Black Sabbath	Trashed	D/A
Def Leppard	High 'n' Dry (Saturday Night)	D/A
Sheena Easton	Sugar Walls	X
Judas Priest	Eat Me Alive	X

POP GOES THE METAL

Cyndi Lauper	She Bop	X
Madonna	Dress You Up	X
Mary Jane Girls	In My House	X
Mercyful Fate	Into the Coven	O
Mötley Crüe	Bastard	V
Prince	Darling Nikki	X
Twisted Sister	We're Not Gonna Take It	V
Vanity	Strap On 'Robbie Baby'	X
Venom	Possessed	O
W.A.S.P.	Animal (Fuck Like a Beast)	X

Nine of the 15 songs were flagged for sexual content, with two falling into each of the other three categories. Venom and Mercyful Fate, two of the more obscure acts on the list, were the ones flagged for occult content, rather than more familiar targets such as the Mötley Crüe, Black Sabbath, or Ozzy Osbourne.

This was part of their apparent strategy: to single out the worse of the worst and depict it as the norm for the recording industry — and metal bands in particular. Hence the inclusion of Venom, which had composed songs with titles like "Sons of Satan" and included a drummer who went by the stage name of Abaddon, a demonic name that meant "doom" or "destroyer."

Venom were the godfathers of black metal, but U.S. radio stations didn't play their songs, and they weren't widely known outside the metal underground.

Also cited was an even more obscure band called the Mentors, whose 1985 album included song titles like "Golden Showers," "Clap Queen," "My Erection is Over," and "Wine You, Dine You, Sixty-Nine You." None of these songs was ever going to get radio airplay or wide distribution. Most of the Mentors' records were sold at their concerts or via mail order, not at record stores, and the album in question had sold just

7,500 units in a market where you needed to move 500,000 copies to be considered a success.

But that wasn't the point. The point was to make people pay attention, and they did.

The irony was, the PMRC was using shock tactics to attack bands for using shock tactics. Another strategy was to spotlight ambiguous lyrics and interpret them in the most disturbing way possible. When Gore accused Twisted Sister vocalist Dee Snider of singing about sadomasochism in the band's song "Under the Blade," Snider responded that "the only sadism, bondage and rape is in the mind of Ms. Gore."

Snider said Gore had edited and misquoted the words. Then, she'd misinterpreted them on top of that: "The lyrics she quoted have absolutely nothing to do with these topics," he said. "On the contrary, the words in question are about surgery and the fear that it instills in people."

Ultimately, the PMRC withdrew its call for specific ratings after talking with the Record Industry Association of America, which agreed instead to slap generic "Parental Advisory" stickers on releases with explicitly sexual or violent content. The move was agreed to a month before a Senate hearing was even held on the matter, but the hearing went ahead anyway, and the PMRC got what it wanted: publicity for its cause.

Susan Baker would later admit as much: "It gave us more exposure," she told *Newsweek* in 2015, "which is what we were hoping for."

PMRC leaders made a point of saying they weren't calling for government regulation, which begged the question as to why a Senate hearing was necessary. The most reasonable reply was to make a show of force and portray the issue as one that merited government — and public — attention.

POP GOES THE METAL

Tipper Gore

John Denver

When the time for that hearing came, Nebraska Sen. J. James Exon, a Democrat, remarked: "I have been around here a while, and I have been through many hearings in many committees. This is the largest media event, both in this room and the people waiting outside, that I have ever seen."

Three musicians from very different backgrounds — Frank Zappa, John Denver, and Twisted Sister's Snider — agreed to appear, and all of them spoke out against the stickers.

Zappa said the PMRC ratings system amounted to "the equivalent of treating dandruff by decapitation."

Denver, whose wholesome image made him a powerful advocate for free speech, pointed out that some newspapers had refused to print ads for his movie *Oh God*, a comedy featuring George Burns in the title role. Evidently, they thought the very idea of an actor depicting the Almighty was blasphemous.

Denver also recalled that several radio stations had banned his song "Rocky Mountain High" because programmers thought he was talking about drug use. Lyrics could be interpreted in a number of ways, he suggested, and could be misconstrued easily, based on a listener's biases.

It was a point driven home by Snider, who arrived dressed in a sleeveless black T-shirt, black trousers and a chrome belt, and who introduced himself as a non-smoking, non-drinking Christian with a 3-year-old child. In contrast to Denver, he was expected to be combative.

And he was.

He wasn't expected to be articulate.

But he was that, too.

He noted that Twisted Sister's "We're Not Gonna Take It" had been included among the "Filthy Fifteen" for its allegedly violent content, but said the song's lyrics weren't violent at all. And he was right. Defiant and rebellious, yes. But there wasn't any violence there. Snider accused the panel of hearing what they expected to hear, having confused the lyrics with the band's popular MTV video, which showed a verbally abusive father getting his comeuppance in slapstick fashion.

Dee Snider

It was funny.

In fact, Snider — who first appears in the video in a high-speed spin move that recalls Taz from Looney Tunes — said the video was "simply meant to be a cartoon with human actors playing variations on the Roadrunner/Wile E. Coyote theme."

"Each stunt," he said, "was selected from my personal collection of cartoons."

The United Way of America had even sought and received permission to use the video in a program to illustrate the changing American family. They were interested in it because of its "light-hearted way of talking about communicating with teenagers."

If anyone had a problem with the lyrics on one of the records they'd purchased, Snider said, there was an easy solution: Return it for a refund.

Denver warned the senators that putting stickers on LPs or banning them outright might have the opposite effect than what they intended: "That which is denied becomes desired," he pointed out. "That which is hidden becomes interesting."

Especially for teenagers.

When the rating system went into effect, kids predictably sought out the records with stickers because they were more likely to be cool or edgy. But that didn't make them easier to get. Even though Tipper Gore had gone out of her way to say the labels weren't censorship, they still wound up encouraging censorship in practice. Some retailers relegated stickered albums to the back of the store, others refused to carry them at all, and still others only did so if the artists recorded sanitized versions of the songs that led to the warning. Those "clean" CDs weren't labeled as such, so buyers often thought they were getting the original recordings.

Parental Guidance

Being included in the "Filthy Fifteen" wasn't the end of the matter for Judas Priest, which released a song called "Parental Guidance" to protest the idea of stickers.

"I don't really feel that we as a band have done anything that can be misconstrued as harmful or damaging," vocalist Rob

POP GOES THE METAL

Halford said in 1986. "God forbid, we should ever want to do that. That would end our career overnight."

As it turned out, their career almost *did* end because someone accused them of doing just that.

In 1990, Judas Priest was named in a civil lawsuit alleging that the band was responsible for an attempted double-suicide. Two young men, ages 18 and 20, had shot themselves with a sawed-off shotgun at a church playground in Nevada five years earlier.

One of them, Raymond Belknap, had died, while the other, James Vance, had survived and written a letter to his mother four months later. It read: "I believe that alcohol and heavy metal music, such as Judas Priest, led us or even 'mesmerized' us into believing that the answer to 'life was death.'"

Vance's mother responded by suing the band, saying the pair had shot themselves because they'd heard subliminal messages ("Let's be dead" and "Do it") on Priest's song "Better By You, Better Than Me." It wasn't a new song: In fact, it dated back more than a decade, having been recorded for their 1978 album, *Stained Class*.

One other thing wasn't new, either: Vance's troubled state. His home life had never been anything close to ideal. He'd run away 13 times; his mother admitted that she'd hit him on more than one occasion; and he, in turn had assaulted her more than once. He'd even tried to choke her when he was all of 8 years old.

Vance and Belknap had been smoking pot and drinking heavily before they shot themselves, but did the family sue their dope dealer or the liquor company? Besides, how easy would it have been to find something that sounds like either of those two brief phrases in the backward static of virtually any album?

The case went to trial anyway. Vance was supposed to

testify, but he died of a methadone overdose in a psychiatric ward before he could take the stand. The band members, meanwhile, were left to defend themselves. Of course, they hadn't done any backward masking or recorded any hidden messages. It was easy enough, they maintained, to hear what you were looking for when you played a record backwards at various different speeds.

They demonstrated this by playing parts of *Stained Class* backward and coming up with absurd phrases that sounded like "Help me keep a job," "Hey, Ma, my chair's broken" and "I-I-I asked her for a peppermint."

"We wanted to prove to the judge that these sounds can be manufactured in the mind more than anything else," Halford said. "If you can drop a seed of what something might be, then you can convince your brain that that's exactly the sound or phrase you're listening to."

The judge's demeanor, Halford said, seemed to change as he heard that argument, realizing that the supposed presence of the phrase "Do it" was a "trick of the mind more than anything else."

The case was dismissed, but the band had to pay $250,000 in legal fees.

And Priest wasn't the only, or even the first metal artist to be blamed for a young man's suicide.

By 1986, fans had been listening to a track called "Suicide Solution" on Ozzy Osbourne's first album for five years without thinking much about it. The lyrics, written either by Osbourne himself or by co-writer Bob Daisley, depending on whom you believe, told a cautionary tale about the dangers of drinking: the "solution" in question being a solution in the *liquid* sense. That is to say, alcohol.

POP GOES THE METAL

Most listeners didn't need an interpreter to understand the opening refrain — "Wine is fine but whiskey's quicker / Suicide is slow with liquor / Take a bottle and drown your sorrows / Then it floods away tomorrows."

Osbourne said as much: "The song wasn't written for suicide. It was about a friend of mine who killed himself on alcohol and drugs, meaning solution as a liquid, not as solution as a way out."

The friend, as Ozzy told it, was AC/DC singer Bon Scott. By Daisley's account, the lyrics had been meant for Osbourne himself, who had his own history of alcohol abuse.

Ozzy Osbourne

Either way, John McCollum's father had a different interpretation. McCollum had killed himself with his dad's .22-caliber pistol after listening to the song, and his parents blamed Osbourne for the tragedy.

So they sued.

The plaintiffs' lawyer pointed to Osbourne's association with dark themes in an attempt to buttress their case.

"The satanic influence of heavy metal is well-known," the

family's attorney, Thomas Anderson, said. "Record albums of Ozzy Osbourne reflect the pentagram, which is symbolic of the devil, an upside-down cross and many other satanic symbols."

The lyrics to "Suicide Solution" didn't say anything about guns, though, so the plaintiffs couldn't make their case based on that song alone. They contended, however, that McCollum had also been listening to "Paranoid," a Black Sabbath song that contains the lines, "Can you help me? Oh, shoot out my brains."

It seemed like a stretch, and the presiding judge must have agreed, because he dismissed the case in August of 1986.

And those Parental Advisory stickers? They're still around, but who buys CDs anymore? It's hard to put a sticker on a song that's streamed digitally (although you can still see them there), the lyrics are available online anyway, and you can access pretty much any song you want with the press of a button. Or you can watch the video on YouTube.

Nobody really cares anymore.

Unfortunately for fans, a lot of people stopped caring about pop metal, too.

PARENTAL ADVISORY EXPLICIT CONTENT

PART III:
RE-VERSE
Cutting the Power

Every Rose
Has Its Thorn

The Bottom Drops Out

Even as mainstream metal hit its peak in popularity, things were already beginning to change. The fan sitting at home watching *Headbangers Ball* or hearing yet another Bon Jovi song top the charts wouldn't have noticed it, but change starts small, whether it's the start of something new or the beginning of the end.

There had always been a disconnect between the fans at home watching slick 3-minute videos and all the mayhem, the mischief, and the madness that was happening on the Strip and in the psycho circus that was the typical concert tour.

Sure, fans went to concerts and lit up to such an extent that a 15,000-seat arena smelled like everyone had gathered round a marijuana bonfire. And yes, a few women near the front got to go backstage after the show... on the understanding that they'd provide brief but intimate "companionship" for someone(s) in the band.

But bands were doing stuff a lot harder than pot and were "doing," in the crude vernacular, a lot more than one woman backstage. And elsewhere.

When Crüe drummer Tommy Lee was asked whether he'd had sex with 1,000 women, he responded that the number was higher than that. "That's for damn sure." Kiss co-founder Gene Simmons said he'd been with more than 4,000.

Some rockers — such as Simmons, Ted Nugent, and Dee Snider — avoided the substance abuse that went along with the stereotypical "lifestyle." But in general, whether it was sex, drugs, or rock 'n' roll, it was always, in Lee's words, "bigger, better, faster, harder, louder."

Bigger was *always* better.

Aerosmith frontman Steven Tyler said he'd made millions. When asked where it had gone, he said: "Up my nose. I must've snorted up all of Peru."

In the world of metal, women who'd made a major impact could almost be counted on one hand (Joan Jett, Lita Ford, Girlschool; maybe Vixen, Wendy O. Williams and Doro Pesch). Testosterone was on overload, even in bands who dressed themselves up in spandex, heels and eyeliner.

Simmons and Stanley bragged, with some justification, that no one could top Kiss' show. Nikki Sixx said he and the other members of Mötley Crüe would go watch other bands perform and come away saying, "We can top that."

When everything always had to be bigger, things could spiral out of control pretty fast. In a 2006 interview with VH1, Blackie Lawless — himself one of the more extreme figures on the scene — described it as "kind of a gigantic frat party in your senior year that was going on every night. There was blatant hedonism. I mean, it's everything you ever heard, and 10 times more."

In 1988, filmmaker Penelope Spheeris brought the reality of that hedonism to the screen in vivid terms.

POP GOES THE METAL

When Spheeris got caught in traffic on the Sunset Strip and saw everything that was going on around her, she decided it was time for a sequel to her 1981 documentary on the punk rock scene, *The Decline of Western Civilization*.

When she made that sequel, it blew up the wall that had separated the heartland from the hedonism.

It was like a less-mature version of *Animal House* with guitars — and without the comedy.

On second thought, there *was* comedy.

It just wasn't necessarily intended. Band members made bad jokes, usually involving sex, then laughed at their own humor like Beavis and Butt-Head.

The Decline of Western Civilization Part II: The Metal Years introduced its viewers to Gene Simmons, his bat-lizard makeup long-since removed, as a nearly 40-year-old man ogling a much younger, swimsuit-wearing woman in a lingerie shop. Yes, this was the same guy who'd immortalized a woman who made sculptures of rock stars' erect penises in a song called "Plaster Caster." But it was one thing to hear that kind of blatant sexuality from a guy in his 20s on vinyl and another to see it from a middle-aged dude on the screen.

The film showed band members pouring beer over each other's head, talking about picking their noses, picking up women and why they didn't have (or want) regular jobs. They bragged about their sexual exploits and about sponging off women. They talked about why groupies were the best thing about being in a band, and about why they were the "fleas and ticks of rock 'n' roll."

W.A.S.P. singer Lawless would have been a natural choice to appear in the movie. But the band's guitarist, Chris Holmes, recalled Spheeris telling him that Lawless wanted money to appear, and she didn't have it, which is why she contacted him.

Lawless, however, tells a different story. By his account, Spheeris wanted to film a one-on-one debate between Lawless and PMRC co-founder Tipper Gore, which Lawless said was supposed to be the centerpiece of the film. But, he continued, Gore's husband — Tennessee Sen. Al Gore — decided to run for president, so she pulled out the day before the debate was to be filmed. (Al Gore ended up losing in the Democratic primaries to Mike Dukakis.)

Either way, Lawless wasn't interviewed for the film, but Holmes was. The obviously drunk guitarist appears floating in a pool on a chaise lounge as his mother looks on.

"I'm a full-blown alcoholic," he says.

"Just when he's awake," his mother adds.

He predicts he'll probably be dead in 10 years and pours vodka into his mouth straight from the bottle (although half of it rolls down his chin).

When Lawless saw the scenes with Holmes, he got on the phone to Spheeris and asked her not to use them. But it was too late: The prints had already been sent to the theaters.

Spheeris talked to established rockers like Ozzy Osbourne (in the kitchen), Paul Stanley (lying in bed, surrounded by women), and Lemmy from Motörhead, as well as club owners like longtime fixture Bill Gazzarri of Gazzarri's and newcomer Riki Rachtman of the Cathouse.

Also interviewed were the members of a band called Odin, whose lead singer, Randy O, is anointed by Gazzarri as the next David Lee Roth. He's shown in concert as well as in a hot tub (where he explains why he wears pants with holes in the back). He talks about having been suicidal at times, but also declares his intention to become the next Jim Morrison or Robert Plant.

He's asked: What if it doesn't happen?

"It's gonna happen," he says.

Most of the rockers interviewed had the same attitude. There was no Plan B. If they didn't make it, they'd end up in a drainage ditch or on skid row.

If the rockers come off looking less than stellar in the film, their critics — represented not by Tipper Gore, but by probation officer Darlyne Pettinicchio — seem just as clueless, if not more.

Pettinicchio talks about a program called Back in Control, which she says is meant to help parents regain control of their kids. She extolls the benefits of "demetaling," a system designed to stop young people from listening to heavy metal. It comes off as a kind of deprogramming effort, which involves nothing more than denying kids access to heavy metal music and clothing (not exactly the most original or sophisticated plan ever developed).

Pettinicchio adopts a serious tone in describing how the heavy metal "horns" sign represents the devil and even creates three 6's that are visible from different angles. Don't tell that to fans of the University of Texas football team, who use it as a tribute to their Longhorns.

Ronnie James Dio — supposedly one of the first to use the sign in a rock 'n' roll context — said he got it from his Italian grandmother, who used it to ward off the evil eye. Gene Simmons also claims credit for it. Before that, a cartoon version of John Lennon was shown flashing the sign on the cover of the Beatles' *Yellow Submarine* album. And the Buddha used it to *expel* demons, not conjure them up.

You Give Love a Bad Name

Even as pop metal hit the peak of its popularity, external pressures were building: Music snobs had always found it to be shallow and derivative, and they only amplified their criticism as it became more popular.

Fans didn't care. At first.

Metal fans have a history of dismissing the critics as part of their natural distrust of mainstream judgments. But when metal *itself* became mainstream, it seemed to some like nothing less than open betrayal. The complaint that bands had sold out, abandoning their roots when dollar signs started flashing, had been part of metal culture for years. It had been one reason the first wave of Kiss fans (at least, some of them) had deserted the band when its songs became more formulaic and merchandising replaced the music as Job One.

When metal acts got successful, it exposed a disconnect that had always been there, but which fans chose to ignore. As long as the bands were struggling, they had something in common with their followers. Clueless record companies and radio stations rejected bands for playing metal, just as clueless teachers, parents, etc. dismissed teenage fans for listening to it. But when those same record companies and radio stations began to embrace pop metal, it shattered that sense of commonality. Marginalized teens still felt marginalized, and it seemed like their heroes had left them behind.

It was a double-edged sword: Popularity made bands rich, but it was the kiss of death to their fans.

The only antidote, for metal bands that had "made it," was to use that newfound popularity to amplify their message of defiance by appearing even more dangerous and extreme than before. And sometimes, even that didn't work. Twisted Sister's video to "Be Chrool to Your Scuel" was banned by MTV, but that didn't blunt the band's freefall from metal standard-bearer to has-been within just a couple of years. It may not have helped that frontman Dee Snider started hosting a show called *Heavy*

POP GOES THE METAL

Metal Mania (the precursor to *Headbangers Ball*) on the video music channel that same year.

You couldn't have it both ways, fans seemed to be saying. Mainstream was plainstream. If metal was morphing into a new version of "corporate rock," where did that leave the kids?

Even Snider's impressive speech to the Senate panel on record labeling couldn't save him and, in fact, it might have hurt him even more. Here was a literate guy telling "the man" that he was a dad who didn't drink and didn't smoke. To rockers paying attention (and, admittedly, a lot of them weren't because they either didn't care or knew the deck was stacked against them), Snider might have seemed like an imposter: a sheep in wolf's clothing who was trying to beat the enemy on its own terms. Metal fans, by and large, took a different approach: Light up, flip the bird, and turn up the music so they didn't have to listen to adults and their B.S.

To many, pop metal seemed like a compromise, especially as it gained acceptance on MTV. Melodies were predictable. Melodies were safe. Melodies were what their parents listened to. Melodies were, therefore, crap.

Blazing guitar solos were no longer enough. As the mainstream embraced pop metal, fans moved away from it, turning instead to the emerging thrash metal movement, led by bands like Megadeth, Pantera, and Slayer. These bands built their sound on influences like Motörhead and Iron Maiden, not Sweet or Slade or Kiss. Hooks and melodies took a backseat to a driving beat and distorted guitars, played at warp speed and with vicious abandon.

(When Metallica itself broke through on MTV with "Enter Sandman," some of *its* fans viewed *that* as a betrayal, too.)

Thrash metal drew on the same punk sensibility that had challenged '70s hard-rock "dinosaurs" like Aerosmith, Black

Sabbath, and Led Zeppelin at the end of that decade, adapting it to fit an expanding metal template. By the early '90s, it would expand to such an extent that it was hard to tell what was metal and what wasn't.

A 1993 article in *Billboard* got right to the point: Whether you called it heavy metal, hard rock, alternative, or even rap, "the traditional lines between these once distinct genres have blurred to the point where crossover is the only constant."

Music marketing executive Munsey Ricci said: "You have heavy artists doing heavy metal and alternative, and then along comes Anthrax doing rap, and Ice-T and Body Count, then the Seattle grunge acts that both the metal and alternative programmers like — and it's all one form of music now. ... Everything's become universal."

Except for melodic metal, which found itself on the outs.

It's common practice to view the '80s in monolithic terms when it comes to pop metal. But the reality is more complicated. The music was evolving throughout the period, and it arrived in two distinct waves. The first wave, spurred by bands like Quiet Riot, Ratt, and Twisted Sister, hit in the early part of the decade but was petering out by 1985, the year of the PMRC hearings.

After that, bands that peaked during the first wave either fell out of favor or had to reinvent themselves.

Van Halen had a new lead singer and was playing increasingly accessible radio rock like "Dreams" and "Love Walks In." There were even more synthesizers on their first album with Sammy Hagar, *5150*, than there had been on David Lee Roth's swan song with the band two years earlier in 1984.

Starting with *Theatre of Pain* in 1985, Mötley Crüe toned down its punk-influenced leather ethos, exchanging it for a (relatively) softer look and sound. The album's hit singles were a power ballad, "Home Sweet Home," and the cover of a 1970s boogie-rock number called "Smokin' in the Boys Room." Both were a far cry from "Live Wire" or "Too Young to Fall in Love," in much the same way that "Beth" had been a departure for Kiss. Even the album cover, in shades of red, purple, and pink, was a sea change from the all-black "Shout at the Devil."

Def Leppard continued to evolve from its heavy beginnings to embrace a more pop-metal sensibility. The band had taken a step in that direction with 1983s *Pyromania*, but then took four years before releasing another album, and when they did, it was a pop-metal masterpiece (*Hysteria*) specifically designed to be the genre's version of Michael Jackson's *Thriller*.

Dysfunctional

Another band that made the transition between these two distinct periods in the 1980s was Dokken.

If there was ever a band primed to hit it big in the '80s, Dokken was it. Frontman Don Dokken knew how to write a strong melody with ample hooks, and guitarist George Lynch came from the same group of Sunset Strip guitar heroes that had produced Eddie Van Halen and Randy Rhoads.

Like Mötley Crüe, Ratt, and Quiet Riot, Dokken had emerged from the L.A. club scene, where Don Dokken caught Lynch and drummer Mike Brown playing in their bands, The Boyz and, later, Xciter. They didn't have a record deal, but Dokken did (with a European label called Carrere). All he needed was a band, so he brought Juan Croucier on board to handle bass and persuaded Brown and Lynch to help him record an album.

Breaking the Chains came out in Europe in 1981 but wasn't released until 1983 in the States. The title track made it to No. 32 on the U.S. Mainstream Rock chart, but the LP itself didn't crack the top 100. Still, it got the band's foot in the door, and there was nowhere to go but up.

Which is precisely what they did. While Twisted Sister and Quiet Riot were on a downward spiral after peaking in 1983-84, Dokken was on the opposite trajectory. Each of their three successive albums sold better than the one before, they all went platinum, and each had multiple top-30 entries on the Mainstream Rock chart.

Videos for songs like "In My Dreams" received significant airplay on MTV. They went with the big-hair look and, for a time, donned colorful euro-glam outfits; they seemed to be hitting their stride when "Dream Warriors" appeared on the soundtrack for *A Nightmare on Elm Street 3: Dream Warriors* (footage from the film was used in the band's music video.)

They weren't Van Halen, Def Leppard, or Bon Jovi, but they were cut from the same cloth and seemed poised to move into that category after *Back for the Attack* went to No. 13 on the album chart in 1987.

They snagged a coveted spot on the Monsters of Rock U.S. tour the following year, slotting in at No. 3 on the bill, behind Van Halen and Scorpions but ahead of Metallica and Kingdom Come. It seemed like the stars were aligned for them to break into the top tier of pop metal.

Then, they broke up, the victims of friction between two creative forces: their singer and their guitarist.

Irresistible force (guitarist), meet immovable object (lead singer).

It was the same old story. To wit:

Guitarist Joe Perry had left Aerosmith in 1979 after a performance at Cleveland's World Series of Rock, on a bill that included fellow heavyweights AC/DC, Ted Nugent, Journey, and Thin Lizzy. Perry had already recorded a solo album, and his wife got into it with bassist Tom Hamilton's wife. Words were exchanged. A glass of milk was thrown. An inebriated Steven Tyler came off stage, saw the whole thing and either told Perry he was fired or agreed when the guitarist said he wanted out.

The so-called "Toxic Twins" would reconcile in time for 1985's *Done With Mirrors* LP.

Rolling Stones guitarist Keith Richards and vocalist Mick Jagger had issues, too. A 2016 feature in the *New York Post*, referencing a memoir by journalist Rick Cohen, appeared under the headline, "Mick Jagger and Keith Richards can't stand each other."

The enmity that grew in Guns N' Roses between Axl Rose and Slash has been just as well-documented. So have feuds between Eddie Van Halen and (first) David Lee Roth (then) Sammy Hagar. But the animosity that built up between Don Dokken and George Lynch rivaled any of those soured partnerships.

Lynch would call Dokken "a very petty human being."

Dokken would say of Lynch: "He thought he was a god, and I disagreed."

Lynch: "Don's ego was just gigantic."

Dokken: "People say to me..., 'Don, you're famous for being an asshole and a prima donna, a control freak.' That was my reputation, because George was putting it out there."

Dokken and Lynch had gotten into it before, but the stress of the Monsters of Rock tour, together with the influence of drugs and alcohol, made the situation too much to handle. After the tour was over, Dokken said he couldn't continue to play with Lynch. He said Brown and bassist Jeff Pilson (who had replaced Croucier after the first album) were welcome to stay on, but they'd need a new guitarist.

When their label, Elektra, heard of the split, they offered the band $10 million to stay together and record two more albums. But Pilson and Brown sided with Lynch, which effectively dissolved the band without its namesake. Don Dokken couldn't even use his own name to form a new band, because the other members owned a stake in the name "Dokken" and sued to prevent him from using it.

They reunited to record two more albums: *Dysfunctional* in 1995 and *Shadowlife* two years later, but by that time, metal's heyday was long past, and Dokken had missed their shot at becoming a mega-selling act. Whether they would have or not would always remain an open question.

Dysfunctional went gold, but *Shadowlife* sounded less like Dokken than an ill-conceived attempt to imitate Foo Fighters or Bush. It didn't make the top 100 and vanished without a trace, after which Lynch and the band parted ways again.

Dokken's assessment on what killed his partnership with Lynch was simple: "When you've got two alpha males in the band, you've got trouble."

Bringin' On the Heartbreak

On the Sunset Strip, there were so many fliers on top of fliers that the city of West Hollywood passed an ordinance banning them. Club owners responded by instituting what they called "pay-to-play" policies: In essence, they forced bands to buy a certain number of tickets, which the musicians had to sell for whatever price they could get.

"The club makes the band buy 100 tickets, and then for the band to get their money back, they have to sell the tickets for eight to ten dollars each," guitarist Greg Leon told *Sleazeroxx*. "If they can't sell them, too bad for the band."

POP GOES THE METAL

Pay-to-play ensured that the bands — not the nightclubs — would be on the hook for less-popular shows, such as those on slow nights like Mondays or Tuesdays.

"I know a few bands that will buy one hundred tickets at eight or ten bucks each just so they can get up on stage and pretend to be rock stars for 30 to 45 minutes," Leon said, "and these bands are better than most."

Bands on the same bill often undercut one another to be sure they got rid of their tickets, meaning that no one who played that particular night made money. Some bands agreed to the clubs' pay-to-play terms but were unable to meet them and had their equipment confiscated.

Suddenly, it was harder for unknown bands to get noticed unless they already had cash to back up their ambition. Most, of course, did not.

In a sense, this was a good thing. There was already a glut of metal-playing wannabes, and record companies had started signing any band they thought might be the next Poison or Bon Jovi. But while imitation may be the sincerest form of flattery, listeners want to be entertained, not flattered, and blatant mimicry gets old after a while.

Originality still counts for something, but if fans' ears are flooded with too much stuff that sounds the same, even the originals will start to sound stale. The baby, as they say, will be thrown out with the bathwater.

That's unfortunate, because, at the end of the 1980s, there were still new bands who also happened to be putting out original stuff. They were still within the pop-metal genre, but they were also something more than clones of Poison or Def Leppard.

They never had the chance to build an audience, though, because just as they were about to hit their stride, pop metal

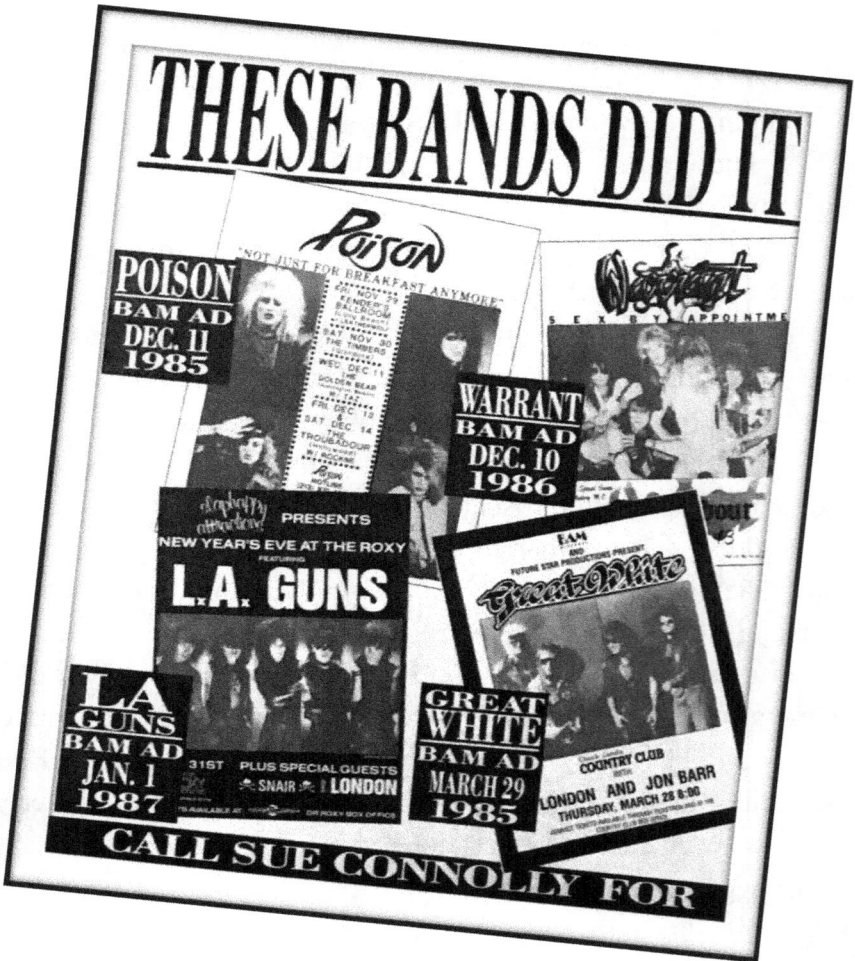

THESE BANDS DID IT

POISON
BAM AD
DEC. 11
1985

Poison
"NOT JUST FOR BREAKFAST ANYMORE"

WARRANT
BAM AD
DEC. 10
1986

PRESENTS
NEW YEAR'S EVE AT THE ROXY
FEATURING
L.A. GUNS

LA
GUNS
BAM AD
JAN. 1
1987

31ST   PLUS SPECIAL GUESTS
SNAIR   LONDON

GREAT
WHITE
BAM AD
MARCH 29
1985

COUNTRY CLUB
LONDON AND JON BARR
THURSDAY, MARCH 28 8:00

CALL SUE CONNOLLY FOR

became a musical casualty on the level of disco a decade earlier. No one went out and burned Twisted Sister albums the way they'd torched Bee Gees records at Chicago's Disco Demolition Night in' 79. But spandex and big hair were about to become as obsolete as bellbottoms and mirror balls to the emerging generation of music fans.

A lot of people don't remember the next wave of pop metal superstars who might have been because, thanks to bad timing,

POP GOES THE METAL

they never were.

Case in point: Lillian Axe.

The band had been around since 1983 but didn't release their first album until 1988. Led by guitarist and primary songwriter Steve Blaze, they weren't a California band; they were the biggest thing in the Big Easy. Neither their eponymous debut nor their follow-up, *Love + War*, on MCA made much of an impact, and MCA dropped the band.

Despite their limited success, the New Orleans band caught on with I.R.S. Records, which released their third album, *Poetic Justice*, in 1992. It featured a hook-heavy gem called "True Believer" and a killer cover version of Badfinger's "No Matter What" — the latter of which came with an MTV-ready video that got some decent exposure. *Poetic Justice* got another boost when it climbed to No. 28 on the Heatseeksers Chart, which Billboard had created a year earlier to spotlight sales by new and developing artists.

The next year's follow-up, *Psycoschizophrenia* would rise even higher on the same chart, peaking at No. 13, but I.R.S. dropped the band, which fell apart as musical tastes changed and wouldn't put out another album (a selection of unreleased songs and demos) for six years.

Lillian Axe lasted a while, but other bands came and went, seemingly without a trace.

Company of Wolves, a blues-rock outfit with a pop sheen, released a self-titled album with Mercury in 1990 backed by a couple of videos: one for a song called "The Distance" and another for the catchy leadoff track, "Call of the Wild."

Their lead singer was Kyf Brewer, who bore a passing resemblance to Kiss' Paul Stanley (without the makeup), and their guitarist was Steve Conte, who would go on to join a reconstituted New York Dolls before teaming up with former

Hanoi Rocks singer Michael Monroe.

They signed with Mercury because their manager was also working with Cinderella and Kiss, both of which were on the label. Conte thought they'd hit their stride at the perfect time, because their record would be coming out between releases by Bon Jovi, Cinderella, Kiss, and Scorpions, so they'd have the playing field to themselves. They weren't trying to be a glam act; their tastes ran more toward Georgia Satellites, Aerosmith and the Stones. They were difficult to classify, which was a problem; and when they *did* get classified, they were lumped into the hair metal category. And that was an even bigger problem.

They started making the rounds for interviews wearing jean jackets, cowboy boots and T-shirts. "We looked rock and roll, but we weren't all glammed up or anything," Conte said in a 2017 interview.

"As the tour went on, we met people who owned boutiques and we met chicks who wanted to do our hair. We loved it. People wanted to give us free shit like purple psychedelic shirts, and we started incorporating all of that shit into our look. By the end of the album cycle, our hair was gigantic and we were wearing psychedelic clothes!"

But hair metal was sinking fast, and Company of Wolves went down with the ship. Mercury dropped them after just one album, although they collected some old demos and released them independently on one disc, and put together another CD with songs they'd written for a never-released Mercury follow-up.

Other bands that emerged around the same time were more in the vein of sleaze metal. Trying to follow in the footsteps of Guns N' Roses probably seemed like a good move for an L.A. band in 1990, and Love/Hate was original enough that they would have been a good bet to find their niche if grunge hadn't come along and spoiled the party.

Skid Row had gotten in just under the wire with 1989's multiplatinum self-titled release, which gave them momentum enough to reach No. 1 with their follow-up, *Slave to the Grind*, two years later. Hits such as "18 and Life" and "Youth Gone Wild" set the band apart from most of the other up-and-comers. It didn't hurt that Sebastian Bach had a four- or five-octave vocal range — and was described by the *L.A. Times* as "heavy-metal's hottest new sex symbol."

But most bands that were trying to launch their careers at the time didn't have a Sebastian Bach out front. Love/Hate did have a bass player called Skid Rose, and they actually toured with Bach's band. But their lead singer was Jim Wilkerson, who went by the stage name Jizzy Pearl.

Love/Hate's first single, "Why Do You Think They Call It Dope?" off their debut album *Blackout in the Red Room*, got some airplay on *Headbangers Ball* and reached No. 46 on the Mainstream Rock chart. The band also got a nod from the *Los Angeles Times* as the best new act since GN'R. But it didn't generate the kind of sales they'd hoped for, so they went back into the studio to try again.

The result was a follow-up titled *Wasted in America*.

Pearl must have felt he needed to go to greater lengths (or heights) to get noticed, because he climbed a hill overlooking L.A. at 3 in the morning on June 1, 1992, and affixed a huge cross to the Hollywood sign.

Then, he tied himself to it.

Firefighters had to go out and get him down, and Pearl was arrested on suspicion of trespassing.

"I hope for their sake it was worth it," TV reporter Mark Brown said, "because this individual is now under arrest."

So was it (worth it, that is)?

Not quite. All four singles released off the album failed to chart, although the title cut barely cracked the top 40 in the U.K. Other albums followed, but by this time, alternative rock was ruling the world and there was little room on the charts for acts like Love/Hate.

A lot of people think the end came with the release of Nirvana's *Nevermind* in 1991, but the curtain really fell on Aug. 8 of the following year, during a co-headlining concert featuring Metallica and Guns N' Roses.

The famously dysfunctional GN'R road show had already hit a pothole the year before in St. Louis, where Axl Rose leapt into the crowd to go after a cameraman who was shooting a video of the show without permission. Rose slammed his open mic down, and it sounded like a gunshot when it hit the stage. He shouted, "I'm going home!" and stomped off stage, with Slash following, saying, "We're outta here."

The crowd went on a rampage, and 60 fans were injured. Rose was charged with inciting a riot; he was later acquitted but had to miss two concerts when a warrant was issued for his arrest.

As always, volatility was the name of the game with GN'R.

The band added Metallica to the bill the following year, but it didn't help. If anything, it got worse.

Everything came crashing down in Montreal, where 55,000 fans turned out to see the two biggest metal bands in the world at the time. Metallica opened the show, and disaster struck when lead singer James Hetfield got confused about where he was supposed to be onstage. During the band's set, huge columns of flame burst skyward from the set. It was part of the show, but what happened to Hetfield wasn't.

He'd somehow wandered into the pyro area, where he was

completely engulfed in 3,200-degree fire. His hair, the skin on his back, his arm, his hand, and his face were severely burned — in some places down to the bone. The band's bass tech, Zach Harmon, later said that if Hetfield had been breathing in, he would have been dead.

The rest of Metallica's set was canceled as Hetfield was rushed to the hospital.

Guns N' Roses was left to calm the waters.

Which was not exactly their forte.

The band, and Rose in particular, were notorious for taking the stage late at their shows — sometimes so late they violated curfews and had to pay fines for violating city ordinances. True to form, they refused to go on early to fill the void left by Metallica's departure. The crowd, naturally, grew restless during the two-hour intermission, but the worst was still to come: Nine songs into their set, the band stopped playing.

Rose went on a tirade about the sound system and declared, "In case anybody here is interested, this will be our last show for a long time."

Then, he bailed.

It was St. Louis all over again. Ten people were injured as fans destroyed escalators and concession stands inside the stadium, then spilled into the surrounding streets, smashing windows, overturning a patrol car and toppling a streetlamp. The moral of the story: When 55,000 fans are denied the opportunity to safely bang their heads, they'll unsafely smash up other things instead.

But something bigger had happened.

Guns N' Roses were, stylistically and chronologically, the connective tissue that bound the '80s and the '90s together. They ditched many of metal's glam trappings, yet still reveled in its bloated excess; their music was wilder and more primal, but it still had the hooks and melodies. Ultimately, they were too volatile to sustain what they had become: the bridge between the hair metal of the '80s and the grunge revolution.

They burned that bridge in Montreal on Aug. 8, 1992, and the fire spread to engulf the metal landscape.

Pagan Rome was burning.

Those godlike frontmen, created in the images of Robert Plant and David Lee Roth, were toppled from their pedestals like marble statues, and so were the guitar heroes whose blazing solos had fanned the flames of their altar fires. Those who still worshipped them went underground, like those who still worshipped the pagan gods at the dawn of the Christian age.

But while Nero may have fiddled, metaphorically speaking (the fiddle hadn't been invented yet) while Rome burned, Axl Rose threw down his mic like a gauntlet for others to pick up — and they wasted no time in doing so.

It was all inevitable.

Nothing lasts forever.

Sad Wings of Destiny

Who framed heavy metal?

Grunge didn't just kill 1980s metal, it obliterated it. Or so the story goes.

And in some ways, it *did* seem to happen suddenly. Propelled by the hit single "Smells Like Teen Spirit," Nirvana's second album, *Nevermind*, started selling 400,000 copies *a week* in the fall of 1991. It would go on to sell upwards of 30 million worldwide.

Another Seattle band, Pearl Jam, had released its debut disc, *Ten*, a month before *Nevermind* hit the stores, and it rocketed to No. 2 on the album charts. It wasn't too long before a couple of other Seattle-based outfits — Alice in Chains and Soundgarden — joined the party.

It was like a seismic shift: Suddenly, West Hollywood was no longer the center of the rock 'n' roll universe.

Seattle was.

Warrant singer Jani Lane illustrated the transformation with a story of two trips he took to meet with the president of his band's label, Columbia Records in New York. The first time, he saw a poster of his band's hit 1990 album, *Cherry Pie*, over the secretary's desk. But by the time he made a return trip two years later to promote Warrant's next album, *Dog Eat Dog*, things had changed. This time, he was greeted by a poster touting Alice in Chains' second album, *Dirt*.

That was one of the first signs, he said, that Warrant had "slipped down the priority ladder."

Not long afterward, the bottom fell out.

"It was like 'every rock band that came out in the '80s sucks, has no reason to live and should not be on this planet, and there's no way they can possibly do anything worthwhile and viable in the '90s,' " Lane said during a 1998 interview. "So let's just burn 'em all at the stake."

Dog Eat Dog made it to No. 25 on the album charts, but none of its four singles cracked the Billboard Hot 100 and only one even managed to make the U.S. Rock chart ("Machine Gun" at No. 36). That was Warrant's last U.S chart appearance, and *Dog Eat Dog* was their last record for Columbia.

The story was similar elsewhere. Poison's fourth album, released in 1993, was their first not to hit the top 10 or reach platinum status in the U.S. Cinderella's string of three straight platinum records was also broken with 1995's ironically named *Still Climbing*, which turned out to be their last release. The more aptly titled *Dysfunctional* marked the end of Dokken's three-album run of platinum certifications, too.

Kix's 1995 album was the first in more than 10 years that failed to chart. Ratt, meanwhile, went on a nine-year hiatus after 1990s *Detonator*, the first of their five albums not to reach platinum status.

And so it went, down the line.

The Sunset Strip scene, which had been going strong since the 1960s, went out with a whimper following pay-to-play.

By 1995, the Z-Rock radio format, which had spotlighted metal from the mid-1980s onward, had switched over to what it called a modern-rock based format. Van Halen and Aerosmith were still on the playlist, but they were the exceptions, not the rule: Mötley Crüe, Poison, Skid Row, and Winger were out; Pearl Jam and Nirvana were in. The network even ditched its slogan, "If it's too loud, you're too old," and replaced it with "Where America Rocks."

Managing director Lee Abrams explained: "Our listeners have grown out of a lot of metal we were playing, and a lot of those '80s bands have worn out their welcome." He said even the network's name had become toxic because it was so closely associated with '80s metal, but he couldn't change it because affiliates had invested so much in merchandise and billboard ads. The *Headbanger's Heaven* show was dropped. One called *Too Much Seattle* was added.

As with all corporate radio, the bottom line was, well, the bottom line. The network was shifting its target demographic group from males ages 16-30 to males 25-34: people more apt to buy groceries and furniture, which (Z-Rock hoped) would pull in more ads for those products.

The revamp didn't work: Z-Rock went off the air on New Year's Eve, 1996.

Nevermind

But even though grunge seemed like an unstoppable force at the time, it proved to be a fleeting phenomenon. With the exception of Pearl Jam, few of the genre's pioneers lasted long.

Alice in Chains' self-titled third album debuted at No. 1 in 1995, but the band went on hiatus after that, and lead singer Layne Staley was found dead of an overdose seven years later. Soundgarden, meanwhile, recorded just one album after 1996 — and waited 16 years to do so.

STEPHEN H. PROVOST

Nirvana followed up the epic success of *Nevermind* with the multiplatinum *In Utero* and a performance on *MTV Unplugged* in 1993. But frontman Kurt Cobain's suicide the following year ended their brief run at the top.

Nirvana drummer Dave Grohl went on to form a much more durable (and, in many ways, more successful) band called Foo Fighters, but it was more a straight-ahead hard rock outfit than anything that could be classified as grunge. For lack of a better term, some commentators started referring to it as "post-grunge."

What was left of grunge became subsumed in a catch-all genre known as alternative rock, which encapsulated everything from post-grunge to rap-rock hybrids (Kid Rock, Linkin Park) to emo and punk-skater bands. The latter found exposure via the Vans Warped Tour, sponsored by skateboard shoe maker Vans, which showcased the likes of Blink-182, Jimmy Eat World and Simple Plan on multiple occasions.

The "alternative rock" tag was also applied to any number of bands that would have been labeled power pop a generation earlier: All American Rejects, Fountains of Wayne, Weezer, Teenage Fanclub and Fastball.

But did grunge *really* kill pop metal, or did it just happen to come along at the right time?

MTV had launched and sustained the hair metal revolution in the 1980s, but less than a year after Nirvana's *Nevermind*, the cable network with "Music" in its name took a tentative step away from "all music, all the time" with the debut of its first reality show, *The Real World*. Even that title was telling when it came to hair metal, which had been built on hype and style. MTV had been the perfect promotional vehicle for flamboyant, loud, in-your-face glam bands. But the channel was already turning down the volume just as the music of T-shirt-and-flannel grunge bands was taking over the world.

Larger than life was out. Down to earth was in.

And down to earth just didn't play as well onscreen. Between 1995 and 2000, MTV cut the number of music videos it played by 36.5 percent. Jon Stewart, later of *The Daily Show*, hosted a talk show on MTV for a couple of years starting in 1993. After the new millennium kicked in, it moved even further away from its original mission with shows like *Punk'd*, *Pimp My Ride*, and *16 and Pregnant*.

"It's very simple," MTV chairman Tom Freston explained in 1995. "MTV is a business over and above the music network. It's a trademark at its core."

But neither grunge nor MTV's burgeoning obsession with reality television would have succeeded in knocking pop metal off the air if the public hadn't been ready for a change. The hair metal trend of the '80s had been built by bands that had scratched and clawed their way to the top through endless self-promotion. It all went back to the "do anything to get noticed" mentality of the Sunset Strip, which itself hearkened back to the initial glam era that had spawned the likes of Alice Cooper and Kiss.

Now, just as Kiss had become cartoonish in the early '80s, the pop metal bands they had inspired started to seem like caricatures of themselves as the decade drew to a close.

In the words of Def Leppard guitarist Phil Collen: "When everything becomes the stereotype, and the stereotype is absolutely pathetic, then it's time to move on."

It had become a way of life for many bands that got their start in Hollywood, which itself had been all about image long before musicians took up that attitude. At the end of the '80s, not only did successful bands like Def Leppard, Bon Jovi and Poison dominate rock radio and MTV's *Dial MTV*, hundreds of less successful (and often, less talented) clones were clamoring to get noticed.

Over-the-top, hard-sell bombast only works for so long before people need a break. And when hair metal descended to what many saw as a new low with the shallow and shamelessly objectifying earworm "Cherry Pie" by Warrant, it was more than even man die-hard fans could stomach.

Keith Cameron described it in *The Guardian* as "the key rock record of 1990..., heaving with sexual innuendos and an aerated production surpassed in sheer artificiality only by the protagonists' poodle-primped tonsorial display." ("Tonsorial" relates to hairstyling, not tonsils, although Jani Lane opens his mouth so wide in the video that you can almost see those, too.)

The Sunset Strip scene had been all about sex, drugs and rock 'n' roll right from the beginning. But "Cherry Pie" took the innuendo to a new level, and you couldn't escape it because that chanting chorus got stuck in your head. Not since Toni Basil's recording of the Chinn-Chapman composition "Mickey" had any chorus been so catchy — and so obnoxious.

Tasked with crafting a song in the vein of Queen's "We Will Rock You" or Aerosmith's "Love in an Elevator," it supposedly took Jani Lane all of 15 or 20 minutes to come up with the lyrics, which he scrawled on the back of a pizza box.

"Cherry Pie" was one of the last metal anthems to hit the charts before grunge took over (Def Leppard managed to have a No. 15 hit with "Let's Get Rocked" two years later), but it's worth noting that the power ballad survived the supposed death of pop metal by several years: Aerosmith hit No. 1 for the only time in its career in 1998 with "I Don't Want to Miss a Thing."

But Aerosmith had been around before the '80s metal boom and would survive its collapse. So would other veteran acts that predated the craze but got caught up in it to a greater or lesser

POP GOES THE METAL

extent: Kiss, Van Halen, Def Leppard, Alice Cooper and Ozzy Osbourne among them.

The bands that were born from the craze were the ones that died with it, with a few notable exceptions like Mötley Crüe (which almost did) and Bon Jovi.

"Cherry Pie" may have been a tipping point, while grunge and MTV might have helped push pop metal over the edge. But blaming any of those things misses a crucial point: It's entirely possible that the trend had simply run its course. Musical tastes, after all, tend to alternate between escapism on the one hand and activism/earnest introspection on the other. By 1990, pop metal had given its audience just about all the escapism it could take. The me-first attitude that had typified the Reagan years began to wane amid the economic downturn of the early '90s, and the nation was ready for a change, both musically and politically.

It shouldn't have come as a surprise.

Looking back at history, musical trends seem to last about five years before being supplanted by the "next big thing." Elvis and the pioneers of rock reigned from the mid-'50s until the early 1960s, when the Beatles ushered in the British Invasion. But the style of music epitomized by British blues and the Merseybeat only remained dominant for three or four years before being overtaken by psychedelia.

The Beatles and the Stones adapted. Chad and Jeremy, the Dave Clark Five, Gerry and the Pacemakers and others fell by the wayside.

Psychedelic rock gave birth to progressive rock on the one hand and the glam/glitter movement on the other. These, in turn, gave way to punk and disco around 1975 — the year the Sex Pistols formed and the Bee Gees released "Jive Talkin'." (It's largely forgotten that the Bee Gees' first hit back in 1967 was widely mistaken for the Beatles, and that their records in the late

'60s had about as much in common with disco as "Enter Sandman" does.)

By the 1980s, New Wave had begun to supplant punk in the U.K., and disco's demise was every bit as sudden and decisive as hair metal's would be a decade later. Perhaps more so.

Don't Cry

Most of these musical forms survived, in slightly different forms and under slightly different names. Power pop was one example, and punk resurfaced in the repertoire of alternative bands like Blink-182, the Offspring and Green Day.

Melodic metal lived on beyond the '80s, as well. You're not likely to find it on the charts, but veteran bands still pack arenas and are among the most profitable touring acts. Guns N' Roses' "Not in This Lifetime... Tour" was the second most-popular tour of the 2010s, behind Ed Sheeran's road show. AC/DC checked in at No. 5, and Bon Jovi was No. 19.

Kiss' "End of the Road Tour" was among the highest-grossing of 2019. Trans-Siberian Orchestra, a hybrid rock-and-classical troupe that's an offshoot of metal band Savatage, ranks at or near the top of touring acts during the holiday season every year. Even Queen continued to tour, filling major arenas, with *American Idol* alum Adam Lambert stepping in for the late Freddie Mercury on lead vocals.

It's ironic that bands who got their start touring to promote album sales aren't making much new music these days because, in the era of streaming music, it's a lot more profitable to go on the road. Gene Simmons put it succinctly in a 2017 interview: "Creating new music so people can download it for free does not appeal to me."

Why bother when you can pack arenas with ticket-buyers

who are willing to pay hundreds of dollars for a seat, forty bucks for a T-shirt and four figures for a meet-and-greet?

Bands in the classic tradition may not be topping the charts, but they're still making good music. In 2000, a band called The Darkness — which might be described as a cross between Judas Priest and Queen — hit No. 2 on the British charts with "I Believe in a Thing Called Love."

Another band from England, the Struts, debuted in 2014 with *Everybody Wants*, an album that sounded like a power-pop version of Queen, while Greta Van Fleet made the first of four straight trips to No. 1 on the Mainstream Rock chart three years later with "Highway Tune." (As much as it might have sounded like it, this was *not* a lost Led Zeppelin track.)

Meanwhile, bands like L.A.'s Steel Panther and Norway's Wig Wam were taking the '80s formula and piling on a little cheese. The result landed somewhere in a nebulous no-man's land between serious and satirical, between Judas Priest and Spinal Tap. A band called Rock Sugar even recorded mash-ups of pop, rock and metal hits for an album called *Reimaginator*. "I Love Sugar on Me" blended Joan Jett and Def Leppard, while "Don't Stop the Sandman" fused Journey's "Don't Stop Believin'" with Metallica's "Enter Sandman."

The music kept evolving, while at the same time revisiting familiar territory.

Power metal bands, many of them based in Europe, were integrating the hooks and melodies of pop metal with the more aggressive style of speed metal. Iron Maiden's "Run to the Hills," the band's first single with Bruce Dickinson on lead vocals, is an early example, its verses galloping full-speed into a killer chorus hook. Bands like DragonForce, Edguy, Gamma Ray, Primal Fear, HammerFall, Silent Force, and Iced Earth took it from there.

Ritchie Blackmore

Many power metal acts set their music against a backdrop of fantasy or epic themes, reminiscent of those explored by Ritchie Blackmore's Rainbow on albums such as *Rising*, from 1976

In an interview four decades after its release, drummer Snowy Shaw of Therion and Dream Evil would describe *Rising* as "the quintessential album that introduced a more Dungeons and Dragons-type fantasy heavy rock to the masses," while Judas Priest vocalist Rob Halford lauded it as "a thrilling

POP GOES THE METAL

album" that "feels as good now as when it first came out."

Priest, one of the founders of power metal, returned to this style on releases like 2008's *Nostradamus*, a concept album built around the life of the 16th-century French visionary.

As for Blackmore, he chose to explore his passion for medieval and Renaissance-era folk music by forming a group with girlfriend Candice Night in 1997. As of 2020, the pair (who married in 2008) had recorded 10 albums as Blackmore's Night, seven of which have hit the top 20 in Germany. Releases like *Autumn Sky* and *Secret Voyage* have topped the Billboard New Age chart, and an 11th album was set for release sometime in 2020.

Symphonic metal, a subgenre related to power metal that came of age in the 21st century, incorporated big hooks with an even bigger sound. Often punctuated with a beauty-and-the-beast approach — operatic female vocals alternating with (often nearly unintelligible) grunts, growls, and snarls from a male counterpart — its distinctive sound has been particularly popular in Europe.

Finland's Nightwish led a parade of symphonic metal bands to prominence in the 2000s, releasing seven straight No. 1 albums in their home country and routinely charting in the top 10 across Europe, despite their relative obscurity in the U.S. Other bands in this subgenre include Epica, Therion, Kamelot, and Sonata Arctica.

In 1999, Edguy vocalist Tobias Sammet founded a project called Avantasia ("avalon" plus "fantasia"), which straddled the line between symphonic and pure power metal. Over the years, it has featured guest performers such as Alice Cooper, Dee Snider, Joe Lynn Turner, Klaus Meine, Geoff Tate, Candice Night, Eric Singer, and Bruce Kulick, to name a few.

STEPHEN H. PROVOST

Days of Future Passed

Mega concert tours.

Power metal.

Symphonic metal.

A newer new wave of heavy metal for the new millennium.

If you're wondering what ever happened to melodic metal, that's just the tip of the iceberg. You may not hear much of it on the radio or see it on MTV anymore, but that doesn't mean it's not around.

In a sense, things have come full circle. MTV's prophecy when it signed on in 1981 with "Video Killed the Radio Star" was true, but only temporarily. Satellite TV had replaced radio, but only for the moment. In the 21st century, MTV was no longer playing metal videos (or many videos at all), but a new phenomenon called satellite radio had emerged to pick up the baton.

In 2008, the XM and Sirius satellite radio networks merged to form Sirius XM. You could find 1980s-era pop metal on Hair Nation (Channel 39), one of several channels dedicated to rock that also included Boneyard (Channel 38). Rebranded as Ozzy's Boneyard in 2012, it featured bands ranging from Black Sabbath to Iron Maiden, AC/DC to Metallica.

In 2017, Sirius XM launched a 24-hour all-music-talk radio channel that carried Eddie Trunk's metal-themed *Trunk Nation* program and a pair of shows that featured former MTV fixtures: former news anchor Kurt Loder, interviewing music figures on *True Stories*, and original VJ Mark Goodman, serving as co-host of a show called *Debatable* with author Alan Light.

So, the next time someone tells you that grunge killed pop metal, ask yourself how many grunge songs you've heard lately. You can still hear plenty of pop metal. You've just got to know where to find it.

As Bret Michaels said, "Rock never really dies. It just goes underground."

STEPHEN H. PROVOST

I Remember You

What Ever Happened To...

As the pop-metal boom of the '80s went bust, some of its biggest names moved on to other things. Some kept making music, while others left the business behind. Still others came to tragic ends, like Quiet Riot's Kevin DuBrow, who died of a cocaine overdose at 52, and Warrant frontman Jani Lane, found dead in a hotel room of alcohol poisoning at 47.

Jizzy Pearl from Love/Hate took DuBrow's spot as lead singer of Quiet Riot after recording an album with L.A. Guns. Robert Mason, who'd done a stint with Lynch Mob, took over for Lane with Warrant.

For others, life went on.

The Van Halen merry-go-round kept on turning, with the band parting ways with Sammy Hagar and recording a couple of songs with David Lee Roth for a greatest hits collection in 1996, then adding extreme vocalist Gary Cherone for *Van Halen III* (not their third album, but a third version of the band) in 1998.

In perhaps the oddest of pairings, Roth and Hagar — who never seemed to get along very well and often had not-so-nice things to say about each other — went on tour *together* in 2002. But that didn't mean they suddenly liked each other: They had to flip coin on Howard Stern's radio show to decide who would headline the opening date.

The tour made them both lot of money, and they seemed to enjoy thumbing their noses in unison at the Van Halen brothers. But they didn't appear on stage together, and they didn't want anything to do with each other on the road, either.

"Believe me, this guy is not your average bear, OK?" Hagar said in an interview. "He's an egomaniac, he is in fantasyland, really believes he's still the rock god of all times, and it's like he's in complete denial."

Roth's take: "Sam throws a party. I *am* the party."

Van Halen, meanwhile, was stuck in neutral. *Van Halen III* had been a huge disappointment, and Cherone was soon without a job. The band went out on tour with Hagar and recorded three new songs with him for a compilation double album in 2004, But by the following year, Hagar was out again, and it wasn't until eight years later that the band recorded its next (and so far last) album, *A Different Kind of Truth*, this time with Roth.

Oddly, it wasn't a different kind of album cover: The train on the cover looked remarkably similar to the steam engine on the front of a 1975 album by the Commodores.

Eddie Van Halen's son, Wolfgang, stepped in to replace longtime member Michael Anthony on bass for the album, while Anthony went on to join Hagar's new band, Chickenfoot. Van Halen stopped putting out new music after that, but Hagar kept making albums and money.

Not that he needed it: His side hustle, a tequila company, proved even more profitable than his recording career. Immortalized in the title of a Van Halen tune, Cabo Wabo Tequila was named for the "Cabo wobble," a stumbling drunken walk of bar patrons in Cabo San Lucas who'd had a bit too much. By 2006, it was making $60 million a year and was the

POP GOES THE METAL

No. 2 selling brand behind Jose Cuervo.

The guy who'd discovered Van Halen in the first place, Gene Simmons, welcomed back former Kiss bandmates Ace Frehley and Peter Criss for an episode of MTV's acoustic showcase, *Unplugged*, in 1995. The two then rejoined the band full time and put the makeup back on to announce a Reunion Tour at the '96 Grammy Awards.

They put out a new studio album (*Psycho Circus* in 1998) and played the Super Bowl pregame show in 1999. But it wasn't long before Frehley and Criss departed again, replaced — in the founders' iconic makeup — by guitarist Tommy Thayer from Black 'n Blue and drummer Eric Singer, who'd played on the band's *Revenge* album.

Kiss made a couple of albums with the new lineup: *Sonic Boom* in 2009 and *Monster* three years later. Meanwhile, Frehley, who'd been criticized by other band members for his drinking, drug use and general flakiness over the years, got sober and became more prolific than the band he'd left. He put out four albums in the span of a decade starting in 2009, as many as he'd released in the 30 years prior to that.

Kiss went on a "Farewell Tour" in 2000 that didn't live up to its name, because the band was still performing in 2020, this time on what it called "The End of the Road Tour."

Def Leppard, Mötley Crüe, Poison, and Joan Jett had been set to tour together that same year, but the coronavirus pandemic forced them to delay those plans. Each of those acts have recorded sporadically in the 2000s, but have toured consistently, because that's where the money is.

Def Leppard's output included an album of covers from the 1970s glam era titled *Yeah!* in 2006, a new studio album called *Songs from the Sparkle Lounge* two years later, and a 2015 self-titled release that recalled their *Hysteria* heyday. Like other big names, they did a Las Vegas residency, late in the summer of 2019.

Mötley Crüe remained as controversial as ever. Vince Neil left in 1992 and recorded a solo album, *Exposed*, the following year. It featured two songwriting collaborations with Tommy Shaw of Styx and Jack Blades of Night Ranger, and it peaked at No. 13 on the album charts. His former bandmates, meanwhile, recorded a self-titled album with new singer John Corabi.

But just as Van Halen fans hadn't taken to Gary Cherone, Crüe stalwarts didn't buy Corabi as a replacement for Neil, who returned for 1997's *Generation Swine*.

With Neil back, though, it was Tommy Lee's turn to jump ship, forming a rap-rock band called Methods of Mayhem, which released one album in 1999 and another in 2010. Lee rejoined Mötley Crüe for a reunion tour in 2004, and Nikki Sixx formed a side project called Sixx:A.M. with guitarist DJ Ashba and singer James Michael (the "A" and "M" in the band's name) in 2007. The band released five albums between then and 2016, when they put out a two-volume project: *Prayers for the Damned* and *Prayers for the Blessed*.

Perhaps Mötley Crüe's highest-profile recent achievement was its publication of *The Dirt*, an autobiography that made the *New York Times* bestseller list in 2001 and was adapted to the screen as a Netflix biopic in 2019.

At the other end of the spectrum, Christian rockers Stryper dropped their yellow-and-black outfits and logo for their 1990 album, *Against the Law*. It didn't sell well, and neither did the next year's follow-up, so the band broke up, with lead singer Michael Sweet going solo.

The band reassembled in 2005 for a new studio album titled *Reborn*, with Michael Sweet producing. Seven more albums followed, with Stryper returning to its original logo, even if they did tone down their wardrobe: The glam suits of the '80s were gone, although the cover of 2013's *Second Coming* did show the band wearing yellow-and-black striped ties.

Michael Sweet sang with Boston for a few years following the death of original singer Brad Delp, and Stryper covered Boston's 1976 classic "Peace of Mind" in 2009 before recording an entire album of secular cover songs in 2011. Bassist Tim Gaines, who had suggested the band's name, was fired in 2017 and replaced by Perry Richardson, formerly of FireHouse.

Sweet also recorded a pair of albums with former Dokken guitarist George Lynch.

The More Things Change

After Lynch and Don Dokken parted ways for the second time in the late 1990s, the three remaining members of Dokken joined forces with former Winger guitarist Reb Beach to record *Erase the Slate* in 1999, and Dokken soldiered on into the new millennium. The band released four more studio albums (three with new guitarist Jon Levin) and, after a somewhat Beatlesque post-grunge detour with 2002's *Long Way Home*, managed to recapture its classic sound.

Lynch and Pilson, meanwhile, joined forces for a harder-edged album of their own in 2003, with Pilson handling vocals.

Dokken's classic lineup would reunite for a brief tour of Japan and one U.S. date, in 2017. And Don Dokken and Lynch would reunite for a show March 6, 2020, in Biloxi, Miss. — the singer's first performance since having neck and spine surgery.

Like other pop metal bands of the 1980s, Poison's fortunes declined in the'90s. Lead singer Bret Michaels wrote, starred in and recorded the soundtrack for *A Letter from Death Row*, a film that featured appearances by Martin and Charlie Sheen.

The album was the first of half a dozen solo releases he'd put out over the next 15 years. *Custom Built* went to No. 1 on three Billboard album charts — Hot 100, Hard Rock, and Independent — when it was released in 2010.

That was a big year for Michaels, in more ways than one.

It was the year he took top honors on Donald Trump's *Celebrity Apprentice* TV show, beating the likes of Ozzy's wife Sharon, Cyndi Lauper, retired baseball star Darryl Strawberry, and, in the finals, Holly Robinson Peete. In the process, he raised $640,000 for the American Diabetes Association.

"All my life I've been a Type 1 diabetic," he said. "I've learned to take things day by day."

It's a good thing, too, because that wasn't the only health issue he'd have to deal with in 2010. In April, shortly after he turned 47, Michaels underwent an emergency appendectomy. Everything seemed to have gone smoothly, but within a few days, he was suffering from headaches and found himself back in the hospital. Diagnosis? A brain hemorrhage. And while he was on the mend from *that*, he had a mild stroke and was told he had a hole in his heart.

He had successful heart surgery at a Phoenix hospital, and he showed his appreciation by donating TVs and a sound system to create a music and hospitality room at the facility.

In 2007, Michaels joined a select group of metal stars with hit reality TV shows. He had two of them, actually. The first, *Rock of Love*, was a *Bachelor*-type show in which women competed to be Michaels' girlfriend (although he didn't marry any of the winners). It lasted for three seasons and was followed immediately by a single season of *Bret Michaels: Life as I Know It*, focusing on his personal life.

It wasn't exactly an original concept.

The Osbournes, featuring Ozzy, Sharon, Kelly, and Jack,

premiered in 2002 and lasted four seasons on MTV. See Ozzy take his son fishing... and throw firecrackers at pelicans. See Sharon throw a ham over the fence at the neighbors. Hear Ozzy talk about the dangers of Viagra. See Sharon suggest using bubbles as part of Ozzy's stage show and hear Ozzy say, "Bubbles? Oh come on, Sharon? I'm fucking Ozzy Osbourne, the prince of fucking darkness!"

Not to be outdone, another prince of (fucking) darkness, Gene Simmons, debuted *Gene Simmons Family Jewels* in 2006 on A&E.

The show aired for seven seasons, but Simmons' partner in Kiss, Paul Stanley, never made an appearance, saying it "wasn't reality."

"To create a life that isn't accurate and for me to be a part of it... and, quite honestly, waste my time?" he told *Rolling Stone*. "You're missing out on living a real life if you're filming a fake one."

(Remember, these are two guys who rose to stardom by creating alter egos in costumes and face paint.)

Twisted Sister singer Dee Snider had his own reality series for one season, too — *Growing Up Twisted* aired in 2010 — and, like Michaels, appeared on *Celebrity Apprentice*. Unlike Michaels, he didn't win, but he did make it through to the eighth week before being "fired."

No matter. He had plenty of other things to keep him busy. He recorded a pair of albums with his own band, Widowmaker, in the early 1990s, and worked as a voice actor in *SpongeBob SquarePants* and a Playstation 2 videogame.

Twisted Sister reunited in 2006 to release one of the more original Christmas albums ever recorded. *A Twisted Christmas* offered a metallic take on traditional carols such as "O, Come All Ye Faithful," which was reworked in the style of "We're

Stephen Pearcy, Warren DiMartini

Not Gonna Take It." There was also a very Twisted version of "The Twelve Days of Christmas," recorded under the new title "Heavy Metal Christmas." Updated lyrics replaced the song's traditional gifts with items such as eight pentagrams, seven leather jackets, six cans of hairspray, five skull-head rings, four quarts of Jack... and, of course, a tattoo of Ozzy.

Ratt didn't record a Christmas album, although they did do that Geico commercial.

Singer Stephen Pearcy quit in 1992 to form a new band, Arcade, which released two albums and included ex-Cinderella drummer Fred Coury. Guitarist Robbin Crosby eventually left the band, as well. He suffered from a pancreatic condition that caused him to gain weight, and he contracted HIV through drug use. It ultimately cost him his life: He died of a heroin overdose complicated by pneumonia and AIDS in June of 2002. At the time of his death, at the age of 42, the 6-foot, 6-inch Crosby weighed 400 pounds.

"What has drug addiction done for me?" he asked in 1999. "It's cost me my career, my fortune, basically my sex life when I found out I was HIV-positive." His life, he said, had become a "maelstrom of hell."

Pearcy eventually returned to Ratt, but two versions of the band emerged: one featuring bassist Juan Croucier and the other helmed by drummer Bobby Blotzer. There was plenty of friction between them, including a lawsuit that reached the 9th U.S. Circuit Court of Appeal, where Blotzer wound up on the losing end.

In 2018, Pearcy and Croucier formed a new version of the band, which appeared in the Geico insurance ad two years later.

Appetite for Destruction

If there seemed to be a lot of drama surrounding Ratt, it was nothing compared to what happened with Guns N' Roses. The band released an ambitious, and massively successful, pair of albums simultaneously under the *Use Your Illusion* title in 1991: They debuted in the top two spots on the Billboard album chart, making GN'R the first band to achieve this feat. The power ballads "Don't Cry" and "November Rain" became hits, with the latter being the longest song ever to appear in the U.S. top 10.

Queen's "Bohemian Rhapsody" had broken all the rules by becoming a hit at 5 minutes, 55 seconds, but "November Rain" ran more than 3 minutes *longer* than that. The video also cost a whopping $1.5 million to make... which was nothing compared to the $5 million that was shelled out to make the video from the even-longer (9:23) "Estranged." That's the same amount of money spent on *My Big Fat Greek Wedding*, and five times as much as it cost to film *Rocky*.

GN'R fired drummer Steven Adler, who responded with a lawsuit (settled a couple of years later). Matt Sorum replaced him. Dizzy Reed joined on keyboards, and guitarist Izzy Stradlin left after the twin *Illusion* albums were released, with Gilby Clarke taking his spot.

Sorum and Clarke both played on the band's 1993 release, an album of cover songs titled *The Spaghetti Incident?* that included a song written by serial killer Charles Manson. It was the last GN'R album for 15 years. In the meantime, the band, for all intents and purposes, broke up and became Axl Rose's baby, with a rotating cast of characters joining Rose and Dizzy Reed for a series of recording sessions that eventually resulted in the 2008 release, *Chinese Democracy*.

One guitarist during this era, Brian Carroll, played behind a mask and with a KFC bucket on his head. Hence his name: Buckethead. Another guitarist, Ron "Bumblefoot" Thal, who would later join the classic prog-rock outfit Asia, was also on the roster for a time. So was DJ Ashba who, at the same time, was playing with Sixx:A.M.

Slash, for his part, formed Slash's Snakepit in 1993 with Sorum and Clarke. In 2000, he teamed up with Sorum and ex-GN'R bassist Duff McKagan to create the supergroup Velvet Revolver, which was fronted by ex-Stone Temple Pilots vocalist Scott Weiland and also included punk guitarist Dave Kushner.

The first of their two albums, *Contraband*, went to No. 1 on the Billboard album chart, with the single "Slither" topping the Mainstream Rock chart and earning a Grammy for 2005's Best Hard Rock Performance.

In 2016, Rose went on the road with AC/DC when vocalist Brian Johnson left the tour on his doctor's advice after suffering hearing loss. The same year, Rose, Slash, and Duff McKagan reunited to kick off a more than three-year "Not in This Lifetime... Tour."

It became the third-highest-grossing tour of all time.

Rock 'n My Country

In 2019, McKagan recorded a country-rock flavored album, "Tenderness," which was produced by country legend Waylon Jennings' son, Shooter Jennings.

He wasn't the metal stalwart to go country. Briefly a member of Black Sabbath, singer Ron Keel had formed Steeler with guitar virtuoso Yngwie Malmsteen and later fronted his own band, Keel. Later on, though, he took a turn back toward Nashville (the Georgia native's first band had been based in Tennessee) and recorded country fare like "My Horse is a Harley" under the moniker Ronnie Lee Keel.

Bret Michaels did the same.

It's not hard to imagine Poison's biggest hit, "Every Rose Has Its Thorn," as a country song, so it's hardly shocking that Michaels three country-flavored studio albums, starting in 2005. That same year, he was a celebrity judge on USA Network's *Nashville Star* — a countrified version of *American Idol*.

Sebastian Bach, formerly of Skid Row, won a music contest on the CMT show *Gone Country 2*, and put out a country single called "Battle With the Bottle" in 2008, while Aerosmith's Steve Tyler moved to Nashville and recorded a country-rock album called *We're All Somebody From Somewhere*, in 2016. It debuted at No. 1 on the country album chart.

Even Bon Jovi took a country turn with its 2007 release *Lost Highway*, the band's last album to go platinum in the U.S. and its last to include a top-30 single, "(You Want to) Make a

Memory," which got to No. 27.

Blackie Lawless' life also took an unexpected turn. The onetime king of the codpiece-clad shock rockers decided to return to Christianity, which he'd left at the age of 18 because he'd become disenchanted with religion. He rediscovered his faith around 2005, comparing himself to the biblical prodigal son. As a result, he doesn't sing "Animal (Fuck Like a Beast)" anymore, in deference to the biblical prohibition against corrupt speech in the Book of Ephesians.

His W.A.S.P. bandmate, onetime vodka-swilling guitarist Chris Holmes, didn't die after 10 years, as he'd predicted in *The Decline of Western Civilization Part II*: Instead, he went into alcohol aversion therapy in 1996 and stopped drinking. As of 2020, he was still performing, having grown a thick beard that made him look like the second coming of Grizzly Adams.

The other up-and-coming bands in *Decline* either came and went or, in most cases, never made it.

London singer Nadir D'Priest kept the Russian flag he tried, and failed, to burn onstage during the film. (The flag, it turned out, had been fireproof.) The band fell apart in 1992, when their manager ditched them in New Orleans without money or transportation, singer D'Priest recalled. He spent three years working on the CD-ROM of the Rolling Stones for their *Voodoo Lounge* tour, which wasn't all bad, he said, because he got to party with Keith Richards. He got clean and sober shortly after that and worked in construction, among other things, then eventually regrouped with London and playing some more gigs.

Seduce broke up, too, with guitarist David Black moving on to post-production work in movies and shampoo commercials.

Bill Gazzarri's enthusiasm for Odin never translated into major success, but Randy O didn't commit suicide, as he'd suggested he might in the film. In 2019, he returned to the Strip to release his debut solo album, the aptly titled *Coming Home*.

Riki Rachtman, whose Cathouse club figured prominently in the film, got sober after his first year running the club and hosted *Headbangers Ball* from 1990 to 1995. The club closed in 1993, and Rachtman moved to Charlotte, N.C., in 2014. Each year, he holds a charity motorcycle run across North America.

As for director Penelope Spheeris, she would go on to direct *Wayne's World*, a film based on the *Saturday Night Live* skit of the same name. The movie starred Mike Myers and Dana Carvey as Wayne and Garth, hosts of a public-access TV show broadcast from Wayne's basement. It was the eighth-highest-grossing film of 1992, and Spheeris went on to direct a film adaptation of *The Beverly Hillbillies* the following year.

And what about that probation officer in *Decline* who demonstrated the evils of the heavy metal "horns," Darlyne Pettinicchio? She actually did all right for herself after the film. As of 2017, she was probation bureau chief with Los Angeles County making a salary of more than $156,000 a year, not counting benefits and other compensation.

Then again, that was nothing compared to what Guns N' Roses grossed on its "Not in this Lifetime... Tour." Over the course of 175 shows, it raked in a cool $584 million.

Outro

Don't Know What You Got (Till It's Gone)

When you're young, you think everything about your life is permanent. You'll always be in school, because school days are slower than molasses and school *years* last an eternity. You'll always be living with your parents, too, despite what they tell you about growing up and moving out one day. Even when you *do* move out and get a job, it feels like you'll be working there in that same office cubicle the rest of your life — statistics be damned.

Eventually, though, you get a different job, then maybe change careers; maybe get married and maybe get divorced; maybe have kids.

Things change.

But some part of you is always stuck back there in your teens and early 20s.

I grew up in the 1970s and '80s, and a part of me still lives there. I remember my mother still listening to big band music and early '50s pop while I'd barricaded myself in my bedroom, listening to Kiss, Queen, and the local album-rock radio station. I didn't understand why she preferred her music, but now I do. It was the soundtrack of her youth, and I had a different soundtrack for mine. Kids today are listening to other kinds of music, and for the most part, I don't get what they see in *their* music, either.

I had trouble coming to terms with the fall of pop metal in the early '90s, but I still enjoyed some of what was left behind. I bought *Superunknown* by Soundgarden, *American Idiot* by Green Day and Weezer's "Green Album." I even started tuning in country stations because the music they played sounded more like what rock 'n' roll used to be. Apparently, I wasn't alone: Bret Michaels re-recorded "Every Rose Has its Thorn" as a duet with Loretta Lynn, and Def Leppard teamed up with Tim McGraw on "Nine Lives." Garth Brooks even went in the opposite direction by covering Kiss' "Hard Luck Woman."

But the major trends left me behind. Kid Rock and Linkin Park were OK, but most pure hip-hop and what passed for pop in the 2010s just didn't do it for me.

Instead, I got into Nightwish and was shocked to when I got tickets to the second show on their 2012 *Imaginaerum* tour for 10 bucks apiece. That's what happens when you're into music no one else is listening to... or at least no one else in the States. When I had to pay more the next time I saw them, it was almost a relief: Some people actually still liked the same music I did.

Of course, most of the tickets I bought — for acts like Aerosmith, Van Halen, Kiss, Yes, Queen, Poison, and Def Leppard — cost a whole lot more. But it was worth it, even if Kiss only had two of the four original players and Queen was touring with Adam Lambert, not Freddie Mercury (RIP). And even if three or four members of Yes weren't touring as "Yes" because they couldn't get along with several other members who were using the name. It wasn't the '80s anymore, but they were still all providing a reasonable facsimile, and that was a whole lot better than nothing.

Like a lot of other people, I still miss MTV when it really was MUSIC Television, and I have zero interest in shows such as *Jersey Shore* and *Ridiculousness* that came to dominate the channel. I miss the days when I could buy a copy of *Circus* to get a pullout poster of Kiss. I miss the days when the music I loved was the centerpiece of popular culture. Those days were fleeting, but they sure were fun while they lasted.

All the hype and hair were secondary.

What was important then, and what's important now, is the music. It's still there, and it's as great as ever.

In the end, that's all that really matters.

STEPHEN H. PROVOST

DATABASE
Names, dates and places

Album Sales

Top-selling melodic metal albums from the 1980s

Album	Band	Sales*	Year
Back In Black	AC/DC	25	1980
Appetite for Destruction	Guns N' Roses	18	1987
Slippery When Wet	Bon Jovi	12	1986
Hysteria	Def Leppard	12	1987
Pyromania	Def Leppard	10	1983
1984	Van Halen	10	1984
Pump	Aerosmith	7	1989
New Jersey	Bon Jovi	7	1988
Dr. Feelgood	Mötley Crüe	6	1989
Metal Health	Quiet Riot	6	1983
5150	Van Halen	6	1986
Permanent Vacation	Aerosmith	5	1987
Open Up and Say...Ah!	Poison	5	1988
Skid Row	Skid Row	5	1989
Shout at the Devil	Mötley Crüe	4	1983
Theatre of Pain	Mötley Crüe	4	1985
Girls, Girls, Girls	Mötley Crüe	4	1987
Blizzard of Ozz	Ozzy Osbourne	4	1980
Diver Down	Van Halen	4	1982
OU812	Van Halen	4	1988

*U.S. sales, in millions; studio albums only; no compilations

Chart-Toppers

Melodic rock and metal No. 1 hits, 1980-1992 *

Single	Band	Wks	Year
Keep On Loving You	REO Speedwagon	1	1981
Jump	Van Halen	5	1984
I Can't Fight This Feeling	REO Speedwagon	3	1985
You Give Love a Bad Name	Bon Jovi	1	1986
Livin' on a Prayer	Bon Jovi	4	1987
Here I Go Again	Whitesnake	1	1987
The Flame	Cheap Trick	2	1988
Sweet Child o' Mine	Guns N' Roses	2	1988
Love Bites	Def Leppard	1	1988
Bad Medicine	Bon Jovi	2	1988
Every Rose Has Its Thorn	Poison	1	1988
I'll Be There for You	Bon Jovi	1	1989
When I See You Smile	Bad English	2	1989
Blaze of Glory	Jon Bon Jovi	1	1990
More Than Words	Extreme	1	1991
To Be With You	Mr. Big	3	1992
I Don't Want to Miss a Thing	Aerosmith	4	1998

*Billboard Hot 100

Power Pop

Selected power pop tracks

Year	Song	Band	Peak
1966	Paperback Writer	The Beatles	1
	Red Rubber Ball	The Cyrcle	2
1967	Carrie Anne	Hollies	9
	My Back Pages	The Byrds	30
	Pictures of Lily	The Who	51
1970	No Matter What	Badfinger	8
1972	Go All the Way	Raspberries	5
	Baby Blue	Badfinger	14
	I Wanna Be With You	Raspberries	16
	Couldn't I Just Tell You	Todd Rundgren	93
	The Ballad of El Goodo	Big Star	—
1973	Tonight	Raspberries	69
1974	September Gurls	Big Star	—
	Know One Knows	Badfinger	—
1975	Fox on the Run	Sweet	5
	I'm On Fire	Dwight Twilley	16
1976	I Only Want to Be With You	Bay City Rollers	12
	Southern Girls	Cheap Trick	—
1977	American Girl	Tom Petty	
1978	Surrender	Cheap Trick	62
	Listen to Her Heart	Tom Petty	66
1979	My Sharona	The Knack	1
	Good Girls Don't	The Knack	1

POP GOES THE METAL

	Girl of My Dreams	Bram Tchaikovsky	37
	Starry Eyes	The Records	56
1979	Girls Talk	Dave Edmunds	65
	Rock N Roll Girl	The Beat	—
	Hearts in Her Eyes	Searchers	—
1980	Tomorrow	Kiss	—
1981	Better Things	The Kinks	92
	From Small Things	Dave Edmunds	—
1983	Slipping Away	Dave Edmunds	39
	A Million Miles Away	Plimsouls	82
1984	You Might Think	The Cars	7
	Do You Want Crying	Katrina & the Waves	37
1988	There She Goes	The La's	49
	Cartoon	Soul Asylum	—
1990	The King is Half-Undressed	Jellyfish	—
	Monument of Me	Merrymakers	—
1991	Baby's Coming Back	Jellyfish	62
1993	Bye, Bye, Bye	Jellyfish	—
1996	The Way	Fastball	4
	Don't Look Back in Anger	Oasis	55
	That Thing You Do	The Wonders	—
1998	Fire Escape	Fastball	86
	Can I Borrow a Kiss	The Knack	—
2001	The Middle	Jimmy Eat World	5
2003	Starlight	Zed	—
	The Last Song	All-American Rejects	—
2004	Welcome to My Life	Simple Plan	40
2005	Perfect Situation	Weezer	51
	I'll Be OK	McFly	—
2009	Back to Me	All-American Rejects	—
2020	Hero	Weezer	—

Anthems

Selected rock and metal anthems

Year	Song	Band	Peak
1955	Rock Around the Clock	Bill Haley	1
1957	Rock and Roll Music	Chick Berry	5
1963	Surfin' U.S.A.	Beach Boys	3
1964	You Really Got Me	Kinks	7
	All Day and All of the Night	Kinks	7
1965	Satisfaction	Rolling Stones	1
	My Generation	The Who	74
1966	Wild Thing	Troggs	1
1968	Born to Be Wild	Steppenwolf	2
1971	Rock and Roll	Led Zeppelin	47
	Baba O'Riley	The Who	—
1972	School's Out	Alice Cooper	7
	Rock and Roll Part II	Gary Glitter	7
1973	We're an American Band	Grand Funk	1
	Smoke on the Water	Deep Purple	4
	Rock & Roll Hootchie Koo	Rick Derringer	23
	Rock the Nation	Montrose	—
1974	It's Only Rock 'n Roll	Rolling Stones	16
1975	Ballroom Blitz	Sweet	5
1976	Saturday Night	Bay City Rollers	1
	Rock and Roll All Nite	Kiss	12
	Shout it Out Loud	Kiss	31
1977	We Will Rock You	Queen	4

POP GOES THE METAL

1978	Rock 'n' Roll Damnation	AC/DC	—
	Long Live Rock and Roll	Rainbow	—
1979	Highway to Hell	AC/DC	47
1980	Back in Black	AC/DC	37
	Living After Midnight	Judas Priest	—
1982	There's Only One Way to Rock	Sammy Hagar	31
	You've Got Another Thing Comin'	Judas Priest	67
	I Love It Loud	Kiss	102
1983	Rock of Ages	Def Leppard	16
	Shout at the Devil	Mötley Crüe	17
	Lick It Up	Kiss	66
1984	Cum On Feel the Noize	Quiet Riot	5
	We're Not Gonna Take It	Twisted Sister	21
	Rock You Like a Hurricane	Scorpions	25
	I Can't Drive 55	Sammy Hagar	26
	Turn Up the Radio	Autograph	29
	Bang Your Head	Quiet Riot	31
	Mama, Weer All Crazee Now	Quiet Riot	51
	I Wanna Rock	Twisted Sister	68
	You Give Love a Bad Name	Bon Jovi	1
1987	Livin' On a Prayer	Bon Jovi	1
1988	Bad Medicine	Bon Jovi	1
	Nothin' But a Good Time	Poison	6
1989	Born to Be My Baby	Bon Jovi	3
1990	Cherry Pie	Warrant	10
	Up All Night	Slaughter	27
1992	Let's Get Rocked	Def Leppard	15

Ballads

Selected rock ballads and power ballads

Year	Song	Band	Peak
1971	Without You	Harry Nilsson	1
	Imagine	John Lennon	1
	Stairway to Heaven	Led Zeppelin	—
1972	Layla	Derek & Dominoes	10
1973	Goodbye Yellow Brick Road	Elton John	2
1974	Angie	Rolling Stones	1
1975	All By Myself	Eric Carmen	2
	Lady	Styx	6
	Only Women Bleed	Alice Cooper	12
	Free Bird	Lynyrd Skynyrd	19
1976	Dream On	Aerosmith	6
	Beth	Kiss	7
	Somebody to Love	Queen	13
	Hard Luck Woman	Kiss	15
1977	Love Hurts	Nazareth	8
1978	Dust in the Wind	Kansas	6
1979	Babe	Styx	1
1981	Keep On Loving You	REO Speedwagon	1
	Waiting for a Girl Like You	Foreigner	2
1982	Open Arms	Journey	2
1983	Faithfully	Journey	13
	Still Lovin' You	Scorpions	64
1984	I Want to Know What Love Is	Foreigner	1

POP GOES THE METAL

1984	Sister Christian	Night Ranger	5
	Bringin' on the Heartbreak	Def Leppard	61
1985	Can't Fight This Feeling	REO Speedwagon	1
	Goodbye	Night Ranger	17
	Alone Again	Dokken	64
	Home Sweet Home	Mötley Crüe	89
1986	Amanda	Boston	1
	Carrie	Europe	3
	Nobody's Fool	Cinderella	13
1987	Love Bites	Def Leppard	1
	Alone	Heart	1
	Is This Love	Whitesnake	2
	When the Children Cry	White Lion	3
	Wanted, Dead or Alive	Bon Jovi	7
	Never Say Goodbye	Bon Jovi	11
	I Won't Forget You	Poison	13
	Honestly	Stryper	23
	You're All I Need	Mötley Crüe	83
1988	Sweet Child 'o Mine	Guns N' Roses	1
	I'll Be There for You	Bon Jovi	1
	The Flame	Cheap Trick	1
	Angel	Aerosmith	3
	When It's Love	Van Halen	5
	Wait	White Lion	8
	Don't Close Your Eyes	Kix	11
	Don't Know What You Got (Till It's Gone)	Cinderella	12
1988	Reason to Live	Kiss	83
1989	Every Rose Has Its Thorn	Poison	1
	When I See You Smile	Bad English	1
	Heaven	Warrant	2

1989	Patience	Guns N' Roses	4
	I Remember You	Skid Row	6
	Close My Eyes Forever	Lita Ford/Ozzy	8
	Without You	Mötley Crüe	8
	Love Song	Tesla	10
	Headed for a Heartbreak	Winger	19
	I'll See You in My Dreams	Giant	20
	Sometimes She Cries	Warrant	20
	The Ballad of Jayne	L.A. Guns	33
1990	More than Words Can Say	Alias	2
	Something to Believe In	Poison	4
	Forever	Kiss	8
	Silent Lucidity	Queensrÿche	9
	Fly to the Angels	Slaughter	19
	Love Walked In	Thunder	—
	I'll Be Waiting	Talisman	—
1991	More Than Words	Extreme	1
	To Be With You	Mr. Big	1
	Wind of Change	Scorpions	4
	Love of a Lifetime	FireHouse	5
	Miles Away	Winger	12
	Heartbreak Station	Cinderella	44
1992	November Rain	Guns N' Roses	3
	When I Look Into Your Eyes	FireHouse	8
	Don't Cry	Guns N' Roses	10
	Love is on the Way	Saigon Kick	12
	Have You Ever Needed Someone So Bad	Def Leppard	16
	Where You Goin' Now	Damn Yankees	20
1993	Bed of Roses	Bon Jovi	10
	Two Steps Behind	Def Leppard	12

POP GOES THE METAL

	Amazing	Aerosmith	24
1994	Always	Bon Jovi	4
1995	Can't Stop Lovin' You	Van Halen	30
1998	I Don't Want to Miss a Thing	Aerosmith	1

Stage Names

Metal stars and their real names

Stage Name	Birth Name	Band
Joey Allen	Joseph Alan Cagle	Warrant
Michael Anthony	Michael Sobolewski	Van Halen
Sebastian Bach	Sebastian Bierk	Skid Row
Reb Beach	Richard Earl Beach Jr.	Winger
Steve Blaze	Steve Nunenmacher	Lillian Axe
Marc Bolan	Mark Feld	T. Rex
Geezer Butler	Terence Butler	Black Sabbath
Vinnie Chas	Vincent Pusateri	Pretty Boy Floyd
Ronnie James Dio	Ronald Padavona	Dio
Joe X. Dubé	Jeff Grobb	Starz
Jon Bon Jovi	John Francis Bongiovi	Bon Jovi
Lizzy Borden	Gregory Harges	Lizzy Borden
Bun E. Carlos	Brad M. Carlson	Cheap Trick
Eric Carr	Paul Caravello	Kiss
Alice Cooper	Vincent Furnier	Alice Cooper
Peter Criss	Peter Criscuola	Kiss
Nadir D'Priest	Antonio Munoz	London
Bobby Dall	Robert Kuykendall	Poison
C.C. DeVille	Bruce Johannesson	Poison
Razzle Dingley	Nicholas Dingley	Hanoi Rocks
Billy Dior	Billy McCarthy	D'Molls
Taime Downe	Gustave Molvik	Faster Pussycat
Jackie Fox	Jacqueline Fuchs	Runaways

POP GOES THE METAL

Oz Fox	Richard Martinez	Stryper
Rik Fox	Richard Suligowski	Steeler
Ace Frehley	Paul Frehley	Kiss
Jay Jay French	John French Segall	Twisted Sister
Lizzy Grey	Stephen Perry	London
Tracii Guns	Tracy Ulrich	L.A. Guns
Joan Jett	Joan Marie Larkin	Runaways
John Paul Jones	John Baldwin	Led Zeppelin
Kari Kane	Cary Ayers	Pretty Boy Floyd
Jani Lane	John Oswald	Warrant
Blackie Lawless	Steven Duren	W.A.S.P.
Jake E Lee	Jakey Lou Williams	Badlands
Tommy Lee	Thomas Lee Bass	Mötley Crüe
Oni Logan	Leonardo Gimenez	Lynch Mob
Mick Mars	Robert Alan Deal	Mötley Crüe
Duff McKagan	Michael McKagan	Guns N' Roses
Punky Meadows	Edwin Meadows Jr.	Angel
Bret Michaels	Bret Michael Sychak	Poison
Michael Monroe	Mattie Fagerholm	Hanoi Rocks
Ozzy Osbourne	John Osbourne	Black Sabbath
Vince Neil	Vince Neil Wharton	Mötley Crüe
Jizzy Pearl	James Wilkinson	Love/Hate
Iggy Pop	James Osterberg Jr.	The Stooges
Dane Rage	Dane Scarborough	London
Dizzy Reed	Darren Reed	Guns N' Roses
Rikki Rockett	Richard Allen Ream	Poison
Axl Rose	William Bruce Rose	Guns N' Roses
Skid Rose	Chris Rose	Love/Hate
Gene Simmons	Chaim Witz	Kiss
Eric Singer	Eric Mensinger	Kiss
Nikki Sixx	Frank Serafino Ferrana	Mötley Crüe

STEPHEN H. PROVOST

Chris Slade	Christopher Rees	AC/DC
Slash	Saul Hudson	Guns N' Roses
Dee Snider	Daniel Snider	Twisted Sister
Mark St. John	Mark Norton	Kiss
Paul Stanley	Stanley Eisen	Kiss
Izzy Stradlin	Jeffrey Dean Isbell	Guns N' Roses
Nasty Suicide	Jan-Markus Stenfors	Hanoi Rocks
Sylvain Sylvain	Sylvain Mizrahi	New York Dolls
Joey Tempest	Rolf Larsson	Europe
Matt Thorr	Matt Thorne	Rough Cutt
Johnny Thunders	John Genzale	New York Dolls
Mike Tramp	Michael Trempenau	White Lion
Steven Tyler	Steven Tallarico	Aerosmith
Vinnie Vincent	Vincent Cusano	Kiss
Sandy West	Sandy Pesavento	Runaways
Chip Z'nuff	Gregory Rybarski	Enuff Z'nuff

Formerly Known As...

Bands and their former names

Band	Former name(s)
Autograph	Wolfgang
Europe	Force
Guns N' Roses	Hollywood Rose
House of Lords	Giuffria
Kiss	Wicked Lester
Kix	Shooze, The Generators
Lillian Axe	Oz/Stiff
Lion	Lyon
Love/Hate	Dataclan
Night Ranger	Ranger, Stereo
Poison	Paris
Quiet Riot	Mach 1, Little Women
Ratt	Mickey Ratt
Steelheart	Red Alert
Stryper	Roxx Regime
Trixter	Rade
Twisted Sister	Silver Star
Van Halen	Genesis, Mammoth

Timeline

Key dates in pop metal history

1960s

1964   Whisky a Go Go opens on the Sunset Strip, Jan. 11

The Kinks release proto-metal anthem, "You Really Got Me," Aug. 4, followed by the similarly rocked-out "All Day and All of the Night," Oct. 23

1968   Blue Cheer releases *Vincebus Eruptum*, including the distorted proto-metal "Summertime Blues," Jan. 16

Deep Purple makes live debut, Denmark, April 20

Iron Butterfly releases "In-A-Gadda-Da-Vida," June 14

Led Zeppelin makes live debut, Copenhagen, Sept. 7

1969   Led Zeppelin releases self-titled debut album, Jan. 12

1970s

1970   Black Sabbath releases self-titled debut album Feb. 13

Los Angeles FM rock radio station 95.5 adopts KLOS call letters, March 22

1971   Alice Cooper's "School's Out" peaks at No. 7 on Hot 100, July 29

1972   Van Halen plays as "Mammoth," Pasadena, Oct. 28

1973   Aerosmith releases self-titled debut, Jan. 5

Kiss performs first concert, Popcorn Club, Queens, Jan. 30

Alice Cooper's *Billion Dollar Babies* hits No. 1 on

POP GOES THE METAL

Billboard album chart, April 21

Deep Purple release "Smoke on the Water," May

Singer Ian Gillan leaves Deep Purple, June 29

1974 Kiss releases self-titled debut album, Feb. 18

Van Halen plays first gig at Gazzarri's, April 4

Guitarist Ritchie Blackmore quits Deep Purple to form
Rainbow, June 21

Sweet releases *Desolation Boulevard* in U.K., November

1975 AC/DC releases debut album, *High Voltage*, Feb. 17

Aerosmith releases breakthrough *Toys in the Attic*, April 11

The Rocky Horror Picture Show hits theaters, Aug. 15

Kiss releases double-live album *Alive!* Sept. 10

1976 Kiss releases *Destroyer*, March 15

Judas Priest releases *Sad Wings of Destiny*, March 23

Deep Purple breaks up, July 19

Kiss' "Beth" hits No. 7, Dec. 4

1977 Cheap Trick releases self-titled debut album, February

Kiss plays Madison Square Garden, with Sammy Hagar
opening, Feb. 18

Marvel launches Kiss comic book, June 30

Led Zeppelin's North American Tour cut short by death of
singer Robert Plant's son, July 26

1978 Van Halen releases debut album, Feb. 10

Cheap Trick releases their breakthrough *Live at Budokan*,
which eventually goes triple-platinum, February

Aerosmith, Van Halen, Ted Nugent among 11 bands to
play at Cotton Bowl in First Texxas Jam Music
Festival, July 1

AC/DC releases *Highway to Hell*, July 27

Kiss members release 4 solo albums on same day, Sept. 18

NBC airs *Kiss Meets the Phantom of the Park*, Oct. 28

1980s

1980 Girl, with Phil Collen and Phil Lewis, releases debut album,
  Sheer Greed, January

AC/DC vocalist Bon Scott, 33, dies Feb. 19

Judas Priest releases *British Steel*, April 14

Black Sabbath begins first tour with Ronnie James Dio
  on lead vocals, April 29

Kiss, drummer Peter Criss, part ways, May 17

Led Zeppelin plays last concert, in West Berlin, July 7

AC/DC releases *Back in Black* with Brian Johnson
  on lead vocals, July 25

Rainbow, Scorpions, Judas Priest play first Monsters of
  Rock Festival, Castle Donington, England, Aug. 16

Ozzy Osbourne releases solo debut, *Blizzard of Ozz*,
  Sept. 20

Led Zeppelin drummer John Bonham, 32, dies Sept. 25

1981 Nikki Sixx forms Mötley Crüe, Jan. 17

Starwood closes, June 13

MTV launches Aug. 1

Dokken's debut, *Breaking the Chains*, released in U.S.,
  Sept. 18

Mötley Crüe releases debut, *Too Fast for Love*, Nov. 10

1982 Ozzy Osbourne bites head off bat, Des Moines, Jan. 20

Joan Jett's "I Love Rock 'n' Roll" tops chart, March 20

Guitarist Randy Rhoads, 25, dies in air crash March 19

Ozzy Osbourne marries his manager, Sharon Arden, July 4

Judas Priest releases *Screaming for Vengeance*, July 17

Kiss begins 10th anniversary tour, with Vinnie Vincent
  replacing Ace Frehley on guitar, Dec. 29

POP GOES THE METAL

1983   375,000 people attend Metal Day at US Festival, May 29

Kiss appears without makeup on MTV, Sept. 18

Quiet Riot's *Metal Health* tops album chart, Nov. 26

1984   Van Halen releases *1984*, Jan. 9

Bon Jovi releases self-titled debut album, Jan. 21

Van Halen hits No. 1 with "Jump," Feb. 25

This is Spinal Tap mockumentary hits theaters, March 2

Ratt releases debut, *Out of the Cellar*, March 23

Twisted Sister releases *Stay Hungry*, May 10

Mötley Crüe frontman Vince Neil arrested after car crash
     kills Hanoi Rocks drummer Razzle Dingley, Dec. 8

1985   Guns N' Roses debuts at the Troubadour, March 26

David Lee Roth leaves Van Halen, April 1

Ozzy Osbourne, Judas Priest among acts at Live Aid
     concert for famine relief, July 1

Senate holds hearing on PMRC warning labels, Sept. 19

1986   *Dial MTV* premieres, Feb. 17

Van Halen releases *5150* with Sammy Hagar, March 2

Mötley Crüe drummer Tommy Lee marries TV star
     Heather Locklear, May 10 (d. 1993)

Documentary *Heavy Metal Parking Lot* filmed, May 31

David Lee Roth releases solo debut, *Eat 'Em and Smile*,
     July 7

Poison's releases debut album, *Look What the Cat
     Dragged In*, Aug. 2

Ozzy Osbourne cleared in fan-suicide case, Aug. 7

Bon Jovi releases *Slippery When Wet*, Aug. 18

Z Rock, syndicated hard-rock radio format, debuts, Sept. 1

Cathouse opens on Sunset Strip, Sept. 23

Run-DMC's cover of Aerosmith's "Walk This Way,"
     with Steven Tyler and Joe Perry, hits No. 4, Sept. 27

Stryper releases *To Hell With the Devil*, Oct. 24

Bon Jovi's "You Give Love a Bad Name" hits No. 1, Nov. 29

1987 L.A. rock radio stalwart KMET signs off, Feb. 14

Bon Jovi's "Livin' on a Prayer" tops singles chart, Feb. 14

Whitesnake releases self-titled album, April 7

Guns N' Roses releases *Appetite for Destruction*, July 21

Aerosmith releases comeback album *Permanent Vacation*, Aug. 25

"Here I Go Again" by Whitesnake hits No. 1, Oct. 10

Nikki Sixx of Mötley Crüe revived after being pronounced DOA from overdose, Dec. 22

1988 *Decline of Western Civilization Part II* released, June 17

Guns N' Roses tops Hot 100 with "Sweet Child O' Mine," Sept. 10

Kix releases *Blow My Fuse*, Sept. 19

Poison's "Every Rose Has Its Thorn" hits No. 1, Dec. 24

Bill & Ted's Excellent Adventure released, Feb. 17

1989 Bon Jovi's "I'll Be There for You" tops singles chart, May 13

Mötley Crüe album *Dr. Feelgood* debuts at No. 1, Sept. 1

"Sweet Child O' Mine" by Guns N' Roses wins first MTV Best Heavy Metal Video awards, Sept. 6

Great White, Damn Yankees first pop-metal acts on *MTV Unplugged*, March 30

1990s

1990 Judas Priest cleared in fan-suicide case, Aug. 24

Warrant releases *Cherry Pie*, Sept. 11

1991 Def Leppard guitarist Steve Clark, 30, dies Jan. 8

New York Dolls guitarist Johnny Thunders, 38, dies April 23

Riot at Guns N' Roses concert in St. Louis, July 2

POP GOES THE METAL

Bill & Ted's Bogus Journey released, July 19

"November Rain" by Guns N' Roses, the longest top-10
Song at nearly 9 minutes, peaks at No. 3, Aug. 29

AC/DC, Metallica, Pantera, Black Crowes play concert in
Moscow before 1.6 million fans, Sept. 28

Guns N' Roses releases two *Use Your Illusion* albums
simultaneously, debuting at Nos. 1 and 2, Sept. 17

Kiss drummer Eric Carr, 41, dies Nov. 24

1992 Vince Neil, Mötley Crüe part ways, Feb. 14

Wayne's World released, Feb. 14

Riot at Guns N' Roses/Metallica show in Montreal, Aug. 8

1993 *Beavis and Butt-head* premieres on MTV, March 8

David Lee Roth busted in pot purchase, April 16

Dazed and Confused film released, Sept. 24

1994 Bon Jovi guitarist Richie Sambora marries Heather
Locklear, Dec. 17 (d. 2007)

Mötley Crüe releases self-titled album with John Corabi
on vocals, March 15

1995 Tommy Lee marries Baywatch star Pamela Anderson,
Feb. 19 (d. 1998)

1996 Original Kiss members reunite at Grammys, Feb. 28

Sammy Hagar, Van Halen, part ways, June 16

First Ozzfest tour kicks off in Ottawa, with Ozzy, Slayer,
Danzig and 10 other bands on two stages, Sept. 25

Z Rock radio format discontinued, Dec. 31

Vince Neil rejoins Mötley Crüe for *Generation Swine*
album, June 24

1997 Sweet vocalist Brian Connolly, 52, dies Feb. 9

Judas Priest releases *Jugulator*, first album in seven years
and first of two with Tim "Ripper" Owens, Oct. 16

1998 *Van Halen III* released with former Extreme vocalist

Gary Cherone, March 17

Drummer Cozy Powell (Rainbow, Black Sabbath, Whitesnake), 50, dies April 5

"I Don't Want to Miss a Thing" becomes Aerosmith's first No. 1 hit, 25 years after first album, Sept. 5

Kiss releases *Psycho Circus* with original lineup, Sept. 22

1999   *Detroit Rock City* film released, Aug. 13

2000s

2000   *Almost Famous*, film based on experiences of *Rolling Stone* reporter Cameron Crowe, opens, Sept. 13

2001   Mötley Crüe publishes "The Dirt," May 22

Rock Star, film inspired by Judas Priest singer Tim "Ripper" Owens, debuts, Sept. 7

Kiss plays at closing ceremonies of Winter Olympics in Salt Lake City, Feb. 24

2002   Sweet drummer Mick Tucker, 54, dies Feb. 14

The Osbournes premieres on MTV, March 5

David Lee Roth, Sammy Hagar kick off tour, May 29

Ratt guitarist Robbin Crosby, 42, dies June 6

2003   Jon Bon Jovi heads owners group for new Arena Football League team in Philadelphia, the Soul, July 10

2004   Van Halen kicks off tour with Sammy Hagar, June 11

2005   Final episode of *The Osbournes* airs, March 25

2006   *Gene Simmons Family Jewels* debuts on A&E, Aug. 7

Runaways drummer Sandy West, 47, dies Oct. 21

2007   Bon Jovi releases country-rock LP *Lost Highway*, June 8

First Rocklahoma festival opens, including Ratt, Poison, Quiet Riot, Dokken, Skid Row, Twisted Sister, over four days in Pryor, Okla., July 12

Rock of Love with Bret Michaels debuts on VH1, July 15

Quiet Riot vocalist Kevin DuBrow, 52, dies Nov. 25

2008 Sirius XM satellite radio merger approved, July 19

AC/DC releases worldwide No. 1 album *Black Ice*, Oct. 20

That Metal Show debuts on VH1, Nov. 15

2009 Kiss releases *Sonic Boom*, first of two studio albums with
former Black 'n Blue guitarist Tommy Thayer

Guns N' Roses releases "Chinese Democracy," Nov. 23

2010s

2010 Ronnie James Dio, 67, dies May 16

2011 Warrant vocalist Jani Lane, 47, dies Aug. 8

2012 Van Halen releases its first album in 14 years, *A Different
Kind of Truth*, with David Lee Roth, Feb. 7

Guitarist Ronnie Montrose, 64, dies March 3

Jon Lord (Deep Purple, Whitesnake), 71, dies July 16

2013 Vixen founder, guitarist Jan Kuehnemund, 51, dies Oct. 10

2015 Twisted Sister drummer A.J. Pero, 55, dies March 20

VH1 ends *That Metal Show* after 127 episodes, May 9

2016 Guns N' Roses "Not in This Lifetime... Tour" reunites Slash,
Axl Rose, Duff McKagan, April 1

Classic Dokken lineup releases first new song in 20 years,
"It's Just Another Day," after a brief reunion.

Axl Rose joins AC/DC for European tour, May 7

Volume debuts on Sirius XM as first all-talk radio channel
devoted to music, Oct. 17

2017 AC/DC rhythm guitarist Malcolm Young, 64, dies Nov. 18

2020 Sweet bassist Steve Priest, 72, dies June 4

STEPHEN H. PROVOST

References

"20 questions with Steve Whiteman, 12/31/02," metalsludge.tv, Dec. 31, 2002.

"39 years ago: Nikki Sixx forms Motley Crue," loudwire.com, Jan. 17, 2020.

"40 years ago Def Leppard record The Def Leppard E.P. at Fairview Studios," deflepparduk.com.

"40 years ago Def Leppard release first record (The Def Leppard EP)," deflepparduk.com.

"100 greatest guitarists," Rolling Stone, Dec. 18, 2015.

"1976 Readers' Poll," Creem, March 1977.

"1998 Jani Lane on the death of 80s hair metal and realizing grunge was in!" youtube.com.

"A La Carte: The Band," alacarte.rocks.

"About Starz," starzcentral.com.

Abraham, Willard. "Coping/Teen Talk," Baltimore Evening Sun, p. D8, Sept. 17, 1990.

Abraham, Willard. "Heavy-metal music doesn't ruin lives," Petaluma (Calif.) Argus-Courier, p. 17, May 25, 1985.

Abraham, Willard. "Teens love their heavy metal music," Newark (Ohio) Advocate, p. 7, Aug. 11, 1990.

Aledort, Andy. "Learn Randy Rhoads' warm-up exercises and more in this complete 1982 guitar clinic," guitarworld.com, March 19, 2020.

"Alice Cooper – In His Own Words," superseventies.com.

Almond, Steven. "Heavy metal gains credibility," Pensacola News Journal, p. 4D, Sept. 22, 1989.

"And here's the news," Los Angeles Times, Calendar p. 73, April 4, 1982.

"And the Cradle Will Rock," Van Halen News Desk, vhnd.com.

"Angel to appear at the Vegas Rocks! Hair Metal Awards," melodicrock.com.

Atkinson, Terry. "Breaking out of bar-band gigs," Los Angeles Times, pt. IV, p. 8, Dec. 27, 1977.

Atkinson, Terry. "Pop Briefs," Los Angeles Times, Nov. 5, 1978.

Atkinson, Terry. "Riffs run rampant in Van Halen debut album," Los Angeles Times Calendar, p. 80, March 5, 1978.

Bangs, Lester. "Pretties for You," rollingstone.com, July 12, 1969.

Barnes, Ken. "Queen II," Rolling Stone, June 20, 1974.

Barton, Laura. "Queen of noise," theguardian.com, Nov. 18, 2007.

Bennett, J. "Guns N' Roses' 'Appetite for Destruction': The story behind the cover art," revolvermag.com, Dec. 1, 2010.

Bienstock, Richard. "Decade of Decadence: A timeline of the Eighties Sunset Strip," rollingstone.com, Oct. 23, 2015.

Bienstock, Richard. "Interview: Phil Collen on the making of Def Leppard's 'Hysteria'," guitarworld.com, Oct. 12, 2012.

Bienstock, Richard. "Twisted Sister: An Unpublished History," guitarworld.com, March 19, 2009.

Billboard.com/charts.

Bishop, Marlon. "? and the Mysterians: The migrant kids who inspired punk rock," latinous.org, March 25, 2016.

Borzillo, Carrie. "Z-Rock wants to get out of your face," Billboard, July 22, 1995.

Boss, Kit. "Satellite programming strikes blow against local radio," Tallahassee Democrat, p. 7C,
Aug. 1, 1986.

Bosso, Joe. "Steve Hackett: How I invented finger tapping," musicradar.com,
April 30, 2012.

Brady, Shaun. "TIDAL Playback: Paul Stanley of Kiss," tidal.com, March 4, 2020.

Brackett, Nathan. "The New Rolling Stone Album Guide," Simon & Schuster, New York, 2004.

Brannigan, Bianca. "The Roxy, Rainbow Bar named West Hollywood Landmarks,"
lacurbed.com, Nov. 5, 2019.

Branst, Lee. "Stryper mixes Christianity and heavy metal," San Pedro News-Pilot, p. E14,
July 6, 1984.

Callwood, Brett. "Glycerine queen, forever!" City Slang, metrotimes.com, April 25, 2012.

Campbell, Mary. "Love-Hate singer Jizzy Pearl finds competition makes band stronger,"
Fond du Lac Commonwealth Reporter, p. 10, Sept. 20, 1990.

Campbell, Mary. "Rat emerges from cellar and attic," Baxter (Ark.) Bulletin, p. 12,
June 22, 1984.

Cameron, Keith. "Nirvana kill hair metal," The Guardian, June 11, 2011.

Cartwright, Garth. "Sandy West: Drummer in teenage rock group who overcame the
'bimbo' tag to lasting effect," theguardian.com, Oct. 25, 2006.

Chen, Min. "Entertainment or Death: How Mötley Crüe's 'Home Sweet Home' lit the way
for all power ballads to follow," proxymusic.club, Oct. 15, 2019.

Cherkis, Jason. "The Lost Girls," highline.huffingtonpost.com.

Childers, Chad. "38 years ago: Iron Maiden introduced metal to MTV," loudwire.com, Aug. 1, 2019.

"Christian rock music on the rise," Santa Cruz Sentinel, p. 7, July 30, 1984.

"Circus Magazine is no more," blabbermouth.net, May 18, 2006.

Clark, Nick. "Badfinger: last act in a rock 'n' roll tragedy," independent.co.uk, April 26, 2013.

Cooper, Candy. "Judas Priest trial," San Francisco Examiner, reversespeech.com, Sept. 29, 1989.

Criss, Peter. "Makeup to Breakup: My Life In and Out of Kiss," Scribner, New York, 2012.

Crook, David. "Warner/Amex plans 'video radio,'" Los Angeles Times, pt. VI, p. 2, March 4, 1981.

Crowe, Adell. "Rock stars defend raunchy songs," Burlington (Vt.) Free Press, p. 1, Sept, 20, 1985.

"Darlyne R Pettinicchio," calsalaries.com, 2017.

"David Bowie setlist, May 30, 1983," setlist.fm.

"David Lee Roth pissed off at Van Halen (1986)," youtube.com.

Deb. "Interview with Blackie Lawless of W.A.S.P.," Metal Flakes, earcandy_mag.tripod.com,
May 20, 2001.

"Deep Purple In Rock – 50 years of the definitive hard rock classic album," getintothis.co.uk,
June 5, 2020.

Deriso, Nick. "Before they were Kiss: The history of Wicked Lester," ultimateclassicrock.com,
Sept. 29, 2014.

Deriso, Nick. "The death of Randy Rhoads," ultimateclassicrock.com, March 19, 2016.

Deriso, Nick. "Patty Smyth is happy to have turned down Van Halen job," ultimateclassicrock.com,
Feb. 19, 2014.

"Don Dokken discusses his forthcoming release "The Lost Songs: 1978-1981," eddietrunk.com,
July 3, 2020.

"Don Dokken: 'George Lynch thought he was God, and I disagreed,'" blabbermouth.net,
Aug. 12, 2004.

POP GOES THE METAL

"Drummer out of danger after arm amputation," Columbus (Ind.) Republic, p. 2, Jan. 5, 1985.

"Drummer's severed arm reattached," The Miami News, p. 3, Jan. 2, 1985.

Duff, S.L. "Retail reaction: Metal's selling bigger and better than ever despite media blackout," Billboard, May 10, 1986.

Earles, Andrew. "Power pop: The '70s, the birth of cool," magnetmagazine.com.

"East senior auditions for video DJ position," Columbus (Ind.) Republic, p. 7, June 3, 1981.

Elliott, Paul. "Dokken: The hair metal band that hated itself," loudersound.com, Oct. 2, 2015.

Elliott, Paul. "Exploding cod-pieces, raw meat and God: an audience with W.A.S.P.'s Blackie Lawless," loudersound.com, Nov. 10, 2015.

"Episode 31: Steve Blaze (Lillian Axe)," brainfartinterviews.com, Feb. 8, 2019.

Feldman, Paul. "Rock singer arrested in fatal car crash," Los Angeles Times, pt. II, p. 1, Dec. 10, 1984.

Fortham, Ian. "The death of Razzle: the story of Vince Neil and a car crash," loudersound.com, Dec. 8, 2016.

Frolik, Joe. "Van Halen's selling itself," Austin American-Statesman, p. D7, Nov. 20, 1978.

Furek, Maxim W. "The Death Proclamation of Generation X," iUniverse, Inc., New York, 2008.

Galluci, Michael. "David Coverdale hopes to end fight with Robert Plant," ultimateclassicrock.com, June 15, 2013.

Gault, Anna. "Kiss and tell: Kiss frontman Gene Simmons bedded 4,000 women – including Scots groupies," thescottishsun.co.uk, Nov. 29, 2017.

"Gene Simmons talks about 'Rock School,'" blabbermouth.com, Aug. 29, 2005.

"George Lynch Discusses Early Guitar Influences Dokken – Lynch Mob Guitarist," livetojam, youtube.com, March 23, 2011.

Giles, Jeff. "The day Joe Perry quit Aerosmith," ultimateclassicrock.com, July 28, 2015.

Goodwyn, Tom. "Vince Neil on jail sentence: 'Courts wanted to make an example of me'," nme.com, Feb. 22, 2011.

"Go All The Way by The Raspberries," songfacts.com.

Goldstein, Patrick. "Gene Simmons Takes a Spin as a Record Mogul," Los Angeles Times, July 17, 1988.

Goldstein, Patrick. "MTV softens hard edge on heavy-metal image," Los Angeles Times, March 3, 1985.

Goldstein, Patrick. "Skid Row's Sebastian Bach embroiled in AIDS Row," Los Angeles Times, Jan. 21, 1990.

Goldstein, Toby. "Before the Riot was Quiet, the metal was glitter," Creem Close-up: Metal Rock 'n' Roll, October 1985.

Goth, Greg. "Drummer says 'Christian band' is wrong label for Stryper," San Bernardino County Sun, p. D1, Feb. 2, 1989.

"Greg Leon interview," sleazeroxx.com, March 25, 2007.

Grow, Kory. "PMRC's 'Filthy Fifteen: Where are they now?" rollingstone.com, Sept. 17, 2015.

"Guitar World Magazine names 'Greatest Guitarist of All Time,' 957thehog.com, Feb, 21, 2019.

Hanifan, C.E. "Pop goes the world," Wausau Daily Herald, p. 32, April 17, 2003.

Harper, Leah. "Suzi Quatro: 'It was only when we got the pictures back that I realised it was a sexy outfit'," theguardian.com, Dec. 17, 2019.

Harrington, Richard. "Joan Jett's passion is rock, more rock," The Capital Times (Madison, Wis.),

p. 43, Jan. 15, 1987.

Harris, Larry. "And Party Every Day: The Inside Story of Casablanca Records," Backbeat
Books, New York, 2009.

Hartmann, Graham. "11 most epic codpieces in rock + metal," loudwire.com, April 17, 2017.

Hartmann, Graham. "Dee Snider won't vote for Donald Trump, wonders why Vince Neil didn't do
serious jail time," loudwire.com, Feb. 19, 2016.

"Heavy metal singer sued on suicide," Napa Valley Register, p. 15, Jan. 14, 1986.

"Heavy: The Story of Metal Part III: Looks That Kill," youtube.com.

Hiatt, Brian. "Kiss Forever: 40 Years of Feuds and Fury," rollingstone.com, March 26, 2014.

Hilburn, Robert. "Homegrown Punk," Los Angeles Times, Jan. 4, 1977.

Hilburn, Robert. "Pasadena's Van Halen: Slow Start, Strong Finish," Los Angeles Times, pt. IV,
p. 9, July 11, 1978.

Hilburn, Robert. "Under the rock, an exciting crop of newcomers," Los Angeles Times Calendar,
p. 93, Nov. 27, 1977.

Hilburn, Robert. "X and PiL: Rock from the fringe," Los Angeles Times Calendar, p. 60,
May 10, 1981.

Himmelsbach-Weinstein, Erik. "The music festival that time forgot: Inside Steve Wozniak's
US Fest," lamag.com, June 28, 2017.

"History of MTV," metalitch.com.

Hogan, John. "Cadillac's connection to Kiss endures 40 years later," freep.com, Oct. 8, 2015.

Hochman, Steve. "Some rockers opt for change in lifestyle," Los Angeles Times, p. F1,
Nov. 26, 1991.

Holloway, Alan. "Dee Snider, 'The Twisted Sister,'" rockunited.com, Dec. 7, 2007.

Horn, John. "MTV zips past music videos to revamp format," Indiana Gazette, p. 23, Sept. 6, 1989.

"How a suicide pact was almost the end of Judas Priest," Metal Hammer, loudersound.com,
April 22, 2020.

"How did The Horns become the symbol of heavy metal?" blog.drooble.com, Jan. 25, 2017.

"How some area pastors hear the music," Green Bay Press-Gazette, Scene p. 1,
March 27, 1988.

Howrey, Jeff. "Runaways are fabricated pop," Daily Utah Chronicle, p. 8, Oct. 13, 1976.

Hyman, Dan. "After all these years, Cheap Trick's Rick Nielsen still wants you to want him,"
vice.com, April 6, 2016.

"In two exclusive interviews with Rock Candy Mag, it's clear that Don Dokken and George Lynch
still can't get along, rockcandymag.com, Aug. 1, 2019.

Ives, Brian. "When the PMRC's 'Filthy Fifteen' targeted metal: Dee Snider looks back,"
loudwire.com, June 13, 2018.

Kaufman, Spencer. "Brian Johnson recalls meeting Bon Scott at a gig before replacing him in
AC/DC," ultimateclassicrock.com, June 13, 2011.

Kourasanis, Jakam. "Richie Ranno (Starz) Interview, medium.com/@JakamKourasanis,
Dec. 2, 2015.

Jackson, Jeanne and Kruse, Lisa R. "Critics fault influence of 'black metal," Asbury Park (N.J.)
Press, p. 1, Nov. 12, 1989.

"Jimmy Page reportedly refused to appear on 'That Metal Show' because 'he wants nothing to do
with the term metal,'" ledzepnews.com, May 6, 2018.

"Jizzy Pearl on the Hollywood Sign," Eyewitness News, June 1, 1992, youtube.com.

POP GOES THE METAL

Josi, Christian. "Stephen Pearcy's new memoir is awesome. Period," huffpost.com, May 9, 2013.

Kaufman, Gil. "Ratt guitarist Robbin Crosby dies," mtv.com, June 10, 2002.

Kelley, Ken. "Cinderella's Tom Keifer says Gene Simmons discovered band, not Jon Bon Jovi," ultimateclassicrock.com, July 22, 2014.

Kennedy, Bud. "Denton radio station changes its format from country to 'Z-Rock,'" Fort Worth Star-Telegram, Sect. 6, p. 11, July 3, 1987.

"Kiss' Gene Simmons on how he discovered Van Halen," metalwani.com, October 2017.

"KISS Land of Hype and Glory 1978," youtube.com.

Klosterman, Chuck. "Paradise City," Spin Magazine, September 2002.

Knapp, Gary. "Building the American Dream," AuthorHouse, Bloomington, Ind., 2007.

Konow, David. "Bang Your Head: The Rise and Fall of Heavy Metal," Three Rivers Press, New York, 2002.

Knutsson, Robert. "38 år sedan," kissarmysweden.net, April 11, 2010.

Krome, Kari. "Memories of Rodney Bingenheimer's English Disco as the Installation Opens Inside ltd los angeles," thelosangelesbeat.com, Sept. 24, 2015.

Kudler, Adrian Glick. "A totally incomplete history of trouble at the Chateau Marmont," lacurbed.com, July 30, 2019.

Lang, Derrik J. "Back on road," McAllen (Tex.) Monitor, p. 2D, June 5, 2010.

Lanham, Tom. "Starz: Band that should have made it makes comeback," eastbaytimes.com, Dec. 16, 2005.

Latta, David. "Age Shall Not Weary Her: Suzi Quatro Bathes in Rock 'n' Roll's Fountain of Youth," davidlatta.com, Sept. 27, 2011.

Leaf, David; Sharp, Ken. "Kiss: Behind the Mask – Official Authorized Biography," Hachette Book Group, New York, 2003.

Leogrande, Ernest. "Wear Watcha Want," New York Daily News, Aug. 29, 1972.

Ling, Dave. "The story of Starz, the band who grabbed defeat from the jaws of victory," loudersound.com, Oct. 21, 2016.

Ling, Dave. "The Sweet: is it finally time to give them the credit they deserve?" loudersound.com, Oct. 25, 2017.

Lifton, Dave. "Quiet Riot's Kelly Garni said he once tried to kill Kevin DuBrow," ultimateclassicrock.com, March 5, 2019.

Lifton, Dave. "The History of Pete Ham and Badfinger," ultimateclassicrock.com, April 24, 2015.

Linder, Doug. "The McMartin Preschool Abuse Trial: A Commentary," law.umkc.edu, 2003.

Little, Michael. "Angel on his shoulder," washingtoncitypaper.com, May 31, 2002.

"Lita Ford: Wikipedia: Fact or Fiction?" loudwire.com.

Locker, Melissa. "Nikki Sixx says goodbye for good: Inside the end of Motley Crue," Feb. 5, 2014.

Locker, Richard and Deibel, Mary. "Parents against pornrock lyrics get results," Elmira (N.Y.) Star-Gazette, p. 10, Sept. 11, 1985.

"Low budget films that more than made their money back," editorchoice.com.

Mackay, Emily. "The strangest tales from rock's most mythical hotels," bbc.co.uk, April 10, 2017.

Magahern, Jimmy. "Rock band credits God for its success," Tampa Bay Times, p. 7E, March 21, 1987.

Makabe, R.G. "Satanic symbols find teen audience," Auburn Journal, p. 1, Sept. 13, 1985.

Manisco, Patricia. "Suddenly an innocent victim," Los Angeles Times, South Bay section, Dec. 20, 1984.

Marshall, Clay. "Rikki Rockett remembers Poison's 'Open Up and Say... Ah!'," ultimateclassicrock.com, May 3, 2018.

Marti, Ines. "Freddie Mercury: 'I'm not gonna be a star, I'm gonna be a legend," highxtar.com, Nov. 3, 2018.

Martin, Pat. "Rock radio: Stations throw metal onto junkpile," Billboard, May 10, 1986.

Martino, Alison. "It's All Happening! Rodney Bingenheimer's Long Gone '70s-Era Disco Returns," Los Angeles Magazine, lamag.com, Sept. 7, 2015.

Masley, Ed. "Alice Cooper bandmates reflect on their historic past," azcentral.com, March 3, 2011.

Masley, Ed. "Gratitude keeps Bret Michaels rocking," Arizona Republic, p. C6, Nov. 14, 2019.

Matovina, Dan. "Without You: The Tragic Story of Badfinger," Frances Glover Books, San Mateo, Calif., 2000.

Maxwell, Jessica. "Fifth-four hours: Things to do from 6 p.m. Friday Jan. 28 to midnight Sunday Jan. 30," Los Angeles Times, Jan. 25, 1977.

Means, Andrew. "Thoughtful lyrics, teamwork brighten Rainbow's outlook," Arizona Republic, p. G2, March 22, 1981.

Meares, Hadley. "Glitter, glam, grit," la.curbed.com, March 21, 2019.

Merlan, Anna. "The Seedy Backstory of the Runaways and Their Rapist Svengali Producer," jezebel.com, July 9, 2015.

Merryweather, Cherry. "Top 10 disturbing facts about the 'Night Stalker' Richard Ramirez, listverse.com, Jan. 16, 2020.

"Metal Evolution: Glam Metal," youtube.com.

Michaels, Mark. "Interview with bassist Rick Fox (Steeler, W.A.S.P., Sin)," thecosmickview.blogspot.com, July 22, 2019.

Montgomery, Nikki. "90s At 9 'Cherry Pie' Is So Obviously Dirty, But Can You Prove It?" rock947.com, Sept. 4, 2018.

"Moorhead has KMET-FM jocks playing 'Hit-or-Miss' on LP cuts," Billboard, July 29, 1972.

Morse, Tim. "Classic Rock Stories," St. Martin's Griffin, New York, 1998.

"Motley Crue singer won't go to jail," Santa Rosa Press-Democrat, p. 4, June 11, 1985.

"Mötley Crüe singer gets 2-week jail sentence," Santa Fe New Mexican, p. A10, Jan. 19, 2011.

"MTV is changing heavy metal tune," Detroit Free Press, p. D1, Feb. 15, 1985.

"Music" (calendar), LA Weekly, p. 95, Nov. 1-7, 1985.

Newton, Steve. "Autograph guitarist Steve Lynch talks Van Halen, two-handed tapping, and The Right Touch," earofnewt.com, Nov. 8, 1985.

"No Life 'til Metal: The Twisted Sister Collection," nolifetilmetal.com.

Obrecht, Jas. "A legend is born: Eddie Van Halen's first interview," musiciansfriend.com,

"Odin frontman Randy O to release debut solo album Coming Home," hairbandheaven.rocks, Aug. 18, 2019.

Ohland, Gloria. "Rocking 'round the clock on television," Philadelphia Inquirer, p. 26, Aug. 3, 1981.

Olsen, John P. "Billboard New Age Chart musicians; Blackmore's Night," newagemusicworld.com, March 19, 2011.

Orf, Chris Hansen. "Outrageous stage antics made Alice Cooper a superstar," eastvalleytribune.com, Oct. 31, 2007.

"Outcomes of high profile day care sexual abuse cases in the 1980s," pbs.org.

Paige, Earl. "Chains in heavy push for metal," Billboard, Oct. 13, 1984.

Paltrowitz, Darren. "Angel's Punky Meadows on 2020 plans, almost joining Kiss, & more," thehypemagazine.com, Dec. 22, 2019.

Parks, John. "George Lynch talks T&N, Michael Sweet, Randy Rhoads, his film Shadow Train and much more," legendaryrockinterviews.com, Dec. 22, 2012.

"People, etc.," Tucson Citizen, p. 33 Jan 26, 1985.

Polcaro, Rafael. "The tragic story of Randy Rhoads death," rockandrollgarage.com, March 24, 2019.

"Pop Picks," Los Angeles Times Calendar, p. 67, Nov. 17, 1985.

Prato, Greg. "Frankie Banali of Quiet Riot," songfacts.com.

Prince, Nancy. "CHS Students Creators Of New Singing Group," Cortez High School Newspaper, Oct. 16, 1964.

"Profile: Gary Glitter," news.bbc.uk, Aug. 21, 2008.

Pruitt, Sarah. "Babysitters accused of satanic crimes exonerated after 25 years," history.com.

Puterbaugh, Parke. "Diver Down," Rolling Stone, June 10, 1982.

"Quiet Riot singer died of overdose," news.yahoo.com, Dec. 10, 2007.

"R&R Street Talk," Radio & Records, p. 28, Aug. 9, 1985.

"Radio Station KABC-FM now called KLOS," Valley News, p. 24, March 30, 1971.

"Rainbow 'Rising' at 40," metalshockfinland.com.

"Ratings stalled, MTV turns to spinoffs," The Charlotte Observer, p. 10A, Feb. 19, 1995.

Reiff, Corbin. "30 years ago: Vince Neil punches Izzy Stradlin at MTV's VMAS," ultimateclassicrock.com, Sept. 6, 2015.

Renoff, Greg. "The History of Eddie Van Halen and Keyboards," ultimateclassicrock.com, Jan. 26, 2015.

Renoff, Greg. "How David Lee Roth really left Van Halen," ultimateclassicrock.com, Aug. 10, 2015.

Reynolds, Simon. "Alice Cooper: 'Rock music was looking for a villain,'" theguardian.com, June 12, 2014.

Rojas, Aurelio and Sisk, K. Mack. "Richard Ramirez' 'Highway to Hell,' Ukiah Daily Journal, p. 12, Sept. 8, 1985.

"Rick Allen plans comeback," Mansfield (Ohio) News-Journal, p. 2, Jan. 9, 1985.

Rivadavia, Eduardo. "About Xciter," itunes.apple.com.

Roberts, Janey. "Why Queen should not have printed 'No Synthesizers' on liner notes," classicrockhistory.com, 2019.

"Rockers shake Senate hearing on raunchy lyrics," Reno Gazette-Journal, p. 5, Sept. 20, 1985.

"Rocket interviews George Lynch," themetalden.com, March 15, 2009.

Robinson, Jonnie. "Geordie" A regional dialect of English," bl.uk, April 24, 2019.

Roxon, Lillian. "The Dolls Will Be Heard From," New York Daily News, Sept. 3, 1972.

"Rudy Sarzo talks passing of Randy Rhoads," bravewords.com, Jan. 9, 2016.

"The Runaways Rock Japan 1977 HD," archive.org.

Schael, Eric. "When Led Zeppelin started breaking records set by the Beatles," cheatsheet.com, April 20, 2019.

Schaffner, Lauryn. "Joe Elliott: Def Leppard was 'so far removed' from hair metal," loudwire.com, June 20, 2019.

Schleuss, Heinz. "Rock 'n' roll with real soul," Escondido Times-Advocate, p. 3, Dec. 21, 1987.

Schonfeld, Zach. "Parental Advisory Forever: An oral history of the PMRC's war on dirty lyrics," Newsweek, Sept. 19, 2015.

Schwinden, Richard L. "Twisted Sister, 1982-87," patch.com/minnesota/roseville, April 14, 2016.

Sharma, Armit. "Gene Simmons: 'Creating new music so people can download it for free does not appeal to me," musicradar.com, Nov. 7, 2017.

Sharp, Ken. "Down to Earth: How Angel fell from grace," loudersound.com, Oct. 27, 2016.

Simmons, Gene. "Kiss and Make-Up: A Memoir," Crown Publishers, New York, 2001.

Simpson, Dave. "Hair! Despair! Nightmares! What happened to 1980s metal also rans?" theguardian.com, Oct. 15, 2015.

"Singer defends suicide song," Hanover (Pa.) Evening Sun, p. 2, Jan. 22, 1986.

"SiriusXM launches Volume: First-ever 24/7 music talk radio channel – where music is the conversation," prnewswire.com, Sept. 29, 2016.

Smith, Kyle. "Mick Jagger and Keith Richards can't stand each other," nypost.com, May 11, 2016.

Spitz, Marc (with Brendan Mullen). "We Got the Neutron Bomb: The Untold Story of L.A. Punk," Three Rivers Press, New York, 2001.

Stark, Phyllis. "Guilty plea entered in Stern sabotage; KRFX GM finds Simpson bad company," Billboard, July 8, 1995.

"Stars rock hearing on labeling," Hartford Courant, p. A3, Sept. 20, 1985.

"Starz/Stories guitarist Richie Ranno," fullbloommusic.com.

Strauss, Duncan. "Poison: With name like that, it better be good," Los Angeles Times, pt. VI, p. 2, April 18, 1986.

"Stryper," annecarlini.com.

"Suzi Quatro Rocks On!" abc-mallorca.com, March 6, 2008.

"Swaggart plans to step down," The New York Times, Oct. 15, 1991.

"Sweet is ready for America," The Salina (Kansas) Journal, p. 21, June 11, 1978.

"Sweet – 'Scene: All That Glitters' Documentary," Official Sweet Channel, youtube.com.

"Ted Templeman: 'If I'd tried to put Sammy Hagar in Van Halen in 1977, I'd have made the biggest mistake in rock history," vhnd.com, May 16, 2020.

Testa, Bart. "News of the World," Rolling Stone, Feb. 9, 1978.

"The best rock documentary you've never heard of," smithjournal.com.au, June 13, 2016.

Thompson, Dave. "Welcome to My Nightmare: The Alice Cooper Story," Omnibus Press, 2012.

Tianen, Dave. "Heavy metal hymns," Green Bay Press-Gazette, Scene p. 1, March 27, 1988.

"TimesTalks: Joan Jett," New York Times Events, youtube.com, Oct. 1, 2018.

Transcript of 1985 Senate PMRC hearing, joesapt.net.

Triplett, Gene. "Wrestling with Roth and Hagar," The Oklahoman, July 19, 2002.

Trunk, Russell A. "Stryper," annecarlini.com.

Uykucuoglu, Berk. "David Lee Roth reveals how did Gene Simmons discover Van Halen in 1976," metalheadzone.com, Feb. 25, 2020.

"Van Halen 'Jump' fun facts!" Van Halen News Desk, vhnd.com.

Van Matre, Lynn. "Van Halen's Roth tests solo waters," Chicago Tribune, Jan. 31, 1985.

Verna, Paul. "Pay-to-play club gambit causing internal controversy," Senate Reports, Nos. 419-484, Jan. 3-Oct. 9, 1992.

Wake, Matt. "An'80s glam-metal survivor tells all," al.com, July 10, 2019.

Wake, Matt. "Happy 30th anniversary to the Cathouse, Hollywood's most decadent rock club," laweekly.com, Sept. 14, 2016.

Waksman, Steve. "This Ain't the Summer of Love: Conflict and Crossover in Heavy Metal and Punk," University of California Press, Berkeley, 2009.

Wall, Mick. "Stick to your guns," Kerrang, April 21, 1990.

POP GOES THE METAL

Walters, Barry. "David Bowie, Sexuality and Gender," billboard.com, Jan. 14, 2016.

Warburton, Nick. "Wainwright's Gentlemen," thestrangebrew.co.uk.

Ward, Steven. "Andy Secher, Hit Parader," rockcriticsarchives.com.

Ward, Steven. "Running away with the Circus (XII): Ben Liemer," rockcriticsarchives.com.

Wardlaw, Matt. "'5150' is better than 'Eat 'Em and Smile,'" ultimateclassicrock.com, Oct. 23, 2013.

Matt Wardlaw, Matt. "Revisiting the influential, short-lived and expensive US Festival," ultimateclassicrock.com, Sept. 3, 2015.

Warner, Brian. "Sammy Hagar: Unlikely tequila mogul and centimillionaire," celebritynetworth.com, March 9, 2014.

Watts, Chelsea Anne. "Nothin' But a Good Time: Hair Metal, Conservatism, and the End of the Cold War in the 1980s," graduate thesis, University of South Florida, Nov. 30, 2016.

Whalen, Andrew. "Mötley Crüe and the real story of Nikki Sixx's overdose: Going beyond 'The Dirt,' Newsweek, June 26, 2020.

Whitaker, Sterling. "Ozzy Osbourne nearly passes out during Rand Rhoads' audition," ultimateclassicrock.com, May 10, 2013.

White, Adam. "Z-Rockin' at retail," worldradiohistory.com, March 20, 1987,

"Who was Nicholas 'Razzle' Dingley & how long did Mötley Crüe's Vince Neil serve in jail for the fatal car crash?" radiox.co.uk, March 30, 2019.

Wiederhorn, Jon. "Judas Priest's Rob Halford reflects on 25th anniversary of subliminal message lawsuit," yahoo.com, Aug. 24, 2015.

Wien, Gary. "Company of Wolves," newjerseystage.com, May 22, 2017.

Wilding, Philip. "What happened the night James Hetfield caught fire," loudersound.com, Oct. 6, 2019.

Williams, Cameron. "How MTV changed the world with its industry of cool," sbs.com.au, Feb. 13, 2017.

Williams, Timothy. "Rock guitarist accidentally shoots woman," latimes.com, June 12, 1993.

Woods, Rebecca. "Black Sabbath: 'We hated being a heavy metal band," BBC News, Feb. 4, 2017.

Young, Charles M. "Van Halen," Rolling Stone, May 4, 1978.

Yozwiak, Steve. "428 cited at Van Halen concert for marijuana, booze violations," Arizona Republic, p. 7, May 18, 1984.

"Ziggy Stardust vs. David Bowie: How the LGBT Community can relate," exhibits.library.villanova.edu.

STEPHEN H. PROVOST

Illustrations

- **DOKKEN** guitarist George Lynch at the video shoot for "Burning Like a Flame," by perfectrx, CC BY 2.0, https://www.flickr.com/photos/perfectrx/33582524302/in/photostream/, *p. 105*

CHAPTER 6

- **DAVID LEE ROTH** performs with Van Halen in 1978, by Carl Lender, CC BY 2.0, https://commons.wikimedia.org/wiki/File:David_Lee_Roth_-_Van_Halen.jpg, *p. 119*
- **WHISKY A GO GO** on the Sunset Strip, 2006, by Tim McGarry, CC BY 2.0, https://www.flickr.com/photos/tim_mcgarry/394866452/in/photostream/, *p. 122*

CHAPTER 7

- Ad for **DEF LEPPARD** in November 1987 issue of *Hit Parader*, author collection, *p. 130*
- **BRIAN JOHNSON** with AC/DC Nov. 3, 2008, at St. Paul, Minn., by Matt Becker, CC BY-SA 3.0, https://is.wikipedia.org/wiki/AC/DC#/media/Mynd:Brian_Johnson.jpg, *p. 141*

CHAPTER 8

- Ad for **REO SPEEDWAGON** concert televised on MTV from the Sapulpa (Okla.) Herald, Aug. 6, 1981, *p. 154*

CHAPTER 9

- Ad for the **US FESTIVAL**, Los Angeles Times, April 24, 1983, *p. 169*
- **TOWER RECORDS** at 8844 W. Sunset Blvd., West Hollywood, 2006, by Matt Dillon, CA BY-SA 3.0, https://commons.wikimedia.org/wiki/File:Tower_Records_Sunset.jpg, *p. 177*
- Flier for **GUNS N' ROSES** concert at the Troubadour in West Hollywood, July 20, 1985, author collection, *p. 183*
- Ad for **LIXXARRAY** concert April 27, 1991, at the Roxy, author collection, *p. 188*

CHAPTER 10

- Classified ads from November 1987 issue *Hit Parader*, author collection, *p. 205*

About the author

During a 30-year career in journalism, Stephen H. Provost worked as a managing editor, copy desk chief, columnist and reporter at five newspapers. Now a full-time author, he has written on such diverse topics as American highways, dragons, mutant superheroes, mythic archetypes, language, department stores and his hometown. He currently lives in Virginia. And he loves cats. Read his blogs and keep up with his activities at stephenhprovost.com.

Also by the author

Works of Fiction

    Memortality (The Memortality Saga, Vol. 1)

    Paralucidity (The Memortality Saga, Vol. 2)

    The Talismans of Time (Academy of the Lost Labyrinth, Vol. 1)

    Pathfinder of Destiny (Academy of the Lost Labyrinth, Vol. 2)

    The Only Dragon

    Identity Break

    Feathercap

    Nightmare's Eve

Works of Nonfiction

    Yesterday's Highways (America's Historic Highways, Vol. 1)

    America's First Highways (America's Historic Highways, Vol. 2)

    Highway 99 (California's Historic Highways, Vol. 1)

    Highway 101 (California's Historic Highways, Vol. 2)

    A Whole Different League

    The Legend of Molly Bolin

    Fresno Growing Up

    Martinsville Memories

    50 Undefeated

    The Osiris Testament (The Phoenix Chronicles, Vol. 1)

    The Way of the Phoenix (The Phoenix Chronicles, Vol. 2)

    The Gospel of the Phoenix (The Phoenix Chronicles, Vol. 3)

    Forged in Ancient Fires (The Phoenix Principle, Vol. 1)

    Messiah in the Making (The Phoenix Principle, Vol. 2)

    Requiem for a Phantom God

    Media Meltdown in the Age of Trump

    Please Stop Saying That!

STEPHEN H. PROVOST

Praise for other works

"The complex idea of mixing morality and mortality is a fresh twist on the human condition. ... **Memortality** is one of those books that will incite more questions than it answers. And for fandom, that's a good thing."

— Ricky L. Brown, Amazing Stories

"Punchy and fast paced, **Memortality** reads like a graphic novel. ... (Provost's) style makes the trippy landscapes and mind-bending plot points more believable and adds a thrilling edge to this vivid crossover fantasy."

— Foreword Reviews

"The genres in this volume span horror, fantasy, and science-fiction, and each is handled deftly. ... **Nightmare's Eve** should be on your reading list. The stories are at the intersection of nightmare and lucid dreaming, up ahead a signpost ... next stop, your reading pile. Keep the nightlight on."

— R.B. Payne, Cemetery Dance

"**Memortality** by Stephen Provost is a highly original, thrilling novel unlike anything else out there."

— David McAfee, bestselling author of 33 A.D., 61 A.D., and 79 A.D.

"Profusely illustrated throughout, **Highway 99** is unreservedly recommended as an essential and core addition to every community and academic library's California History collections."

— California Bookwatch

POP GOES THE METAL

"As informed and informative as it is entertaining and absorbing, **Fresno Growing Up** is very highly recommended for personal, community, and academic library 20th Century American History collections."

— John Burroughs, Reviewer's Bookwatch

"Provost sticks mostly to the classics: vampires, ghosts, aliens, and even dragons. But trekking familiar terrain allows the author to subvert readers' expectations. ... Provost's poetry skillfully displays the same somber themes as the stories. ... Worthy tales that prove external forces are no more terrifying than what's inside people's heads."

— Kirkus Reviews on **Nightmare's Eve**

"… an engaging narrative that pulls the reader into the story and onto the road. … I highly recommend **Highway 99: The History of California's Main Street**, whether you're a roadside archaeology nut or just someone who enjoys a ripping story peppered with vintage photographs."

— Barbara Gossett,
Society for Commercial Archaeology Journal

STEPHEN H. PROVOST